DELAWARE POLITICS AND GOVERNMENT

*Politics and Governments
of the American States*

Founding Editor

Daniel J. Elazar

Published by the University of
Nebraska Press in association
with the Center for the Study
of Federalism at the Robert B.
and Helen S. Meyner Center
for the Study of State and Local
Government, Lafayette College

WILLIAM W. BOYER AND EDWARD C. RATLEDGE

Delaware Politics and Government

UNIVERSITY OF NEBRASKA PRESS
LINCOLN AND LONDON

Library of Congress
Cataloging-in-Publication Data
Boyer, William W.
Delaware politics and government /
William W. Boyer and Edward C. Ratledge.
p. cm.—(Politics and governments of
the American states)
Includes bibliographical references and index.
ISBN 978-0-8032-1345-6 (cloth : alk. paper)—
ISBN 978-0-8032-6220-1 (pbk. : alk. paper)
1. Delaware—Politics and government.
I. Ratledge, Edward C. II. Title.
JK3716.B67 2009
320.4751—dc22
2008043540

Set in Times by Bob Reitz.
Designed by Joel Gehringer.

To the memory of
Dr. John A. Munroe (1914–2006)
colleague, friend, and
eminent historian of Delaware

CONTENTS

ILLUSTRATIONS

MAP OF DELAWARE, 14

FIGURES

Preface

When most Americans think about Delaware, they may focus on its smallness and the conservative business image it projects. And surely these are two characteristics that help to condition the government and politics of this small state. But there are many other dimensions of Delaware's political culture that also contribute to an understanding of its complexity and uniqueness, including its location, sectionalism, economic and ethnic diversity, and historical development from a colonial past. We have welcomed the challenge and opportunity to demystify Delaware by explaining how its government and politics compare with the rest of the nation.

In a sense this book had its beginning when one of us, as a University of Delaware political science professor emeritus, was writing a book on the public policy problems of this small state, while the other, as an economist/demographer, was serving as the long-time director of the university's Center for Applied Demography and Survey Research, which has conducted many public affairs research projects for Delaware government and nongovernmental entities. We are indebted to the staffs of the center and the university's Morris Library for assisting us with our collaborative effort.

We owe special debts of gratitude to: the late Daniel Elazar, for his seminal studies of political culture of the states that have informed our analysis; Lafayette University professor John Kincaid, the former series editor, for his initial guidance; and to three readers who suggested helpful revisions of our draft manuscript—former University of Delaware professor Robert Denhardt, now director of Arizona State University's School of Public Affairs; long-time State of Delaware administrator Thomas Eichler; and political science professor Gene Halus of Saint Joseph's University.

We wish, too, to acknowledge others who have contributed to our study, in one way or another, including: Matthew Boyer, James Flynn, Edward

Freel, Janet Johnson, the late Kenneth Koford, Karen Kral, Jerome Lewis, Steven Peuquet, Joseph Pika, Peter Ross, Alexander Settles, Leland Ware, and Yun Zhuo.

We should like to add that, regardless of the assistance we have received, we alone are responsible for the contents of this study.

DELAWARE POLITICS AND GOVERNMENT

CHAPTER ONE

Delaware in Transition

Delaware is a small state, but as realtors are often heard to say, the three things that matter are "location, location, location." The location of Delaware on a peninsula just south of Philadelphia in the midst of the Boston–Washington megalopolis is central to the state's development. It is also midway between Washington, the center of the nation's political power, and New York City, the center of the nation's financial muscle. Delaware plays a role on both of these stages. Since the state lies on a peninsula split by a canal, the lower two counties have a different character and orientation than the northern county, which sits in the I-95 corridor. Delaware is referred to as the "First State" because it was the first to ratify the U.S. Constitution, which ensured that small states would have more political power than warranted by their diminutive size.

THE SMALLEST STATE?

The word "Delaware" comes from the name given the river (Delaware River) in honor of Lord De La Warr, the first governor of colonial Virginia.[1] Only Rhode Island, at 1,045 square miles,[2] has less land area than Delaware, and only five states much larger in area have less population according to the 2000 U.S. census: North Dakota (635,867), South Dakota (781,919), Vermont (623,908), Alaska (670,053), and Wyoming (515,004). Delaware can claim to be the smallest state when the factors of land area (1,982 square miles—forty-ninth in the nation) and population (783,600 in the 2000 census—forty-fifth) are combined.

Delaware is located in the northern and eastern third of the low-lying Delmarva Peninsula that separates the Delaware and Chesapeake estuaries. It shares the greater part of the peninsula with eastern Maryland on its western and southern borders, while its short northern semicircular border adjoins Pennsylvania. Delaware is ninety-five miles long from north to south, and its width from east to west varies from nine miles in central New Castle County to thirty-five miles at the southern boundary. It comprises three counties— mostly metropolitan New Castle County (438 square miles) in the north, more rural Kent County (594 square miles) in the center of the state, and mostly rural Sussex County (950 square miles) in the south. Except for low foothills in the north of New Castle County, the state is flat, with a curving eastern coastline of some three hundred miles featuring sandy beaches in the southern half of Sussex County along the Atlantic Ocean and marshes to the north along the navigable Delaware Bay and Delaware River.

From its inception, Delaware has developed significant differences in lifestyle between northern New Castle County ("upstate") and the land south ("downstate"), including a healthy contest for political power and influence within the state. Since the opening in 1829 of the fifteen-mile-long Chesapeake and Delaware Canal, which bisects New Castle County and connects the Delaware River and the Chesapeake Bay, upstate has been commonly known as "north of the canal" and downstate as "south of the canal." North of the canal is wealthier and more commercial, populous, urban, and northern in orientation, and it adjoins the metropolitan area of southeastern Pennsylvania dominated by Philadelphia. This area lies along the northeast axis of railroads and highways linking the megalopolis that stretches from Boston to Washington DC. In contrast, south of the canal has been rural, agricultural, conservative, less wealthy, and clearly more "southern" in orientation.

COLONIZATION

When Delaware first became known to Europeans in the early seventeenth century, it was sparsely populated by Lenape and Nanticoke Indian tribes, most of whom withdrew from Delaware by the middle of the eighteenth century to avoid the increasing numbers of European settlers. Meanwhile, the Dutch had established the first European settlement, on what is now known as Lewes Creek, but all thirty-two settlers were soon killed by Indians.[3]

Swedes established the first permanent European settlement in 1638 in what is now the east side of the city of Wilmington, where its twenty-five colonists erected Fort Christina. At its height, New Sweden's residents probably numbered no more than one thousand. The Swedish colony was conquered in 1655 by a strong Dutch force, led by Peter Stuyvesant from New Amsterdam (New York). To secure labor, the Dutch began importing

African slaves and trading with the English in Maryland. Dutch-English rivalry in western Europe opened the way for English conquest of New Amsterdam in 1664. Delaware then was ruled from New York. In 1673–74, during the third Anglo-Dutch war, the Dutch briefly reconquered English possessions in the region. After the 1674 peace treaty ended the war, Delaware was among the lands restored to the English, who ruled Delaware through the next hundred years.

In 1682 the "Counties of New Castle, Kent and Sussex on the Delaware" became an appendage of Pennsylvania when William Penn, its proprietor, sought access to the ocean. These "Lower Counties" elected delegates that year to the Pennsylvania assembly, the beginning of representative government for them. However, the three counties later chose to discontinue their association with Pennsylvania, resulting in their formation in 1704 as a separate British colony, with their representatives meeting in the northern town of New Castle.

When King Charles II gave the grant of land named Pennsylvania to William Penn in 1681, he specified that its boundary would be twelve miles from New Castle, thereby creating the unusual circular boundary that eventually became the permanent line between the two future states of Delaware and Pennsylvania and allowing Delaware to claim the Delaware River to the low water mark of New Jersey—a boundary still being disputed (see chapter 3).

The Delaware counties had little significance in Britain's total imperial picture. It, along with Pennsylvania, was governed as proprietary colonies—as distinguished from royal colonies—with governors appointed by Penn's proprietors. The governor for colonial Delaware normally resided in Philadelphia. Although he could veto any bill passed by the Delaware assembly, he seldom did so, preferring to resolve differences by compromise. Moreover, Delaware's legislative measures, unlike Pennsylvania's legislation, did not have to be submitted to England for approval. Accordingly, colonial Delaware in these respects enjoyed almost as much self-government as did the colonies of Connecticut and Rhode Island, where governors were elected.[4]

Neighboring Maryland was ruled as a royal colony until 1715, when Lord Baltimore regained his colonial possessions. Boundary disputes between Maryland and the Lower Counties persisted for over a century, involving several agreements and surveys authorized first in 1685 by the English Privy Council, and later by the English court of chancery. The southern boundary of the Lower Counties was surveyed and marked in 1750–51, but the north-south border—later part of the Mason-Dixon Line—was not fixed as

Delaware's western boundary until after the 1763–68 surveys conducted by surveyors Charles Mason and Jeremiah Dixon, who had been brought over from England to settle the matter. Indeed, the long boundary dispute with Maryland was not finally settled until 1775, in time for Delawareans to be swept up with, and ultimately to join, other colonies in the American Revolution.

REVOLUTION, INDEPENDENCE, AND CONSTITUTIONALISM

Delawareans joined other colonists to protest British policies by sending delegates to the so-called Stamp Act Congress in New York in 1765 and later to the First and Second Continental Congresses of 1774 and 1775. Delaware supported measures to create the Continental Army commanded by George Washington, contributed arms and troops, and adopted on June 15, 1776, its resolution suspending all royal authority in Delaware. On July 2, 1776, in one of the best-known events in Delaware history, delegate Caesar Rodney hurried to Philadelphia to cast the Delaware delegation's decisive vote to join the other colonies in making a unanimous decision for independence, proclaimed July 4 by the Declaration of Independence.

In mid-July the Delaware assembly provided for the election of ten delegates from each of the three counties to draft a constitution that, when adopted by the convention on August 27, became not only Delaware's first state constitution but also the first state constitution in the United States framed by an elected constitutional convention. Major features of this constitution and Delaware's subsequent constitutions—of 1792, 1831, and 1897—are discussed in chapter 4.

In October 1777 British troops captured Wilmington and seized Delaware's president, while the British fleet sailed from the Chesapeake to the Delaware River. Thus, it was no longer safe for Delaware's assembly to continue meeting in nearby New Castle. Moreover, downstate assemblymen from Kent and Sussex Counties had chafed at the leading political role of New Castle County. Finally, Dover in Kent County near the center of the state became Delaware's permanent state capital in October 1781.

Although Delaware was next to the last state to ratify the Articles of Confederation, which merely provided a legal basis for the union of thirteen states, Delaware became by unanimous vote of its constitutional convention on December 7, 1787, the first state to ratify the United States Constitution. Delaware's designation as "the First State" remains a matter of considerable pride among Delawareans. The state's quick action was afforded by the lack of opposition to the constitution, primarily because little Delaware was assured equal status with larger states by the provision that gave each state two senators regardless of its population. Since 1823 it has been authorized to be represented by a total of only three members in the Congress—two in the Senate and one in the House.

Delaware remained a conservative tidewater state during most of the nineteenth century, somewhat isolated from the stress of evolving western migration, urbanization, and industrialization of other coastal states. Aside from a few British skirmishes off the Delaware coast, the War of 1812 did not disturb Delaware's tranquility.

During the first years of the new national Congress, two political parties gradually emerged in the United States: the Federalists and the Republicans. A similar division developed in Delaware, where the southern two counties, Kent and Sussex, supported the Federalists, while the greatest strength of the Republicans, later known as the Democratic-Republican Party, was in northern New Castle County, which included the nascent commercial area of Wilmington. Downstate versus upstate sectionalism within Delaware was to influence Delaware politics through the nineteenth and most of the twentieth century. One party would normally control Kent and Sussex Counties while the other party controlled New Castle County.

In the early 1820s the Democratic-Republicans won control of the Delaware legislature. The Federalists reestablished their control in 1823, continuing in power until 1827 when they split into two factions—one supporting Andrew Jackson and known as the Jacksonians (which soon became known as the Democratic Party), and the other supporting John Quincy Adams (known as the Whigs). In no other state had the Federalists lasted longer than in Delaware. Meanwhile, leaders of the Democratic-Republicans in Delaware also split on which candidate to support, Jackson or Adams, causing the two old parties to be replaced by new parties, as will be discussed in chapter 5.

According to the 1850 census, New Castle County had almost 47 percent of the total population of Delaware. During the next decade, Delaware's immigrant population, concentrated mostly in New Castle County, increased by 87 percent. Together with migration to Delaware from northern states, Delaware was developing a stronger socioeconomic connection to the North. As the Civil War approached, however, many prominent Delawareans remained sympathetic to the South. The average Delawarean remained strongly unionist, not because he favored abolition of slavery, but because he rejected secession. Perhaps most important was the fact that none of Delaware's surrounding states, even the border state of Maryland, opted for secession. Although some Delawareans offered their services to the Confederacy, the proportion of Delaware's total population that served in the Union Army was greater than that contributed by any other northern state.

The proslavery Democratic Party continued to be the majority and controlling party in Delaware until the 1890s, when Republicans replaced the Democrats as the dominant political party in the state.

TWENTIETH-CENTURY CHANGES

Delaware had changed dramatically since 1800. As the twentieth century dawned, downstate continued to be primarily agrarian, but fewer Delawareans made a living from farming than from manufacturing. Wilmington had become an industrialized city of 75,000 inhabitants, with over 40 percent of the state's population, while New Castle County as a whole contained almost 60 percent of the state's population. This concentration of population and financial power alarmed downstate Delawareans who were concerned about diminution of their political power.

With few exceptions Republicans, supported by African American voters, retained control of Delaware until 1936, when amid the Great Depression the state elected its first national Democratic ticket since 1912 and its first Democratic governor since 1897. After 1936 there was a fairly equal sharing of political power by the two parties. First one party and then the other party dominated the state's political life. Meanwhile, party politics increasingly replaced personalistic politics.

Perhaps the most salient twentieth century themes impacting the state's political development were the emergence of a diversified, greatly expanded population and a drastically changing economy. These two important themes merit closer examination in this introductory chapter.

DIVERSIFYING POPULATION

According to the 2000 census, Delaware's total population had reached 783,600, a substantial increase of 117,432, or about 17.6 percent, over the 1990 census, the highest percentage increase in its region and fourth highest among states east of the Mississippi River. Delaware was ranked in 2004 as the eighth fastest-growing state in the nation with a population of 843,524—an increase of nearly 60,000 in four years. The state's total population in 2007, according to the U.S. Census Bureau, was 864,764,

1. Delaware Population by County, 1790–2030

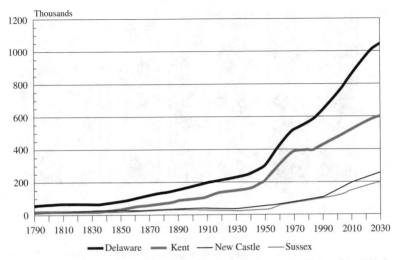

Thousands

Source: Center for Applied Demography & Survey Research, University of Delaware. Delaware Population Consortium, October 2007.

a further increase of 81,164 or 10.4 percent since the year 2000. But even such growth was not enough for Delaware to gain a second seat in the U.S. House of Representatives. Delaware's 2000 population density (persons per square mile) was 401.1, the seventh highest among the states, up from 340.8 in 1990.[5]

New Castle County had a population of 528,218 in 2007, or 61 percent of the state's population. Delaware's largest city, Wilmington, had a 2007 population of 72,868, well down from its 1940 peak of 112,504. The 2007 population of Newark, the third largest city, was 29,992. These politically significant figures meant then that almost half of the state's population lived in suburban New Castle County outside the cities of Wilmington and Newark.

On the other hand, New Castle County's prominence was somewhat mitigated by the fact that the population growth rate of Sussex County was almost three times that of New Castle County during the 1990s. Sussex emerged as the fastest growing county, adding 43,409—a whopping increase of 38.3 percent since 1990, reaching a total of 156,638 in 2000. Its 2007 population was recorded as 184,291—an increase of nearly 28,000 in only seven years. Retirees accounted for a large part of the increase, attracted by the combination of low property taxes, no sales tax, large pension exclusions from state income taxes, a relatively low cost of living, and proximity to beach resorts—a combination with which neighboring states could not compete. The greatest boom was in the beach area of eastern Sussex County, which attracted many upper

2. Delaware Race Distribution, 1950–2030

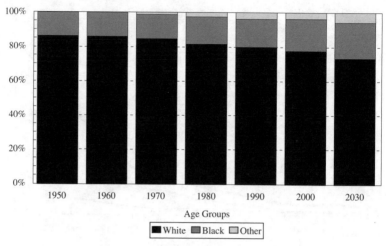

Age Groups

■ White ■ Black □ Other

Source: Center for Applied Demography & Survey Research, University of Delaware. Delaware Population Consortium, October 2007.

income residents, including retirees. Meanwhile, the 2000 census showed that Kent County had added 15,704, or an increase of 14.1 percent since 1990, for a total of 126,697, compared with New Castle County's increase of only 13.2 percent. Kent County's 2007 population showed a continuing increase to 152,255. The faster growth rates of the southern two counties, portending political change, are discussed in subsequent chapters.

According to the 2000 census, whites represented 76 percent of Delaware's population, while the black or African American population was 20 percent. ("African Americans" and "blacks" are used interchangeably in this book.) Most black Delawareans (105,052, 67 percent of the state's total black population of 157,152) lived in New Castle County. Forty percent of African Americans lived in Wilmington—41,976, or 58 percent of Wilmington's total population.

Asians composed the third largest (18,944) and fastest growing 2000 census group in Delaware (up from 9,067, an increase of 109 percent since 1990). They represented 2.4 percent of the state's population in 2000. Asians were more affluent than Delaware's general population. Their median household income was $65,190, rising 57 percent from the 1990 census, compared with $47,381 for the state as a whole, a rise of 36 percent. Median household incomes among other groups were: whites, $50,496 (up 38 percent); blacks, $35,517 (up 46 percent); and Hispanics, $36,290 (up 29 percent).

Delaware's American Indian population was 2,731 or 0.3 percent of the state's population according to the 1990 census. Nanticokes, estimated to be over 700, far outnumbered other Delaware tribes, including Cherokee, Delaware, Blackfoot, Iroquois, and others.

The largest ethnic group, according to the 2000 census, comprised Hispanics, a total of 37,277, or 4.8 percent of Delaware's population (compared with 2.3 percent, counted by the 1990 census).

Although most Hispanics lived in New Castle County (26,293, or 5.3 percent of the County's population in 2000), the Hispanic population of Sussex County was 6,915, or 4.4 percent of Sussex's population. These immigrants were attracted by plentiful jobs in the poultry industry, construction, and tourism.

Delaware's minority population in 2000 made up about one-fourth of the state's population. Minorities accounted for more than 31 percent of Delaware's population in 2007, attributed to a 50.1 percent increase in the state's Hispanic population since 2000, together with a 45 percent jump in its Asian population and a 18 percent in its black population. There were proportionately more non-Hispanic blacks, many more Hispanics as a whole, and more than twice as many non-Hispanic Asians as there were in 1990, making Delaware one of the more diverse states in the Northeast.

In 2000 there were 63,262 Delawareans over the age of five who spoke a language other than English at home (up 46 percent since 1990); this was 8.1 percent of the state's population.

Other interesting 2000 census statistics helped characterize Delaware's diversifying population. "Atomization"—the breaking of the population into smaller units—continued a trend in Delaware and the nation. In 2000, 74,639 Delaware householders lived alone (an increase of 29 percent over 1990), 27,071 of whom were sixty-five years and older. Of a total of 204,590 family households, 38,986 were headed by single women (a rise of 34 percent). The size of the average Delaware "household," moreover, continued to fall from 3.4 in 1950, to 2.63 in 1990, and to 2.54 in 2000.

Finally, the 2000 census showed that Delaware was aging. There were 133,925 persons aged sixty and older living in Delaware, or 17 percent of the state's population; this was an increase of 23,287, or 21 percent, from 1990. According to the Delaware Population Consortium, 52 percent of the projected 250,000 growth of Delaware's population between 2000 and 2030 will occur among the state's senior citizen population.

CHANGING ECONOMY

Farming had been the heartbeat of Delaware's nineteenth-century economy, as it was in the rest of the United States. Significant increases in agricultural

3. Acres of Delaware Farmland, 1920–2027

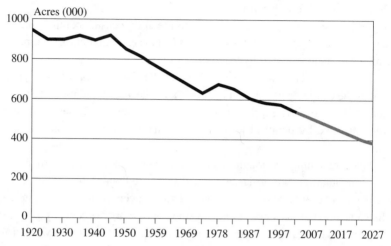

Acres (000)

Source: Center for Applied Demography & Survey Research, University of Delaware. U.S. Bureau of Census, Census of Agriculture.

productivity through the twentieth century, however, allowed people to leave the farms for other more valuable jobs.

In the early 1900s T. Coleman du Pont, then president of the DuPont Company, built a concrete divided highway the length of the state with his own money, which presaged a revolution in agricultural production in southern Delaware by enabling farmers to transport their products to distant urban centers. Within a few years Sussex County became the largest poultry-producing county in the nation, a position it still held in 2002. More and more land was cleared to produce corn and soybeans to feed broiler chickens.[6]

Agriculture was to continue to constitute a major part of Delaware's economy into the twenty-first century. The chicken industry alone in 2002 produced nearly 1.5 billion pounds of broilers, constituting 80 to 90 percent of Delaware's total agricultural production. Forty-six percent of the state's land area (580,000 acres) was being used in 2002 to produce poultry and other products.[7]

But this was only one side of the story of Delaware agriculture. Much of Delaware's best farmland has been taken over by housing, commercial development, and industrial parks (see chapter 12). Farmland decreased nearly 40 percent after 1950, while net farm income plummeted by 45 percent.

As many farms became economically unviable, their owners were more than willing to sell to developers at the price of residential land. Residential home construction became the most prevalent and profitable use of the land.

By the end of the twentieth century, agriculture represented only 1.5 percent of the state's total GSP and less than 1 percent of employment in Delaware.[8]

Until the 1970s, manufacturing dominated Delaware's economy. Manufacturing had gained some importance even in colonial Delaware when shipbuilding, tanning, iron making, and milling were enterprises in Wilmington and its vicinity. In the early 1800s the new nation—freed from colonial restraints—experienced the so-called Industrial Revolution, which introduced water-powered factories and mills in northern New Castle County that manufactured gunpowder, textiles, paper, and iron manufactures.

Most significant in consequences was E. I. du Pont's 1802 establishment of a powder works plant on the Brandywine River north of Wilmington. By 1995 the DuPont Company had become a diversified global corporation. DuPont began to cut 40,000 employees worldwide and shed various businesses in 1989, which dropped its employment numbers 27 percent to about 100,000 employees worldwide in the late 1990s including about 15,000 in Delaware, a number that fell further to about 8,200 in 2005.[9] Among other prominent chemical companies in Delaware in the late 1990s were the faltering Hercules Company (which merged with the Ashland Company in 2008) and the expanding British-based AstraZeneca.

After chemicals, prominent manufacturing enterprises in Delaware were transportation equipment, primarily Daimler-Chrysler and General Motors automobile assembly plants in New Castle County (the former announced in 2007 that in 2009 it would idle its Newark plant, which had numbered 1,200 employees in 2007); food production; scientific instruments; plastics; printing; and publishing.

In the midst of the nation's economic recession in the early 2000s, Delaware manufacturers continued to shed jobs at a rapid rate. In 1951 manufacturing accounted for nearly 44 percent of the state's total jobs, a proportion that fell to 13 percent in 2001, a pattern that has been repeated across the United States and even across the world.[10] Manufacturing jobs declined as technology and worker productivity accelerated.

Although Delaware's manufacturing employment has continued to diminish, manufacturing output continues to increase—it has become more efficient and productive, remaining a dominant sector in terms of wages and contribution to the state's economic output. Delaware's export sales of merchandise in 2000 totaled $5.9 billion, up 22 percent from 1999 and well above the 12.6 percent rise in total U.S. exports over the same period. In 2000 Delaware recorded export sales of $7,514 for every person residing in the state, the highest per capita export value of any state and 52 percent above the 1993 per capita value of $4,942. Chemical products remained the

4. Delaware Employment by Sector, 1939–2007

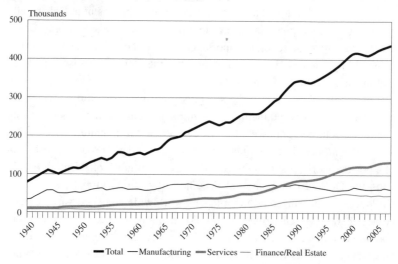

Source: Center for Applied Demography & Survey Research, University of Delaware.

state's leading export category, accounting for $4.5 billion, or more than three-quarters of Delaware's total exports in 2000. Other significant exports were plastic and rubber products, machinery, fabric mill products, paper products, and computers and electronic products.[11]

Delaware's economy since the early 1950s, along with the nation as a whole, experienced a major structural shift from "goods-producing" industries (e.g., agriculture, manufacturing, and construction) to services (e.g., financial, professional, and business services). Just as manufacturing surpassed agriculture as Delaware's foremost economic sector toward the end of the nineteenth century, services surpassed manufacturing toward the end of the twentieth century.

In fact, many jobs in manufacturing simply transferred to the services sector as Delaware companies subcontracted data processing, human resources, and other functions in order to focus on their core businesses. One of the fastest growing sectors in Delaware's economy is business and professional services.

As will be discussed in subsequent chapters, Delaware's economy received a major boost in the early 1980s through a rapid expansion of the financial services sector. Following the passage of Delaware's Financial Center Development Act in 1981, many major banks relocated their credit card operations to Delaware in reaction to the extremely high interest rates coupled with caps existing in other states.

Another shift in the economy appeared to be emerging as the twenty-first century was underway when, in late 2004, a national business magazine rated Delaware as the top state in biotechnology resources, featuring the five-year-old Delaware Biotechnology Institute next to the University of Delaware—a partnership among government, academia, and industry to promote Delaware as a home for biotechnology.[12]

CONCLUSION

The foregoing overview of less than four centuries establishes that Delaware has developed from a sparsely populated, agrarian, and relatively insignificant polity to a densely and diversely populated, agrarian, and financial and legal center, and a commercial hub of America's eastern seaboard. It also establishes that from its tranquil inception to its bustling present, Delaware has experienced marked differences between its concentration of population, commerce, and wealth north of the canal and the less-favored, but rapidly changing, area south of the canal.

These various characteristics have affected and defined Delaware's political culture and development, to which we now turn.

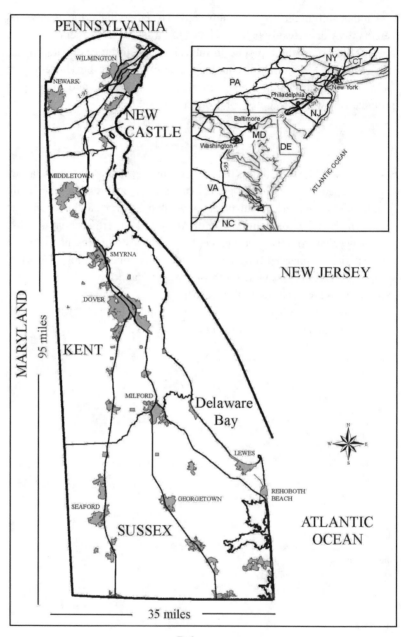

Delaware

CHAPTER TWO

Political Culture of the "First State"

Every state develops a "political culture" that consists of its norms and symbols of political engagement. This culture is generally defined as the orientations and expectations of politicians and the general public about the purpose and conduct of government. Political culture, then, is a concept that includes a polity's character and how people choose to govern themselves.[1]

Delaware has a political culture that has been shaped by its colonial roots, the evolution of the state's economy, competition with other states, and the personal nature of politics in a small state. Even globalization has affected the nature of politics in Delaware over the past quarter of a century. That culture is still evolving today, as these dimensions change over time.

Daniel Elazar's pathbreaking study of political culture in the United States provides the conceptual underpinning of this book.[2] His study helps us achieve a penetrating understanding of Delaware's political culture as a thematic context for our analysis of Delaware's politics and government.

ELAZAR'S THREE POLITICAL CULTURES

According to Elazar, the general political culture of the United States as a whole is rooted in two shared but contrasting, and sometimes conflicting, conceptions of the American political order. On the one hand, the political order may be conceived as a "marketplace" in which basic political engagements derive from bargaining among groups and individuals who act from self-interest. On the other hand, the political order may be conceived as a "commonwealth" in which people cooperate to have the best government based on their moral principles or values.

Elazar proceeds to distinguish the fifty states of the nation in terms of three descriptive political subcultures he labeled as *moralistic, traditionalistic,* and *individualistic*. Although Elazar represents these political cultures as ideal types, they can explain much of the variations in the politics and governments among different American states. These cultures exist together in the United States, side-by-side or overlapping in some states, while each is strongly tied to specific states and sections of the country.

The *moralistic political culture* emphasizes the commonwealth conception of democratic government, in which people and politicians perceive politics and government as advancing the public interest and placing moral obligations on citizens, public service, and the marketplace. Public participation and public service are core values. Politics is not considered a proper realm for private economic gain, and there is little tolerance of government corruption. At the same time, the moralistic political culture is strongly committed to active government intervention in the economic and social life of the community. Examples of states strongly tied to a moralistic political culture are Maine, Vermont, Michigan, Wisconsin, Minnesota, North Dakota, Utah, Colorado, and Oregon.

The *traditionalistic political culture* emphasizes a paternalistic, elitist and hierarchical conception of the commonwealth, in which government acts positively but is limited primarily to continuing the maintenance of a social order that places family ties or social position above personal ties. Those at the top of the social structure try to dominate politics and government. Traditionalistic political culture acts to confine real political power to a relatively small and self-perpetuating group drawn from an established elite that inherits the right to govern through family ties or social position. Other citizens are not expected to be active, or participate, even minimally in politics. States strongly tied to a traditionalistic political culture include Virginia, Tennessee, South Carolina, Georgia, Alabama, Mississippi, Louisiana, and Arkansas.

Of fundamental interest to us here is the fact that Elazar places Delaware squarely within the *individualistic political culture*. The individualistic political culture, according to Elazar, emphasizes the conception of the democratic order as a "marketplace." Political life within an individualistic political culture is based on a system of mutual obligations rooted in personal relationships, which can be direct in simple societies but are usually too complex to maintain face-to-face ties. Mutual obligations are harnessed through political parties that are competitive but not overly so. Politicians pursue office as a means of controlling the actions of government in terms of both programs and regulation. Public participation in the political system is indirect, and deciding issues by referendum is rare or nonexistent. Since the individualistic political culture eschews ideological considerations, both citizens and politicians look upon political activity as mainly the province of professional politicians to whom the public has delegated their authority and responsibility. Besides Delaware, examples of other states strongly tied to an individualistic political culture are New Jersey, Maryland, Pennsylvania, Ohio, Indiana, Illinois, and Nevada.

Elazar draws a number of observations from his analysis, some of which appear important for our study of Delaware. He considers twenty-five, or fully half of the fifty states, including Delaware, as strongly tied to one or the other of the three political cultures. The other twenty-five states are characterized by a dominance of a synthesis or an amalgam of more than one political culture. For example, New York is dominated by an amalgam of both individualistic and moralistic political cultures, with the individualistic culture more prominent; California conversely is dominated by moralistic and individualistic political cultures, but the moralistic culture is more prominent; and North Carolina is dominated by traditionalistic and moralistic political cultures, with the traditionalistic culture dominating.

Elazar observes that, in general, the states of the far North, Northwest, and Pacific Coast are dominated by a moralistic political culture; the states of the greater South are dominated by the traditionalistic political culture; and the states stretching across the middle sections of the country in a southwesterly direction are dominated by the individualistic political culture. Migration and other population changes, according to Elazar, help explain cultural differences among the states. It follows, moreover, that the dominance within a state of one or another political culture, or an amalgam of political cultures, may change over time.[3]

THE CHEMICAL CAPITAL OF THE WORLD

During the first half of the last century, Delaware's political culture could be characterized—to use Elazar's distinction—as an amalgam of traditionalistic and individualistic political cultures, with the traditionalistic culture the more influential. From an early gunpowder enterprise on the Brandywine River, the du Ponts had built a statewide and worldwide chemical conglomerate.

Led by the DuPont Company, the chemical industry became the economic backbone of Delaware. While some manufacturing facilities were located in Delaware, their corporate headquarters and research divisions were their prized assets.

The DuPont Company, affectionately known as "Uncle Dupie," never employed more than 10 percent of Delaware's workforce, yet its jobs were well paid with excellent benefits (and nonunion). Many Delawareans spent their entire careers with DuPont. The company was the state's largest employer, a major taxpayer and economic force. It was also a major political force directly and indirectly through the du Pont family. Pierre S. du Pont IV became governor in 1976 and served two terms. The company also encouraged its employees to run for political office (successfully) and to serve on boards and commissions. The du Pont family built schools, hospitals, colleges, roads, newspapers, banks, and parklands, and they created a host of charities. Taken together, the company and family had enormous influence on the economic and political development of Delaware. The family and company were largely responsible for forming an amalgam of traditionalistic and individualistic political cultures in the state.

In the 1980s, as global competition increased, the DuPont Company itself became a major global corporation, with its sales abroad surpassing sales within the United States. It began to refocus on its core businesses, to downsize, and to take a much less active role in the state's political life, a behavior at the time that was not limited to Delaware's chemical companies but also affected the entire business sector. These shifts moved Delaware away from its traditionalistic vestiges toward a more exclusively pluralistic and individualistic political culture.[4]

THE CORPORATE LAW CAPITAL OF THE WORLD

As the chemical industry grew and then retreated, corporate influence expanded and flourished in Delaware. More than 846,000 entities were incorporated in Delaware by the end of 2007, including 61 percent of the Fortune 500 firms, and over half of the publicly traded companies listed on the New York Stock Exchange.[5] Any enterprise incorporated in Delaware must maintain a corporate office, or have a designated agent, within Delaware.[6]

Delaware's position as the nation's center of corporate law is attributable in part to article 9 of Delaware's 1897 constitution, which abolished incorporation by special act of the state legislature and authorized, by a two-thirds vote of each house, incorporation by a general corporation law of uniform application. Before then, Delaware's legislature had been inordinately engaged in time-consuming granting of corporate franchises secured by "wildcat" lobbyists for fees paid by their clients. Thus, in 1897, the legislature enacted a total of 115 special acts of incorporation. Under article 9, however, the legislature established in 1899, and again in 1967, a comprehensive general corporation law that contributed to Delaware becoming the nation's preeminent center of incorporation.

Accordingly, the General Corporation Law—together with the constitutional foundation that authorizes that law and mandates that it may only be changed by an extraordinary two-thirds vote of the legislature—helps to foster Delaware's reputation as the nation's leading corporate law center.[7]

There are a number of reasons why Delaware is the foremost choice of corporate America. One is that there is no minimum capital requirement for a Delaware corporation. One may form a Delaware corporation by mail, online, or by phone, and may never even visit the state, even to conduct annual meetings. Such meetings may be held anywhere or not at all should stockholders, directors, or committee members act by unanimous consent. Indeed, one person may hold the offices of corporation president, treasurer, and secretary and be the corporation's sole director, in which case the director may hold meetings alone. One person may even operate anonymously as the sole owner of a Delaware corporation, and choose any name for it. Directors, moreover, have the power to make or alter all bylaws. Delaware corporations may pay dividends from profits as well as from surplus and may conduct any legal business activities.

Another major reason why Delaware corporate law has become a national model, accounting for so many corporations incorporating in Delaware, is the existence of a specialized equity court that focuses on business matters. The Court of Chancery operates without jury trials and is separate from the law courts (see also chapter 8). Because there are no juries, decisions are issued as written opinions, thus evolving a body of corporate law enabling precedents that serve as legal guides for business decisions and behavior.

The Delaware Court of Chancery was created by Delaware's first constitution, the Constitution of 1792. Once the General Corporation Law was enacted in 1899, the Court of Chancery, with only one judge, the chancellor, began hearing cases arising under it, and as a result it developed over time a special expertise in corporate law. Meanwhile, as that court attained national prominence in corporate litigation during the twentieth century, it became necessary for the legislature to authorize its single chancellor to appoint a vice-chancellor. However, the court's workload continued to increase, and in 1949 a constitutional amendment was adopted authorizing further expansion. The court now has one chancellor and four vice-chancellors.[8]

Approximately 80 percent of the Chancery Court's caseload deals with corporate matters, often involving battles of the nation's business giants. The Chancery Court draws on the nation's most highly developed body of corporate law in making its decisions. The court's long-standing national reputation is built largely on its clearly rendered, prompt, and definitive resolutions of corporate disputes. Corporate leaders are comfortable with

Delaware's Chancery Court and its court of appeals—the Delaware Supreme Court—because of the assurance that their business transactions will be judged on established precedent. Most American corporate attorneys have studied Delaware corporate law as law students.[9]

Delaware's image as the nation's corporate law mecca is also enhanced by its reputation as the state having a liability system most protective of business owners from class action litigation. A 2007 U.S. Chamber of Commerce poll of twelve hundred senior attorneys at companies with annual revenues of at least $100 million were asked to rank all fifty states' liability environments affecting important decisions such as where to locate or do business. Delaware was ranked the highest, a ranking it retained in 2008. Moreover, in 2008 Forbes ranked Delaware the third best in the United States for business costs and eleventh overall for business environment. New York and California were ranked at the bottom of the list for business costs.[10]

All corporations incorporated in Delaware pay an annual corporate franchise tax for the privilege of being incorporated in Delaware, ranging from $75 to $165,000.[11] All 293,000 incorporated business entities in Delaware, classified by the Internal Revenue Service as "C" corporations and "S" corporations, must pay the tax, while 563,000 limited partnerships and limited liability companies pay a flat fee of $250. Together they all account for about one-fifth of Delaware's annual state revenue. Because almost all of these businesses impose little or no cost on the state, this revenue allows Delaware to forego a sales tax, thus greatly benefiting the average Delawarean.

In addition, by agreement among the major incorporation capitals in the nation, Delaware is able to claim "abandoned property" held by any business if that business can no longer identify its true owner and in particular the address of that person. By default, the property is claimed by the state in which the business is incorporated. While only a small fraction of abandoned property in the country qualifies under the agreement, so many firms are incorporated in Delaware that abandoned property generates more than 10 percent of Delaware's state government revenue.

LOOKING FOR AN EDGE

In 1977 Delaware's top personal income tax bracket of 19.8 percent for those earning over $100,000 per year was the nation's highest. It was raised to that level during the economic crises of the early 1970s in order to balance the state's budget. At the same time, the corporate income tax was increased to 8.7 percent (sixteenth in the nation).

The 19.8 percent rate was clearly an obstacle for executives wishing to move their companies to Delaware. To address this problem, ten successive tax cuts reduced the tax by the year 2000 to 5.95 percent (twenty-second in the nation) for those earning over $60,000 (see chapter 10).[12] In general, contemporary Delaware tends toward the middle of the states in tax policy, avoiding any negative impact on the state's economy or affecting its growth.

In the early 1980s, with interest rates exploding along with inflation, many credit card issuers were confronted with state caps on interest rates that were implemented in very different times and circumstances. The state of Delaware was presented with an opportunity to gain an edge on those states unwilling to change their interest rate caps. Members of Delaware's corporate legal community were contacted by "money center" banks asking for assistance. This was an unprecedented opportunity to diversify the Delaware economy, create new jobs, and add to tax revenues. With the collaboration of corporate law centers and Delaware's state government, the state's Financial Center Development Act (FCDA) of 1981 was quickly drafted and passed.

Delaware's FCDA deregulated Delaware laws governing bank-issued credit cards. The law granted out-of-state banks a wide range of credit powers that came to affect millions of credit card customers. It gave banks the ability to charge unlimited fees for credit card usage, to foreclose on homes of credit card debtors in case of their default, to charge variable interest rates without any legal ceiling whatever, and to raise interest rates retroactively. According to Professor Elizabeth Warren, who taught contract law at Harvard Law School, the credit card business is "the only business in the world that can change its price after you make a purchase."[13]

One impediment in attracting the credit card banks to Delaware was the bank franchise tax, which was levied at the same rate as the corporate income tax, at 8.7 percent. In order to recognize the large income streams of these new banks, a new series of brackets were introduced so that lower rates were experienced as income levels rose. The FCDA, as amended, reduces the tax rate on a sliding from 8.7 percent for banks with incomes not in excess of $20 million to as low as 1.7 percent on incomes in excess of $650 million. This tax is in lieu of the corporate income tax and the corporate franchise tax.

Changes wrought by FCDA were to prove as important historically for Delaware's economy as Delaware's Chancery Court, the general corporation laws, and even the influence of the DuPont Company itself. In 2004, most of the nation's largest banks owned Delaware operations, including eight of the nation's ten largest credit card issuers, such as MBNA, Bank of America, Discover, Citigroup, and JPMorgan Chase.

Foremost was the very profitable MBNA Corporation, a Maryland transplant in 1982 that was to have a meteoric rise. MBNA became the nation's second largest issuer of credit cards and the state's largest private sector employer, surpassing DuPont in 2001. MBNA grew over 70 percent, from 3,000 Delaware employees in 1991 to 10,300 in 2004, while DuPont cut its ranks 60 percent in Delaware, from 25,000 to 9,900. Announcement of the sale of MBNA to Bank of America (BofA) for $35 billion in July 2005 fueled fears of substantial Delaware job losses. However, BofA eliminated only 794 employees, or 7 percent, from MBNA's then total of 11,002 employees in the first three months after BofA completed its buyout January 1, 2006. More than 1,000 MBNA employees opted for early retirement when executives were preparing the company for sale. The total job loss in Delaware connected with the buyout was approximately 4,500.

By the end of the twentieth century, more than thirty out-of-state banks had brought their credit card subsidiaries to Wilmington. Considering that, according to a 2003 survey, American households kept an average of six credit cards, carrying a total average balance of $9,205—up 210 percent since 1990—the future of banking as Delaware's leading economic sector appeared secure.[14]

Meanwhile, the state's banking industry overall had grown over nine times from a pre-FCDA level of approximately 4,600 employees to roughly 43,000 employees by the turn of the century, totaling about one-tenth of all Delaware employees. In 1980 the state government collected about $2.5 million from the bank franchise tax that yielded more than $175 million by the year 2007—over 5 percent of all state government revenue, compared with about 16 percent revenue yielded by the corporate franchise tax.

During the first few years of the twenty-first century, Delaware's financial services industry experienced some related threats to its continuing leadership, including a national economic recession and aggressive competition among the states. If the past was any guide, however, Delaware's pro-business political culture—notably its unique partnership of business and government—promised to maintain Delaware's position of leadership in financial services.[15]

On the heels of enacting the FCDA, Delaware again tried to gain an edge by broadening its corporate income tax exemption to include "investment holding companies."[16] Such holding companies (i.e., companies that own and control parts or all of other companies) exist only on paper to hold "passive" or "intangible investments"—such as stocks and bonds, patents, and royalty, trademark, or franchise agreements, and the income they generate—which in turn allows them to be exempt from paying any state income tax in Delaware or elsewhere. To qualify for using this Delaware tax "shelter," investment holding companies must be physically located in the state, which means in practice that thousands of company "offices" are located within the slim office towers of Wilmington law firms and banks whose staffs serve as their agents to comply with Delaware law.

By 2004, however, twelve other states had passed laws aimed at Delaware holding companies that were considered "sham" or "shell" corporations whose only purpose is tax evasion. But Delaware retaliated by passing a 2004 law aimed to shield businesses from taxes in other states, whereby so-called headquarters management corporations (HMCs)—unlike investment holding companies—would be required to add jobs or increase spending on services provided by Delaware bankers, lawyers, and accountants. Ostensibly, the new law would thereby benefit Delaware's economy while bolstering companies' arguments for tax exemption in other states. New Jersey Attorney Richard Voll agreed it would be difficult for other states to dispute the legitimacy of HMCs were they to "beef up" their Delaware presence by adding jobs. "You can't get credit because you have a piece of paper in a lawyer's desk," Voll said. "You have to earn it."[17]

Corporate lawmaking in Delaware is the product of a unique partnership of the legal profession and state government. The Council of the Corporation Law Section of the Delaware State Bar Association annually considers drafts of legislation to improve Delaware corporate law proposed by lawyers from influential national and local corporations. In this sense, Delaware permits corporations to write and propose their own legislation, which is continually being considered or debated within the bar association. Corporate authors, both within and outside the state, constantly attempt to hone Delaware laws to give Delaware an edge.

Citizens of the state generally approve of the way business is handled, which is hardly surprising given the longtime stability of the state's economy and the focus on new jobs. A 2001 survey of Delawareans' attitudes toward economic growth revealed that more than 53 percent of respondents statewide who expressed an opinion, felt that government overregulated business—reflecting the probusiness mindset prevailing among Delawareans.[18]

In the same survey, residents of the two lower counties, Kent and Sussex, were significantly more in agreement with the statement that government plays too large a role in regulating business. While these counties have lower incomes, their political culture is even more conservative or individualistic than the more traditional and wealthier New Castle County. Both of the lower counties are growing faster than New Castle County, which may have an impact on the political culture of the state as it continues to evolve.

CONCLUSION

The foregoing analysis unambiguously supports Elazar's inclusion of Delaware within that group of states having an individualistic political culture, because those states draw most heavily on individual values whereby any and all government activity is widely scrutinized. Calls for government action must compete in the "marketplace of ideas" with those desiring no action or alternative approaches. Residents of Delaware and their elected representatives will carefully consider each proposal and its effect on the economy. This is not to say that governmental action that regulates business will always fail. Our subsequent analysis attests the following: the Coastal Zone Act that bars industrial development since the 1970s remains unchanged even today; Delaware, moreover, is the first state to completely ban smoking in public places. Yet Delaware has struggled with helmet laws, strict land-use planning, and laws forbidding discrimination against gays.

Delaware may rightfully claim to be the "corporation capital of the world," because far more companies choose to incorporate in Delaware than elsewhere. There are many reasons for this phenomenon, but no other state can match Delaware in these respects.

What are the challenges for Delaware politics and government? How do the prominence of business and the corporate legal community in Delaware affect government behavior and public policy? What role does north-south sectionalism play in Delaware politics? Remaining chapters help to address these questions.

What we have observed thus far suggests that the political culture in Delaware has evolved from the strong influence in public affairs of the DuPont Company and du Pont family to a diversified, pluralistic, corporate infrastructure that has helped forge a complex economic growth model permeating major public policies in the state. In practical terms, that model infers that creating jobs and keeping the business community and their employees happy will occupy a priority position on the state's public agenda. The business community can generally expect that its concerns, especially as expressed by the corporate legal community, will have weight in public affairs.

CHAPTER THREE

Delaware in the Federal System

The fact that Delaware is the "corporation capital of the world" where more companies have incorporated than anywhere else means that Delaware's business-friendly political culture has been achieved by its successful rivalry with the other forty-nine states to become the nation's preferred corporate home. John Kincaid's study of "competitive federalism" calls such interstate competition "inter-jurisdictional (or horizontal) competition," as distinguished from "intergovernmental (or vertical) competition" that entails competition between the U.S. national government and the state governments.[1]

In this chapter, we analyze Delaware in terms of both interjurisdictional and intergovernmental aspects of competitive federalism and in terms of what may be considered coercive federalism and cooperative federalism. First, we address Delaware's competition with other states in terms of economic development, namely for business firms and tourism. Second, we address Delaware's congressional delegation and especially efforts by some of its members to place themselves and their small state in the national limelight. Third we consider intergovernmental or vertical impacts on Delaware of coercive or regulatory federalism. Fourth, we assess how Delaware engages in cooperative federalism with other states, especially by participating in various associations of state governments and local governments and in interstate compacts and agreements. Fifth, we discuss Delaware's activities in the international arena. And finally, we assess how pervasive is federalism in Delaware, especially in the governance and politics of the state, and how intergovernmental much of Delaware state policy was becoming in the early years of the twenty-first century.

COMPETING WITH OTHER STATES

Delaware attempts to compete with other states in three primary ways: developing an educated and productive workforce, creating a good quality of life, and providing a stable and well-understood business environment. For example, Delaware was able to gain a jump on neighboring Pennsylvania and Maryland by introducing the "video lottery" at its race tracks in the 1990s, attracting many visitors (60 percent of gamblers in Delaware were from other states) who contributed significantly to the development of its economy. By broadly interpreting its constitution, which specifically forbids slot machines but permits lotteries, Delaware reaped a bonanza from video lottery revenue, receiving, for example, $218.8 million in video lottery revenue for fiscal 2007. Pennsylvania passed slots-at-the-tracks legislation in 2004, which had an adverse impact on Delaware in 2007. Maryland, meanwhile, has considered similar legislation and has scheduled a referendum for November 2008. Accordingly, when or if slots become operational in both states, Delaware could initially lose an estimated two-thirds of its slots revenue.[2] Ironically, Delaware's Clean Indoor Air Act of 2002, discussed in chapter 11, which was opposed by the casinos, might be a selling point for attracting nonsmokers to Delaware casinos.

Until recently Delaware has been successful in attracting business—a signal achievement given its diminutive size. Located in the Executive Department of Delaware's state government is the Delaware Economic Development Office (DEDO), which leads the state's efforts in business development and tourism promotion "by enhancing the quality of life and facilitating the retention of and creation of quality jobs." DEDO focuses on recruiting new firms to the state and keeping existing businesses from being pursued by other states.

When it comes to attracting and keeping business, however, smallness has disadvantages. For one thing, there is a smaller labor force, land area, and other infrastructure-supporting resources for business (e.g., energy, water, and transportation) and hence fewer options for location of new business sites. Moreover, larger states (e.g., Texas and New York) have more monetary incentives to offer businesses seeking new locations and hence more government agencies and personnel devoted to serving the interests of existing and prospective businesses. Delaware governor Ruth Ann Minner's $3.1 billion fiscal year 2008 budget allocated only $4.6 million for DEDO. However, DEDO also administers the so-called Delaware Strategic Fund established by the state's General Assembly to help Delaware "to compete for new and existing businesses."[3] A total of $12 million was budgeted for the fund in fiscal year 2008.

How does Delaware overcome disadvantages of its smallness? The previous discussion of Delaware's business-friendly political culture goes far in answering this question. Delaware's smallness facilitates its ability to act faster than other states. In a small state, even small businesses can make a difference. Delaware can focus on attracting and supporting small firms that are in fast-growing industries. Moreover, Delaware's Chancery Court and large body of corporate law favorable to management account for a large number of Delaware attorneys who specialize in working with these laws. Delaware's nationally prominent corporate law firms, concentrated in Wilmington, exert great political weight within the nation and this small state. State legislators and business representatives have formed an ongoing two-way bipartisan cooperative relationship in Delaware that may not easily exist in larger and more populous states where larger government bureaucracies and more partisan politics hinder consensus building. It is this characteristic that moved Celia Cohen to entitle her 2002 book on Delaware politics *Only in Delaware*.[4]

Delaware is so small that most business and government actors know each other personally. Delaware's smallness facilitates the mobilization of all-important political actors, including Delaware's congressional delegation, to address business interests and to make timely decisions. All of those most concerned with a particular issue typically may gather together formally or informally within the confines of a single corporate office or conference room or a state government committee room to reach decisions quickly, if necessary, and these gatherings are rarely secretive. With the assistance of DEDO, even the governor may become pivotally and personally involved with local and out-of-state corporate leaders in such a setting, as did Republican Pete du Pont in the formulation of the landmark Financial Center Development Act of 1981 that successfully competed for credit-card banking, and as Democratic governor Tom Carper did in devising an incentive package in 1998 to attract a major foreign-owned drug company—AstraZeneca Corporation—to locate in northern New Castle County instead of southeastern Pennsylvania. Delaware gained potentially four thousand new high-paying AstraZeneca jobs.[5]

Another factor favoring Delaware in competing for business with other states is Delaware's unique location, situated halfway between the nation's financial center in New York and its regulatory center in Washington, a two-hour train ride in either direction for Delaware entrepreneurs.

Overall, how well does Delaware compete with other states for new and existing businesses? Democratic governor Ruth Ann Minner claimed in October 2003 that Delaware had not suffered from the economic recession then afflicting the country "as drastically as other states." She pointed to Delaware's unemployment rate of 4.6 percent as being lower than the nation's 6.1 percent, and "the creation and retention of 6,100 jobs" since January 2002. She also noted that Delaware was ranked first among the states in the Beacon Hill Institute's Competitive Index. Noting that in any given year nationwide there were eleven thousand economic development organizations chasing fewer than a thousand businesses, Governor Minner cautioned that Delaware should not be complacent. Rather, "more than ever, Delaware needs to focus on retaining and growing businesses."[6]

REACHING FOR STATUS IN CONGRESS

The U.S. Congress is quintessentially federal in its makeup. Each state is represented in Congress equally with two senators in the Senate, and unequally in the House wherein each state's number of representatives is proportionate to its population. Accordingly, Delaware's small population has the least possible congressional representation, having only one representative plus two senators. Nevertheless, Delaware has contributed much more to congressional leadership over the years than have many more populous states with much larger representations in Congress. Having equal representation of 2 senators, it is understandable that Delaware's contribution to Congressional leadership has been more apparent among the total of 100 members in the Senate than in the House where only 1 Delawarean sits among a total 435 representatives.[7]

Delaware voters for many years have understood that seniority is a chief qualification for attaining U.S. Senate leadership status, and have been disposed repeatedly to reelect incumbent senators of both major parties. Thomas F. Bayard, a Democrat from a prominent Delaware political family, served an unprecedented sixteen years in the Senate from 1869 to 1885, during which he was a leading contender—in 1880 and 1884—for the Democratic presidential nomination. After he retired from the Senate, Bayard served as U.S. secretary of state and then the first U.S. ambassador to Great Britain (previous appointments held the title of minister).

The longest Delaware incumbencies in the Senate, however, have been enjoyed by those who have served from 1947 onward and, by virtue of greater seniority, exerted more influence in that august body than had their predecessors, namely Republicans John J. Williams (twenty-four years from 1947 to 1971), William V. Roth Jr. (thirty years from 1971 to 2001), and Democrat Joseph R. Biden Jr. (a record thirty-six-plus years since 1973).

Although John Williams, from agrarian Sussex County, never completed high school, his arithmetic skills—combined with his integrity and sense of right and wrong—became the basis of his fame as one of the most effective investigators in Senate history. His name never appeared on any major legislation, but his patient and thorough search for waste and fraud in federal finance earned him wide respect. Besides his investigation of the then Bureau of Internal Revenue (BIR), his most celebrated triumph was his investigation of influence peddling by Bobby Baker (the secretary to Senate majority leader Lyndon Johnson), who ended up in prison.[8]

Bill Roth, as chairman of the powerful Senate Finance Committee, emulated his predecessor Williams by conducting the most extensive investigation ever of the Internal Revenue Service (IRS, formerly BIR), which disclosed widespread abuses and provided the basis for his authoring the successful IRS Reform and Restructuring Act of 1998. Roth, "the taxpayer's best friend," became widely known as coauthor of the Kemp-Roth tax cuts—President Reagan's economic blueprint—and as creator of the Roth IRA, which allows individuals to invest taxable income that can be withdrawn free of tax in retirement.

When Joe Biden was reelected in 2002 for his sixth consecutive six-year term, he became Delaware's longest serving U.S. senator. During his long tenure, Biden has served as chair of two of the Senate's original standing committees—the Committee on Foreign Relations (2002, 2007–) and the Committee on the Judiciary (1987–1995). As Judiciary Chair, Senator Biden gained perhaps his greatest national television exposure by presiding over the controversial confirmation hearings of Supreme Court nominees Robert Bork in 1987 and Clarence Thomas in 1991. He continued to serve under Republican chairs as the top Democrat on both the Foreign Relations Committee and the Judiciary Subcommittee on Crime. In these capacities, he served as the Democratic Party's chief spokesperson on national security and foreign policy issues, while being instrumental in crafting virtually every piece of crime legislation over the previous decade, including the Violent Crime Control and Law Enforcement Act of 1994 (known as the Biden Crime Law), the Violence against Women Act of 2000, and the law creating the nation's "Drug Czar" who oversees national drug control policy. In 1987 and again in 2008 Biden campaigned briefly for the Democratic presidential nomination.[9]

There is no doubt that Delaware's congressional members, particularly long-time senators, have influenced the federal government's favorable impact on Delaware. For example, Senator Biden's work over twenty years led to the end of federal control and the return to Delawareans of more than 1,180 acres of beach shoreline along the Delaware coast.

OPPOSING FEDERAL REGULATION

Biden's success in ending federal control of part of Delaware's shoreline was a setback in the federal government's decades-long attempts to thwart the state's efforts to manage its own coastal zone.

When Republican governor Russell Peterson (1969–73) pushed enactment in 1971 of the Delaware Coastal Zone Act to ban heavy industry from its shoreline, the Nixon administration exerted extraordinary pressure to stop him. First, President Nixon's commerce department intervened. The assistant secretary of commerce for maritime affairs warned the Delaware legislature that the act "might damage the nation's trade position and undermine President Nixon's program to assure United States leadership in shipping." Then Nixon's secretary of commerce, Maurice Stans, summoned Peterson to Washington and accused him of being disloyal to his country. Peterson responded: "Hell, no. I'm being loyal to future generations of Americans." Finally, the chairman of Nixon's newly created Council on Environmental Quality, Russell E. Train, testified before Congress that the Nixon administration opposed coastal zone management by the states.[10]

Delaware legislator Sherman Tribbitt commented: "It looks like Governor Peterson is in conflict with his President." During his successful campaign to unseat Peterson, Tribbitt, a Democrat, accused Peterson of hampering Delaware's economy by his anti-industry Coastal Zone Act. This perception was one reason Peterson became the first Republican governor in the state's history to lose reelection. Thereafter, political survival in Delaware would require avoidance of an antibusiness image.[11]

During the ensuing years, there were a number of federal attempts to gut the Costal Zone Act. In 1985 President Reagan's justice and commerce departments filed briefs to support a lawsuit brought by the Norfolk Southern Corporation contending that the Delaware's Coastal Zone Act violated the U.S. Constitution's clause that gives Congress the right to regulate interstate commerce. The federal briefs contended that Delaware's "concerns do not outweigh the burden to interstate commerce." The federal courts eventually ruled in favor of Delaware, and the Coastal Zone Act survived.[12] However, the fight did not end there.

One of the more interesting aspects of the relationships between the federal government and Delaware's Coastal Zone Act concerned the dispute following the December 2004 request by British Petroleum (BP) to Delaware's Department of Natural Resources and Environmental Control (DNREC) to permit under Delaware's Coastal Zone Act the construction of a proposed BP liquid natural gas unloading facility in the Delaware River that would extend into the Delaware River from New Jersey's southern shore opposite Delaware's northern shore. Central to the dispute was Delaware's unique semicircular northern boundary established by William Penn's 1862 deed that formed a twelve-mile circle from its center in the city of New Castle, extending the full width of the Delaware River as a part of Delaware to New Jersey's contiguous low-tide line of its western shore. The U.S. Supreme Court had upheld the boundary in 1935, but New Jersey contended a 1905 interstate compact granted it control over facilities on its side of the river. DNREC ruled the BP facility was subject to Delaware's Coastal Zone Act, which precluded BP's projected $600 million liquid natural gas terminal within Delaware's part of the river, a fact disputed by New Jersey, which sought to reap the economic benefits of BP's facility.

At one point, New Jersey officials threatened economic retaliation against Delaware. The chief counsel to New Jersey's acting governor stated: "New Jersey will determine its own destiny and what happens in New Jersey, and Delaware has no right to tell us what we can and cannot do." In May 2005 House Majority Leader Wayne Smith introduced a bill in Delaware's General Assembly that would authorize Delaware's governor "to call upon the Delaware National Guard to protect the territorial integrity of the State of Delaware and to block and/or remove any encroachments upon our boundary."

In August 2005 New Jersey filed suit against Delaware in federal district court. The dispute promised to be a major issue with a variety of dimensions. At stake were billions of dollars in revenues for BP, restrictions on Delaware's Coastal Zone Act, and economic development plans for struggling southern New Jersey communities. Involved were the Federal Energy Regulatory Commission, federal courts, state governments of Delaware and New Jersey, environmental groups, economic development authorities and business leaders, and those who feared BP's proposed facility could be subject to possible accidental explosions or a target for terrorists.

In November 2005 the U.S. Supreme Court agreed to take up the case. Although New Jersey asked the court for a quick ruling, Delaware sought a lengthy fact-finding exercise that would involve historical research. In January 2006 the Supreme Court appointed a special master to conduct the fact-finding exercise. Meanwhile, in June 2006 the Federal Energy Regulatory Commission approved BP's proposed terminal, but the issue remained on hold pending the Supreme Court's ruling. In a ruling released in April 2007, the special master declared that Delaware, "as the sovereign owner" of the "Delaware River bottom," could regulate and police developments extending from the New Jersey shoreline. The U.S. Supreme Court traditionally relied heavily on decisions of its special masters, and it did so in this case by deciding eight to two in favor of Delaware on March 31, 2008.

Another recent environmental threat to Delaware's coastal zone came from the U.S. Army Corps of Engineers. The Corps's history of dredging the Delaware River's federal shipping channel dates back to the late 1800s when the controlling depth of the Delaware River was eighteen feet. During World War II, the depth reached forty feet. In 1992, ostensibly to keep Delaware River ports competitive in the world market, Congress authorized deepening the channel to forty-five feet between Philadelphia and the mouth of the Delaware Bay near Cape Henlopen, a distance of 102.5 miles, all but a few miles of which abutted the Delaware coast line.[13] The project called for Delaware to contribute $10 million, for which more than 10 million cubic yards of the dredged bottom would be used to replenish Delaware's eroding coastal wetlands and beaches. Former governor Peterson raised this question: "Do we want our children playing in river sludge?"[14]

Among Delaware interests supporting the dredging were the Port of Wilmington and the Teamsters. But for various reasons a number of other Delaware interests opposed the dredging, including Green Delaware, the Delaware Nature Society, the Alliance to Dump the Delaware Deepening, the League of Women Voters of Delaware, the City of New Castle, and perhaps most significantly Delaware's entire congressional delegation, comprising Representative Mike Castle and Senator Bill Roth, both Republicans, and Senator Joe Biden, a Democrat. Among the opposing groups' reasons were that dredging would waste tax money; harm Delaware's environment by introducing toxins into the river's fish and crabs, and ultimately into the diets of Delawareans and by dumping dredge spoils along Delaware's beaches and coast; and the Corps's refusal to comply with state requests for specific environmental permits. Finally, a 2002 report by the federal General Accounting Office questioning the project's "economic justification" was enough to put the project on hold, perhaps permanently.[15] In June 2008 the Corps and state of Pennsylvania announced an agreement for dredging the Delaware River from forty to fifty feet. However, required approvals by New Jersey and Delaware were unlikely.

Sometimes Delaware's refusal to comply with federal regulations can be costly. Such was the case in 2003, when the Delaware legislature initially refused to adopt the federal standard of .08 percent as the prohibited blood or breath alcohol consumption level for motor vehicle drivers, with the result that significant federal highway funds for Delaware were withheld. The disagreement revolved on whether .08 would be a "hard floor" whereby drivers could not be arrested for driving while impaired if their blood alcohol levels (BAL) were below .08 percent. The authorization bill passed the Delaware House of Representatives and was assigned to the judiciary committee of the Delaware Senate, whose chairman simply sat on it. His truculence caused a shortfall of withheld federal funding of $2,549,000 for fiscal year 2004. The bill, however, did pass during the next session of the legislature, thus averting further losses of federal highway funds for Delaware.[16]

In August 2005 Governor Ruth Ann Minner dispatched a Delaware Air National Guard unit to Mississippi within twenty hours of that hurricane-stricken state's request for help. She did not need to ask the U.S. Department of Defense (DOD) for permission, since that particular unit was funded by the state and had not been activated by the DOD. Referring to her authority under article 3, section 8 of Delaware's constitution, Minner said "The governor should always have the opportunity to serve as commander-in-chief of our Delaware National Guard." However, she neglected to acknowledge that her authority is constrained by that section's added caveat: "except when . . . called into the service of the United States." Subsequently, Governor Minner engaged in "cooperative federalism" in 2006 by joining all forty-nine state governors in opposing a provision of a bill passed by the U.S. House of Representatives that would authorize the president to call up members of a state's National Guard to active duty without the governor's consent in the event of a natural disaster such as Hurricane Katrina. It should be noted that article 2, section 2 of the U.S. Constitution extends the president's authority as commander-in-chief to include "the militia of the several states, when called into the actual service of the United States," and that under this authority the president had already federalized specific National Guard and Reserve units in support of the post-Katrina action plan of the Federal Emergency Management Agency. The U.S. Army's 82nd Airborne was also deployed in 2005 to bring order to Katrina-stricken New Orleans with the Louisiana governor's required approval. Nevertheless, in their 2006 letter to Congress, the fifty governors called the bill's provision "an unprecedented shift in authority" that would "usurp governors' authority." Clearly, this is an area of *shared* federal and state power subject to modification by the Congress. Political science professor Samuel B. Hoff of Delaware State University commented that the issue was part of the long-time struggle for power between the states and the national government. "It's a federalism issue," Professor Hoff said.[17]

In an interesting twist, in August 2003 Delaware state officials fought for more rather than less federal regulation. They vowed to fight a federal rollback of clean air rules for older factories and refineries, fearing it would leave Delaware with little hope of controlling smog and other pollutants released locally or blown into the state from older plants in neighboring states. The Bush administration had announced it was relaxing clean air rules to allow industrial plants to make upgrades without having to modernize outdated pollution control equipment as previously required. Delaware joined Pennsylvania, New Jersey, and New York in endorsing a multistate objection to the rule changes and also joined other states in a lawsuit challenging the Bush administration's EPA program for controlling new pollution sources.[18] This was another example of Delaware opposing federal regulation by engaging in "cooperative federalism."

COOPERATING WITH OTHER STATES

Joining other states in occasional litigation is one way by which Delaware engages in cooperative federalism. However, as will be discussed in chapter 11, in the mid-1990s Delaware refused to join forty-four other states in suits against tobacco companies to compensate taxpayers for publicly funded treatment of smoking-related illnesses. Nevertheless, Delaware's attorney general did join the attorneys general of forty-five other states in signing the November 1998 multistate out-of-court tobacco settlement (Florida, Minnesota, Texas and Mississippi settled their tobacco cases separately).[19] After the 1998 settlement, the tobacco committee of the National Association of Attorneys General (NAAG) served as the liaison between NAAG and the settling states on the implementation and enforcement of the 1998 settlement agreement. Attorney General Jane Brady, Delaware's first female attorney general, served on NAAG's executive committee and also as chair of the Republican Attorneys General Association and member of the Board of Directors of the National District Attorneys Association. In these capacities, Delaware was well poised to cooperate with other states with regard to common legal and justice concerns.

When Democrat Tom Carper became Delaware's governor in 1993, he put welfare reform at the top of his policy agenda. He wanted to permanently move welfare recipients off of public assistance and into the workforce. He felt that the welfare system perpetuated dependency, diminished self-esteem, and eroded family responsibility.[20] Accordingly, Carper signed legislation in 1995 launching his program "A Better Chance" (ABC) to free recipients from what he called the "welfare trap." In 1999 Carper claimed that ABC had cut the state's welfare rolls by over 40 percent since 1994.[21]

Governor Carper meanwhile became co-chair of the National Governors Association's welfare reform task force and pushed for acceptance of the

Delaware model by both the nation's governors and the federal government. In this he was successful. In August 1996 President Clinton signed into law the federal Personal Responsibility and Work Opportunity Reconciliation Act that required states to have at least 50 percent of their able-bodied, adult welfare clients in the workforce for at least thirty hours per week by the year 2002. States that failed to reach this target would lose 5 percent of their federal welfare block grant funds under the law.

The point emphasized here is that these Delaware-led developments composed an example of both "cooperative federalism" as well as "coercive" or "regulatory federalism." Governor Carper's national leadership led him to be elected by the nation's governors as chair of the National Governors Association (NGA) from 1998 to 1999 and then as chair of NGA's Center for Best Practices in 2000. These distinctions doubtlessly helped Tom Carper to become a U.S. senator in January 2001. Democratic governor Ruth Ann Minner, as the state's first female governor, succeeded Carper and was elected to NGA's executive committee. Thus, leadership in NGA continued to be a prime means by which Delaware cooperated with other states.

There are a myriad of other intergovernmental organizations through which Delaware government and officials cooperate with other states, such as the National Association of Counties (NACO), the National League of Cities (NLC), and the U.S. Conference of Mayors (USCM). Foremost among those at the state level, besides NAAG and NGA, are the National Conference of State Legislatures (NCSL) and the Council of State Governments (CSG).

NCSL is a bipartisan organization that serves state legislators and their staffs by providing research, technical assistance, and meeting opportunities for policymakers to exchange ideas on the most pressing state issues. Delaware hosted the 2005 NCSL annual national meeting.

CSG is perhaps the most important intergovernmental organization for Delaware's state government. CSG is an association of all 50 state governments that promotes policy development, leadership training, and innovative state programming. Indeed, it is the official policy of the State of Delaware, as a member of CSG, to cooperate with other state governments. To facilitate such cooperation, the Delaware legislature passed a law in May 1939 creating the Delaware Commission on Interstate Cooperation, comprising three members of each house of the legislature plus three members of the Governor's Committee on Interstate Cooperation. Among the functions of the nine-member commission are to propose and facilitate the adoption of interstate compacts and uniform reciprocal statutes, administrative rules, and regulations.[22]

A subcommittee of the Delaware Commission on Interstate Cooperation participated in the newly formed Interstate Commission on the Delaware River Basin (INCODEL), the forerunner of the signing of a regional compact in 1961 by President John F. Kennedy and the governors of Delaware, New Jersey, Pennsylvania, and New York that created the Delaware River Basin Commission (DRBC) to oversee with the force of law a unified approach to managing the river system without regard to political boundaries. Members include the four governors and a federal representative appointed by the president. The compact's signing marked the first time since the nation's birth that the federal government and a group of states joined together as equal partners in a river basin planning, development, and regulatory agency. Commission programs include water quality protection, water supply allocation, regulatory review (permitting), water conservation initiatives, watershed planning, drought management, flood control, and recreation.

Another important Delaware interstate compact, created in 1962, is the Delaware River and Bay Authority (DRBA) governed by six commissioners from New Jersey and six from Delaware, and charged with providing vital transportation links between the two states as well as economic development in Delaware and the four southern counties of New Jersey. DRBA operates most prominently the Delaware Memorial Bridge, the Cape May–Lewes Ferry, and five regional airports—three in Delaware and two in New Jersey.

GLOBALIZATION

Delaware's outreach to other polities is not confined to other states but also to other countries. Regardless of U.S. Supreme Court decisions declaring that the federal government alone has full and exclusive responsibility for relations with other countries,[23] the fact is that Delaware is a prime player within the context of globalization. It is now common to refer to the twenty-first century as the century of globalization—of international economic integration. Delaware is a leader among the states in this profound transformation that is taking place.

We have noted that Delaware's population is already multicultural and is fast becoming ever more internationally diverse. And we have also noted that as the so-called corporation capital of the world Delaware incorporates several thousands of non-U.S. firms. But these facts alone do not convey the extent of Delaware's globalization

The Information Technology and Innovation Foundation (ITIF) of Washington DC issued its 2002 State New Economy Index explaining that when the "old economy" emerged in the 1940s, the winners were states whose businesses sold to national markets, whereas in the "new economy" at the beginning of the twenty-first century, the winners are the states whose businesses are most innovative and integrated into the world economy. On this basis, ITIF ranked Delaware's aggregated globalization score first among the fifty states. ITIF's globalization indicators measured twelve items, among them the export focus of the state's manufacturing, namely the value of its exports per manufacturing worker (Delaware ranked seventh); foreign direct investment, namely the percentage of the state's workforce employed by foreign-owned companies (Delaware ranked second); and high-wage traded services (Delaware ranked first).[24]

Among all countries in 2007, the United Kingdom was the leading export market for Delaware goods, followed by Canada and, in descending order, Germany, Japan, and China.[25]

Delaware produces agricultural products that are exported globally to 155 foreign destinations. In fiscal year 2000 Delaware's cash receipts from agriculture totaled $741 million, of which exports were estimated at $103 million. Cash receipts from poultry products reached $64 million. So dominant is export trade in Delaware's poultry production that Russia's decision in 1996 to ban imports of U.S. poultry appeared catastrophic to Delaware producers, especially in Sussex County, which since 1941 had become the country's leading poultry producing county. High Russian officials said the ban would not be lifted until American poultry producers took steps to eliminate deadly salmonella bacteria. Delaware Republican U.S. Senator William Roth, chairman of the Senate's powerful finance committee, responded by urging "immediate . . . retaliation against Russian imports, a freeze on bank loans and credits and suspension of American foreign assistance programs in Russia."[26] Only then did Delaware's so-called "poultry flap" end.

MBNA, formerly one of the nation's largest credit-card banks and Delaware's largest private employer, had begun expanding its business well beyond the nation's borders in the late 1990s and was poised to become a leading credit-card business in England and Europe. And, as we have noted, the DuPont Company, Delaware's second largest private employer, began to see its overseas sales exceed its domestic sales in the late 1980s, and by the late 1990s the company had become one of the world's leading global manufacturing firms. Still Delaware's third largest private employer, AstraZeneca, is a British-owned company; and the state's largest auto assembly plant, DaimlerChrysler, was a joint German-American firm before Daimler withdrew in 2007.

Supported by the Delaware Economic Development Office (DEDO), Delaware public officials have traveled the world boosting Delaware as a place where foreign companies can prosper. Democratic governor Tom Carper (1993–2001) led delegations to seven European countries, Mexico, Canada, Japan, Vietnam, and Taiwan. His successor, Governor Ruth Ann Minner (2001–9), led a delegation in search of investors to Europe and also met in Taipei with Taiwan's president.

The globalization of Delaware is evident also in the state's education sector. For example, during the 2007–8 academic year there were 1,689 foreign students from 102 countries and 607 visiting scholars from 76 countries at the University of Delaware. Moreover, there were 1,700 students participating in study-abroad programs, whereby the university ranked fourth in the nation among doctoral-granting institutions.[27]

CONCLUSION

The foregoing analysis of Delaware in the federal system demonstrates the pervasiveness of federalism in the governance and politics of Delaware and how intergovernmental much of Delaware public policy is becoming.

As a general trend over recent decades, the federal government has been increasingly successful in influencing the states to follow federal policies, goals, and directives through an array of financial and other inducements and sanctions. Some have called this the preemption of state law.

Perhaps Delaware's most distinguishing characteristic or greatest achievement is its rightful claim to be "the corporation capital of the world." We may ask the question whether the federal government could pose a threat to Delaware in this respect.

In the wake of corporate scandals of the early twenty-first century—the so-called "post-Enron" era—there were commensurate calls for the federalization of corporate law, based on a theory that the federal government would be more effective at regulating corporations than individual states. On the other hand, it was difficult to imagine how the federal government could replicate Delaware's long record of corporate case law and its widely respected Chancery Court. Consistency of opinions across ninety-four federal districts would be a major challenge. Yet the threat remained. It also remained for interstate banking, interstate taxation, bankruptcy laws, and a host of other areas that could adversely affect Delaware businesses.

CHAPTER FOUR

The Constitution

The constitutions of a state reflect the people of that state and their views of governance at various points in time. Since constitutions are documents that change as those views change, they leave footprints preserved in time. While Delaware's current constitution—drafted in 1897 and amended through the twentieth century—defines governance today, it is still a work in progress. Its provisions were influenced by various colonial charters and Delaware's three previous constitutions of 1776, 1792, and 1831.

This chapter addresses major features of the current constitution and its predecessors. It also focuses on several broad themes through all of the constitutions that provide understanding of Delaware's changing governance.[1]

LOOKING BACKWARD

Prior to the Delaware Constitution of 1776, the appointed colonial governor appointed in turn most principal public officials including judges, who served at his pleasure, an attorney general, registers in chancery, registers of wills, prothonotaries, and clerks of the peace—all offices that still survive. Since the General Assembly had been in place from 1704, the drafters of the 1776 constitution saw little need to break new ground and they essentially kept existing law in place. In addition, the Constitution of 1776, adopted on September 20 of that year, continued adherence to the common law of England (article 25), and Delaware is still a common law state (see chapter 8). Thus, the 1776 constitution represented a change in sovereignty rather than a change in the form of government. For the first time, however, the importation of slaves from Africa was prohibited, although the status of existing slaves (15–20 percent of Delaware's population in 1790) remained unchanged.

The 1776 convention also issued a Declaration of Rights and Fundamental Rules of the Delaware State (September 11, 1776), but freedom of assembly and speech were notably absent. The document was incorporated by reference in article 30 of the 1776 constitution.

Following the adoption of the U.S. Constitution in 1789, it was imperative that Delaware's constitution be brought into line with federal provisions. Accordingly, the original Declaration of Rights and Fundamental Rules of Delaware was updated and made part of article 1 of the state's 1792 constitution. The two houses of the General Assembly were renamed the Senate and the House of Representatives to conform with the U.S. Congress, and annual elections were provided for members of the House of Representatives and three-year terms for members of the Senate. Representation remained as before, with seven members of the lower house and three members in the upper house chosen in each county. The requirement that five-sevenths of the General Assembly approve any changes to the constitution was reduced to a two-thirds vote of each house, with the governor's approval, in two consecutive sessions of the General Assembly, provided the proposed amendment was published and an election intervened. This process, with the omission of the governor's approval, is the method for amending Delaware's present constitution. Procedures for calling a constitutional convention were also spelled out.

In addition, there were two new and important provisions included in the Constitution of 1792 that are particularly noteworthy. The first strengthened the power of the governor (previously called president) and provided that the governor be elected directly by the people. The second created a separate Court of Chancery, the jurisdiction of which has remained mostly unchanged since 1792.

The constitutional convention that was convened in 1831 could have been characterized as the "too-much-government convention." Forty-six years had passed since the original convention, and there had developed a feeling that the legislature was meeting too often and was too expensive. In addition, complaints about the number of required judges and the difficulty in filling all their positions with qualified people had been frequently expressed.

The convention produced the Constitution of 1831 on December 2. The primary accomplishment was to require the General Assembly to meet biennially instead of annually. This required changing the terms of House members to two years, and increasing the terms for senators and the governor to four years. These provisions reduced the cost of government to some degree and remained unchanged until 1959.

The judiciary was reduced from nine judges to five with lifetime appointments (with good behavior), and court procedures were further elaborated in the 1831 constitution. In contrast with the U.S. Constitution, the Delaware constitution included the structure of the judiciary in full, including key pieces of court procedure. This placed a higher standard for changes in the judiciary, by requiring constitutional amendment as opposed to legislation.

Finally, in an attempt to reduce the number of constitutional conventions, provisions were added to the 1831 constitution that made it somewhat more difficult to call such conventions. A special election was required to be held for that purpose alone. Also required was that the number of people approving the convention should be greater than or equal to the majority of those voting in the largest of the three previous general elections. Obviously, this was a high bar to surmount, because special elections rarely turn out as many voters as a general election. (Removal of the requirement for a special election became effective in 1893).

A curious incident in Delaware's constitutional history occurred in 1852. The question of whether there should be a constitutional convention was submitted to referendum. While a majority of those voting called for the convention, the total number voting did not meet the requirements of the 1831 constitution. Regardless of this irregularity, the convention was called by the General Assembly. In another unprecedented action, the Constitution of 1853 was submitted to the people, who decisively rejected it by a vote of 4,876 to 2,717, with a majority of voters in all three counties against it. Rejection by the voters of the 1853 constitution was in retrospect one factor in making it the only constitution ever submitted to the people of Delaware for their approval.[2]

The failure of the Constitution of 1853 meant that Delaware, as it approached the twentieth century, was in essence still operating under the Constitution of 1792, because the Constitution of 1831, except for minor changes, was almost identical to that of 1792. To deal with this, a referendum was held in 1894, and the General Assembly passed legislation to convene a constitutional convention in December of 1896. The result was adoption of the currently operative Constitution of 1897.

The Constitution of 1897 addressed several very important areas. First, the principle of equal representation for each county was violated for the first time. In the new arrangement Kent County, Sussex County, and New Castle County outside of Wilmington were represented equally in both houses of the General Assembly. (At the time the populations of these three areas were similar). In addition, five seats in the House and two seats in the Senate were allocated to the City of Wilmington. The new arrangement gave New Castle County (with Wilmington included) more than 40 percent of the seats in each house, although the county then accounted for 62 percent of the state's population. Finally, for the first time, each of the representatives and senators was also elected from a well-defined election district (theretofore they had been elected at large within the county).

Another important area addressed by the Constitution of 1897 was voting. The passage of the Fifteenth Amendment to the U.S. Constitution in effect gave the vote to black males. This was recognized by Delaware's 1897 constitution. To further implement this provision, the previous requirement that a voter prove that he had paid taxes (capitation or property) in the county of residence was removed. A requirement was also added that a potential voter be able to read the constitution in English and sign his name. Some pressure was brought to extend suffrage to women, but it was ultimately rejected. The bill of rights remained, as it had since 1792.

Since the Constitution of 1897 was promulgated no constitutional convention has been called. Amendments have been made by the General Assembly according to the procedure defined in the constitution. Several of those amendments are significant and worth noting. Women were given the vote by virtue of adoption of the Nineteenth Amendment to the U.S. Constitution in 1920. The provision of "separate schools for white and colored children" was nullified by the U.S. Supreme Court in 1954. A fully staffed state supreme court was authorized in 1951 for the first time. The three-hundred-year battle for proportional representation in the General Assembly was achieved by federal court decisions in the late 1960s.

Unlike most other states, Delaware always incorporates constitutional amendments directly into the language of the articles they amend, instead of having them listed separately at the end of the document. This has the positive benefit for one not having to wade through any irrelevant predecessors. The history of an amendment is always clearly stated, but one does have to read the laws of the time to see what has been changed. This is annoying to some researchers, but is a feature nonetheless for citizens of the state. The same policy is followed for statutes as well.

With this foregoing background, we now turn to consider in more depth certain important issues in Delaware's governance that have evolved over time. These issues are voting rights, representation, balance of power between state government branches, and what may be termed the issue of public participation.

THE VOTING RIGHTS ISSUE

The Constitution of 1776 did not directly spell out requirements for voting in the state. Instead, in article 5 it retained the qualifications in place during colonial times. The law in place at that time granted the vote to free white male Christians who owned land or other property worth forty pounds.

In 1792 the requirements for voting changed. The requirement that the vote would be reserved for free white men was retained, but the Christian qualification was dropped. A two-year residency requirement was added along with a minimum age qualification of twenty-one years. While property ownership was dropped, an otherwise qualified voter needed to have paid either state or county taxes within six months prior to the election. This might be seen as a property ownership requirement in disguise, but the son of a fully qualified voter between the ages of twenty-one and twenty-two who had not paid taxes was also permitted to vote.

The third constitutional convention altered the language even further but did not break new ground. The Constitution of 1831 reduced the residency requirement from two years to one year, and payment of county taxes alone qualified a person to vote. The minimum age requirement was raised from twenty-one to twenty-two. Convicted felons were excluded from voting, along with idiots, the insane, and paupers. Interestingly, the 1831 constitution also gave the legislature the right to use loss of the right to vote as a punishment for crime without restriction.

The Civil War amendments to the United States Constitution (Thirteenth, Fourteenth, and Fifteenth) required most states to rewrite parts of their constitutions. Delaware was no exception. Prior to the passage of the Fifteenth Amendment, only four states (Vermont, Maine, New Hampshire, and Massachusetts) had allowed free black men of voting age to vote. Pennsylvania initially permitted free black men to vote but then revoked that privilege in 1838. (Meanwhile, New York allowed free black men to vote but demanded higher property and residency requirements; Rhode Island also allowed free black men to vote except in the years of 1822 to 1842.)

While the Fifteenth Amendment made outright disfranchisement based on race illegal, Delaware's other requirements were still enforceable. From 1868 to 1897 Democrats used the taxpaying requirement as a method to deny largely Republican black males from voting.[3] Delaware's assessment and collection laws enacted in 1873 made it the responsibility of the potential voter to make sure he was listed on the county tax rolls for either the property or capitation tax. Furthermore, if the taxpayer was delinquent, his name could be removed from qualified voters for one year.

All of this changed with the passage of the Constitution of 1897—the constitution as amended that still serves Delaware. No longer were black males absolutely excluded from voting. The taxpaying requirements were dropped. However, potential voters were now required to register, to be able to read the Delaware constitution in English, and to write their names. Women continued to be excluded, although the state of Wyoming had become the first state to permit them to vote when it entered the Union in 1890. A proposal to give the vote to women was defeated seventeen to seven at the Delaware convention in 1897, for reasons "ranging from the belief that allowing women to vote would destroy marital harmony to the claim that single women would not wish to register to vote because they would be required to reveal their ages."[4] Delegate William C. Spruance attempted to rationalize the extension of the vote to black males but not to women: "Deficient as the male colored person is, as a general rule, of that intelligence which is desired in the exercise of this right, it is also true that the colored women are vastly inferior to the colored men in that respect. Just think now of the colored women that you know, and you cannot count on your fingers, of all the many you know, those that could be thought fit to exercise this right. I do not want to add to the already large number; I do not want to increase either the number or the proportion of ignorant and unqualified people."[5]

In 1920 the Nineteenth Amendment to the U.S. Constitution was ratified, extending the vote to women. Prior to its adoption, Washington, California, Arizona, Kansas, Oregon, Montana, New York, Michigan, Oklahoma, and South Dakota had granted full voting rights to women. (The Delaware General Assembly did not ratify the Nineteenth Amendment when it was raised in 1920, but did so in 1923)

THE REPRESENTATION ISSUE

Although the "three lower counties" joined together to form the "Delaware State" in 1776, there was little doubt at the time that they intended to retain their individual identities and their equal representation under the 1776 constitution. They were three separate entities with different histories and development paths.

One example of differences between the counties was the fact that many residents of Sussex County were considered to be Tories who defiantly traded openly with the English during the Revolutionary War. At the time, William Killen was serving as the first chief justice of Delaware's Supreme Court. Killen, an anti-England Scotch-Irish immigrant resident of New Castle County, imposed the following sentence upon eight men of Sussex County after their trial and conviction for treason in 1780: "That you return to the prison from whence you came, from thence you must be drawn to the place of execution and when you come there you must be hanged by the neck but not till you be dead, for you must be cut down alive, then your bowels must be taken out and burnt before your face, then your head must be severed from your body and your body be divided into four quarters and these must be at the disposal of the Supreme Authority of the State."[6] Killen's sentence in this instance illustrates an extreme example of the deep-seated, county-based, identity that was to prevail in Delaware over the ensuing years.

Representatives of the three counties, who had been meeting periodically since 1704 to deal with common problems, saw no real need to change the type of representation when they gathered to frame the first state constitution of 1776. They preserved the well-established identities of the three counties, which had roughly the same population at the time. Therefore, each county would have the same number of representatives in the state's two legislative bodies created in the new constitution. This situation would remain exactly the same for the next 120 years.

The constitutions written in 1792 and 1831 did nothing to change the equality of county representation. While the proportions of the population had started to diverge by 1831, with both New Castle and Sussex Counties having become by then larger in population than Kent County, the issue of changing the number and balance of representatives did not really surface. The next constitutional convention of 1852, moreover, failed to address the fact that New Castle County's population had by then become twice as large as the combined populations of the other two counties, and—as noted—this constitution was rejected by the voters in the first and only time a constitution would ever be presented to the people for approval. The representation issue did not arise again until the constitutional convention of 1896–97.

By the time this last constitutional convention convened at the end of 1896, the populations for New Castle, Kent, and Sussex Counties had reached 110,000, 33,000, and 42,000, respectively. Such disproportion was significant to say the least. However, the equality of the counties in the General Assembly had become so firmly established that an equitable solution was not even sought. Instead, representation of New Castle County was divided into two parts, inside and outside of the city of Wilmington. Thus, rural New Castle County was given representation in both houses of the General Assembly equal to each of the other two counties. Then the city of Wilmington was given new seats, but not in accordance with its actual population. One positive feature that did emerge from this "reapportionment" was the development of election districts. Prior to the adoption of the 1897 constitution, all representatives were chosen at large within the three counties. Theoretically, at least, implementation of election districts would bring elected representatives closer, and make them more responsive, to the voters that elected them. In the final analysis, the 1897 changes in representation were the beginning of a process that would lead to "one-person-one-vote" in Delaware seven decades later.

By 1960 the populations for New Castle, Kent, and Sussex Counties were 307,000, 66,000, and 73,000, respectively. The city of Wilmington, having been allocated additional seats in 1897, was now declining in population compared with the significant population rise of suburbanizing New Castle County. In addition, the original election districts within each county, particularly in New Castle, were significantly out of balance. Accordingly, seven New Castle County representatives sued for reapportionment. The General Assembly then made some changes to amend the constitution. Eventually, however, the United States Supreme Court held the relevant amendment and portions of Delaware's 1897 constitution to be in violation of the Equal Protection Clause of the Fourteenth Amendment of the United States Constitution. Following this initial decision, the General Assembly reapportioned again but the federal courts again found those changes unacceptable. After a special census in 1967, an acceptable solution was reached with the courts, and real reapportionment was achieved (see chapter 7).

The changes wrought by ending a scheme that essentially lasted for almost three hundred years were significant. The counties were no longer equal. The urban north was now able to dominate the General Assembly. Residents of the city of Wilmington lost political power along with residents of Kent and Sussex Counties. Reapportionment seemingly changed the entire political landscape of Delaware forever.

THE BALANCE-OF-POWER ISSUE

Other chapters in this book will address the powers of the three branches in turn. It is appropriate here, however, to consider the evolution of their constitutional powers relative to each other.

In 1704 the Assembly of the Lower Counties on the Delaware organized to provide some semblance of representative government for what would eventually become the State of Delaware. Normally residing in Philadelphia, a deputy governor of the colony provided the executive function for the Lower Counties and had the power to approve or disapprove any legislation passed by the assembly. Since the governor's salary was paid by the assembly, he tended to be agreeable, and the three counties remained essentially in charge through the colonial period.[7]

Given the fact that the assembly's colonial relationship was with a compliant, docile, and mostly absent executive, it was hardly surprising that the executive provided by the 1776 constitution would be weak, a circumstance also prevalent in the other revolutionary state constitutions. In fact, the so-called President of the Delaware State was chosen by both houses of the General Assembly. Moreover, he had no veto power and his appointment power was regulated by the General Assembly. He served for a three-year term and could not serve another term until the expiration of a term of an intervening governor. Clearly, there was a fairly strong aversion to a strong executive both at the state and national levels during the revolutionary period. Indeed, no executive had even been provided for the national government under the Articles of Confederation.

Delaware's top judicial appointments were made by virtue of a "joint ballot" of the president and the General Assembly, whereby the former could cast an additional vote in case of a tie. Judges served as long as their behavior was "good," essentially for life. However, the assembly reserved the right to remove both judges and the president from office for "mal-administration, corruption or other means by which the safety of the commonwealth may be endangered."[8] In short, the assembly drove the "ship of state" under the Constitution of 1776.

By 1792, after the recently adopted Constitution of the United States had provided for a fairly strong executive, Delaware's constitutional convention of 1792 was somewhat less paranoid about this issue and was also disposed to provide for a stronger executive. Perhaps the fact that the first president of the State of Delaware had been hauled off to a British prison ship had helped as well.

The governor (no longer the president) was now elected by the people but retained the same three-year term and the restriction against serving a second term before an intervening term of another had been served. The governor's appointment power was increased by granting the governor the authority to seat justices of the peace and by dropping requirements for the assembly to be involved in the appointment process. The assembly retained the right to impeach government officials. The governor was also required to approve any proposed constitutional amendments, but notably he was not given the power to veto legislation.

The 1792 constitution made significant changes in the judiciary, but most had to do with size, scope, and jurisdiction. The "good behavior" requirement was retained. Although the appointment process was moved clearly into the governor's sphere of influence, and probably changed the character of the judiciary, the relationship between the branches was not otherwise changed.

In the 1831 constitution the governor was given a four-year term without any possibility of serving another term. More importantly, the General Assembly now would meet every other year and the terms were extended to two and four years for the House and Senate, respectively, a feature that was to continue to the present. One could infer that the governor thereby gained in power, insofar as the General Assembly was not to meet annually to meddle in the affairs of state. On the other hand, the lengthening of terms for both houses would reduce turnover and increase legislators' experience and influence commensurate with longer incumbency.

The constitutional convention in 1831 continued to fine-tune the judiciary by cutting the number of judges and by providing even more detail concerning the roles and procedures required of the courts. One of the more interesting provisions—presaging the 1897 constitution—gave the General Assembly authority to "enact a general incorporation act" to replace special acts of incorporation.

After more than one hundred years, with the promulgation of the Constitution of 1897 the governor was finally allowed to run for a second term, albeit not to run for a third term. The degree to which this change shifted power within the government is open to debate. Certainly a governor who is reelected has the advantage of not being a lame duck until the sixth year of service. On the other hand, the governor needs the cooperation of the General Assembly to provide a record that will warrant reelection.

Significantly, the governor also gained veto power over all legislation including the power to veto parts of a bill, the so-called line-item veto. The General Assembly retained the right to override the veto with a three-fifths vote in both houses. The governor's appointment power was constrained somewhat by the introduction of a stipulation that most appointments would require the consent of the Senate. In addition, the governor no longer played a role in the constitutional amendment process. Three new elective positions were created that essentially reduced the scope of the governor's power but did little to change the balance of power between the branches.

The 1897 constitution ended the practice of electing representatives at large within the counties. While this change could be viewed as a victory for the voters, it could also be viewed as possibly reducing the control of county delegations over determining candidates for the legislature, or it could be viewed as possibly weakening the legislative branch relative to the executive.

Lifetime appointments with good behavior for judges vanished in the 1897 constitution. The judicial term was set at twelve years, and a sitting judge could reapply at the end of that term along with all others competing for the position. The appointment was now subject to Senate confirmation. Did these changes shift the balance of power? Fixed terms and Senate confirmation could be viewed as possibly encouraging judges to moderate their decisions, inasmuch as their reappointment and confirmation would require them ultimately to depend on their records.

The introduction of "one-person-one-vote" in the late 1960s had the effect of aligning the General Assembly more with the executive, inasmuch as both branches now represented the same electorate. To some extent this reapportionment increased the power of the executive, relative to the General Assembly, but more likely it increased the political alignment between the two branches.

In 1951 a separate and independent Supreme Court was created at long last by constitutional amendment. Delaware finally had a real court, with real judges, and a clear jurisdiction. The days of forming a court of appeals on the fly were over. This was a welcome change for both civil and criminal jurisdictions. It also probably strengthened the judiciary with respect to the other branches, and added to the importance of the appointment process.

THE PUBLIC PARTICIPATION ISSUE

Delaware's Constitution of 1897 is the only currently operative state constitution in the country that was not submitted to the voters for their approval. Viewed from a negative perspective, some would characterize Delaware's constitution as thereby undemocratic. But a positive perspective would characterize the lack of referenda for approval of all four of Delaware's constitutions—of 1776, 1792, 1831, and 1897—as testimony of Delawareans' continuing trust in representative government. Thus, Ralph Moyed, a local liberal columnist, preferred constitution making by the state legislature to approval by referendum, which he equated to "the evil inherent in the lawmaking of the mob."[9]

A reasonable argument can be made that the main reason government by referendum has never gained a foothold in Delaware is because Delawareans have been satisfied with electing their representatives to deal with the business of government; when they were unhappy, they were content with changing their representatives by voting incumbents out of office. Contributing to popular support for representation, as against referenda, is the fact that—in such a small state—citizens have always felt close to their readily accessible representatives, whom they could contact easily and know personally.

Similarly, Delaware's Constitution of 1897 is the only currently operative state constitution that does not require ratification of amendments by the voters. The Supreme Court of Delaware has said: "In this respect, Delaware differs from all other states of the Union which do require approval by the people of proposed changes in their constitutions."[10]

From the very first constitution in 1776, the General Assembly has had the power to alter the constitution. Again, the major reason for this has been that Delawareans have trusted their elected representatives to change their constitution. Accordingly, an amendment of the Constitution of 1897 may be adopted by requiring an extraordinary two-thirds vote in each house of two successive legislatures with an intervening general election. Far from being the easiest state constitution to amend, many Delawareans consider this so-called "two-legged model" to be a higher hurdle than submission to a popular referendum. A century after adoption of the Constitution of 1897, Associate Justice of the Delaware Supreme Court William T. Quillen explained that "precedent did not lie with the referendum principle" in Delaware.[11] The death knell of that principle appeared to have occurred in 1853, when voters resoundingly rejected the proposed constitution. Since then, no other Delaware constitution—nor any amendment for that matter—has been submitted to voters for approval.

Although provision was made in the Constitution of 1897 for a constitutional convention of elected delegates to be called to revise that constitution, no such convention has ever been called. Indeed, since 1897 the constitution has always been amended by the General Assembly rather than being "revised" by convention. In 1968 the General Assembly created the Delaware Constitutional Revision Commission of fifteen members, comprising five members appointed by the governor, five appointed by the president of the Senate, and five by the speaker of the House. In 1969 the commission submitted to the General Assembly a whole new draft constitution in the form of sixty-six amendments, of which twenty-four were approved in 1970 by the assembly and again in 1971. However, some of the amendments were not published as determined by the Supreme Court. As a result, the amendments reintroduced in 1971 in the second leg were not the same. In the final analysis, none of the original twenty-four proposed amendments ever became law.[12]

In a sense, the issue of public participation in constitutional change is a nonissue in Delaware. No organized movement of any political consequence has existed in Delaware to mobilize public participation in constitutional decision making. Defenders of the status quo in Delaware are likely to contend that even major constitutional changes over the past 240 years (e.g., in representation and the separation of powers) have been made through the legislative process without referenda, and that even the United States Constitution was ratified without a popular referendum. If pressed, they could ask, Why change a system that has been operative so long and has worked so well?

CONCLUSION

Several threads or themes emerge from the foregoing analysis of Delaware's constitutional history. One theme is that Delawareans have favored incremental rather than radical change, as evident by their deference to the common law, their continuing trust and acceptance of representative government through the General Assembly, their longtime unwillingness to drop the principle of equal representation by counties, and their rejection or reluctance to act on amendments to the U.S. Constitution. Each of Delaware's four constitutions—of 1776, 1792, 1831, and 1897—revised existing government rather than making fundamental changes. And the Constitution of 1897 continues to be operative, albeit as amended.

Another theme is that since 1682 there has persisted strong identity and political rivalry among Delaware's three counties, the boundaries of which have remained essentially unchanged. This identity doubtlessly derives from the development of Delaware as a union of counties with different colonial roots and diverse economic development through the centuries.

The most apparent theme has been the entrenchment of representative government throughout Delaware's history. Thus, the General Assembly has maintained and even tightened its control over constitutional amendments, which has had the effect of fostering only strongly held incremental change over time. Episodic changes, evoked by referenda, voter initiatives, and recall, are public participation practices inconsistent with Delaware's long history. One point of view contends that these public participative practices are consonant with democratic governance. The point of view prevalent in Delaware, however, is that their political system, devoid of these practices, provides an extremely stable and predictable platform for governance.

CHAPTER FIVE

Political Parties and Elections

This chapter discusses Delaware's two major political parties in history, their similarities, elections, parity and policies, incumbency, campaign finance, bipartisan and consensus politics, and the weakness of third parties.

EARLY HISTORY

It is somewhat of a stretch to date the beginnings of Delaware's current party system to the cleavage between the Anti-Federalists and the Federalists in the days after ratification of the U.S. Constitution of 1787. However, it is possible to see some historic affinities of the present Democratic Party, with its antecedents of Anti-Federalists evolving through Jeffersonians (Democratic-Republicans) and Jacksonians. Likewise, it is also possible to trace the present-day Republican Party back to the Federalists and their Whig successors.

Political change prior to the Civil War was slow in coming to Delaware because of the Federalist Party's remarkable longevity in the state. The election of John Quincy Adams to the presidency by the House of Representatives in 1825 caused a split of Delaware Federalists into a party supporting Adams and a party supporting Andrew Jackson. Those supporting Adams became known as Whigs, while Jacksonians soon became known as the Democratic Party. In the 1850s Delaware's Whigs embraced a nativistic anti-immigration, anti-Catholic movement that made way for the so-called American (or Know-Nothing) Party that swept all three Delaware counties in 1854 and elected both a congressman and a governor. The short-lived American Party met its demise with an unpopular prohibition law its members passed in 1855, which sought to impose total abstinence of liquor upon Delawareans. Accordingly, the Democrats in 1856 resoundingly defeated the American Party, prompting the American Party to reorganize under the name of the People's Party, which advocated protective tariffs and, in turn, became allied with another new party—the antislavery Republican Party.

Even with such successive historic mutations, however, one cannot easily conclude that contemporary Democrats and Republicans resemble their predecessors. And this is true of the party systems in Delaware as well as in the nation, because historically Delaware's parties mirrored in part the national parties, with Republicans generally being the party of business and the Democrats the party of labor.

Although both major Delaware parties have antecedents predating the Civil War, Delaware's present party differentiation dates from the Civil War. The weak Republican Party, which inherited the support of many former Whigs, was then known as the Union Party because it was dedicated to supporting Lincoln and preserving the Union, as were most Delawareans. Its major strength in Delaware was in northern New Castle County. It was the party of opponents to slavery, of industrialists, of Protestant reformers, and of nationalists. On the other hand, the Democratic Party was dominant in rural southern Delaware and was sympathetic to the South and secession. It controlled the state legislature and was supported by Governor William Burton and the state's congressional delegation of Senators James Bayard and Willard Saulsbury and Congressman William Whitely. However, in the end Delaware, like Maryland, did not secede. Indeed, as noted in chapter 1, the proportion of Delaware's population that served in the Union Army was said to have been larger than the proportion of the population of any other northern state.[1]

Delaware's Democratic Party during Reconstruction remained unreconstructed. Lincoln's Emancipation Proclamation of 1863 was directed only to free slaves in the states that were rebelling against the U.S. government and did not apply to Delaware slaves. Delaware Democrats still supported slavery, which persisted only in Delaware, Kentucky, and the Oklahoma Territory until December 1865 when slavery was abolished by adoption of the Thirteenth Amendment to the U.S. Constitution. Not only did the Delaware legislature, then controlled by Democrats, refuse to ratify the Thirteenth, Fourteenth, and Fifteenth Amendments, which offered civil and voting rights to former slaves, but Delaware Democrats also proclaimed themselves the "white man's party" and continued to oppose the Reconstruction policies of the Republican-controlled Congress. The Democratic legislature defiantly declared: "The immutable laws of God have affixed upon the brow of the white races the ineffaceable stamp of superiority, and . . . all attempt to elevate the negro to a social or political equality . . . is futile and subversive."[2]

The Democrats won complete control of the state in 1865 and were able to retain almost uninterrupted control for thirty-three years. This they were able to do by maintaining overrepresentation of Sussex and Kent Counties in the legislature and by nullifying observance of the Fifteenth Amendment in Delaware.[3]

While there were pockets of Republicans in southern Delaware, neither Kent County nor Sussex County as a whole voted Republican until 1888. Although Wilmington voted Republican in every election until 1878, Democrats in New Castle County were augmented by recently arrived Irish immigrant workers who tended to vote Democratic.

In the meantime, the Democratic-controlled state legislature continued to elect Democrats to the United States Senate, most notably the Bayards and the Saulsburys. Historian John Munroe in retrospect agreed with a Republican journalist of that time who labeled these years "the medieval period in Delaware politics," with, according to Munroe, "the Bayards, the Saulsburys, and others acting like feudal lords of this little principality, resolved to keep the peasants—if they were black—in their place and to prevent them from being made use of by the nouveau riche Republican merchants and manufacturers of the cities."[4]

RISE OF THE REPUBLICAN PARTY

Industrialization in the North eventually paved the way for Republicans to gain a foothold throughout the state. The growing influence of industrial and business activity in the Wilmington area, and its association with the Republican Party nationally, helped Republicans win state elections in 1888 that foreshadowed future Republican successes in wresting longtime control from the Democrats. As manufacturing began to surpass agriculture, evidenced by the 1900 census, Republicans gained control of county tax assessments, which theretofore were administered by Democrats to prevent most African Americans from voting. Finally, Delaware's Constitution of 1897 extended the right to vote to African American males.

The rise of the Republican Party in Delaware nevertheless was a painful experience. Voter corruption had long been rife throughout the state, especially in Kent and Sussex Counties. It was common for voters as well as legislators to sell their votes to the highest bidders. The highest bidder of all proved to be John Edward Addicks, a wealthy interloper with deep pockets who had moved to Delaware in 1878 from Pennsylvania. Addicks decided in the 1880s and 1890s that he could "buy" a U.S. Senate seat by taking advantage of rising Republicanism in the small state of Delaware. At that time, the General Assembly was still empowered to select Delaware's two U.S. senators.

By purchasing the necessary votes, primarily of Republican state legislators who had gained control of the legislature, Addicks sought repeatedly to be named one of Delaware's two United States senators. In 1899 he received twenty-one of the necessary twenty-seven votes to be elected; in 1901 he received twenty-two votes. Although he ultimately failed to garner enough votes, coming as close as one vote to being elected, Addicks's efforts split the Republican Party into two factions—so-called Regular Republicans who rejected his bribes and Union Republicans who supported Addicks.

Bitter disputes in the state legislature over electing a U.S. senator caused one or both of Delaware's U.S. Senate seats to remain empty for many years. Remarkably, Delaware's state legislature failed to elect a senator in 1895, 1899, 1901, and 1905, and between 1901 and 1903 both U.S. Senate seats remained vacant, which meant Delaware had no representation at all in that body. Delaware became notorious for these repeated failures, and the story of Addicks became widely covered in the national press. The Seventeenth Amendment of the United States Constitution, adopted in 1913, ended the election of U.S. senators by state legislatures by providing for their direct election by the voters. "The revelation of rampant bribery and corruption made Delaware an illustrative case for Progressive reformers' objective of direct election of United States senators."[5]

The issue of adoption of the Nineteenth Amendment to the U.S. Constitution, which extended suffrage to women, caused Delaware again to become a dubious center of national attention. Suffragists and anti-suffragists from around the nation besieged Delaware legislators for seven months in 1920 over the issue of ratification. Thirty-five states had already ratified the amendment, and Delaware's ratification would have met the Constitution's requirement of three-fourths of the forty-eight states. Republicans then controlled the Delaware Senate by a margin of twelve to five and the House of Representatives by twenty-three to ten.[6] Delaware's Republican governor John G. Townsend and Democratic president Woodrow Wilson both supported ratification. However, Delaware's wealthy gentry and Republicans in the General Assembly were divided on the issue, while Democratic legislators opposed women's suffrage because it would double the number of black voters. Delaware's House of Representatives in the end voted twenty-four to ten against bringing ratification of the amendment to a vote, leaving the honor of the decisive ratification to Tennessee. Accordingly, just as the Democratic-controlled legislature in earlier years refused to ratify the Fifteenth Amendment, the Republican-controlled legislature had now failed to ratify the Nineteenth Amendment. Nevertheless, as soon as both amendments became adopted as part of the U.S. Constitution, they of course applied to Delaware.[7]

The two factions of Delaware's Republican Party were able to significantly out-vote Delaware Democrats in the early years of the twentieth century. Republicans, with few exceptions, supported by African American voters, retained control of Delaware until the 1936 election, when the state elected the first national Democratic ticket (led by Franklin Roosevelt) since 1912 and the first Democratic governor since 1897.

MAINTAINING PARITY

After World War II, Delaware was still somewhat isolated, embedded in the Delmarva Peninsula. Upstate was dominated by manufacturing and business interests, while downstate was dominated by agriculture, with vast farms producing poultry, feed grains, and various vegetables and fruits. Conservative and wealthier upstate and the even more conservative downstate shared power in the state capital, Dover, located in the middle of the state.[8]

The "Big Three" of Delaware politics after World War II were Elbert N. Carvel, a fertilizer salesman from Sussex County; J. Caleb Boggs, a lawyer from Kent County; and John J. Williams, a poultry farmer and feed merchant from Sussex County. Democrat Carvel was elected governor in 1948 and again in 1960. Republican Williams was elected U.S. senator in 1946 and served four terms until 1971, the longest service in that body to that time in Delaware history. Republican Boggs won seven statewide elections, more than anyone previously in Delaware. Boggs first served three terms in the U.S. House of Representatives, from 1947 until 1953, when he became governor and served the allowed maximum of two terms, and then he served two terms in the U.S. Senate until 1973. Although all three were from southern Delaware, each served with the acquiescence or support of New Castle County power brokers.[9]

Social and economic change in Delaware abetted the restoration of the Democratic Party to a position of equality in the 1940s and 1950s. The openings of the Delaware Memorial Bridge in August 1951 and the Chesapeake Bay Bridge in July 1952 proved to be momentous developments. Together they connected Delaware's economy and tourism sectors to the Boston-to-Washington megalopolis of the East. Continuing industrialization created a wave of migration of urbanized workers into the state, who tended to become Democrats. The population of the state soared to over 318,000 in 1950, up from 202,000 in 1910, making Delaware the seventh-fastest-growing state in the nation. The farmland abutting Wilmington began to be transformed by suburbanization. Of 220,000 Delawareans of voting age, 150,000 were in New Castle County alone—a number greater than the total votes ever cast in Delaware prior to 1940. The distinctive rural character of the state was waning. The population explosion of the decade of the 1950s caused a growth rate of 40.3 percent, higher than in all but five other states. Paul Dolan observed in his 1956 book, "Instead of the mass of population being enclosed in small towns and villages or small suburban communities, Delawareans in the main are now to be found in the metropolitan area of New Castle County."[10]

Whereas Republicans in earlier years had dominated New Castle County while Democrats dominated Kent and Sussex Counties, the converse became true in later years, with New Castle County voting Democratic in important elections and Kent and Sussex Counties voting Republican. The tendency of southern Delaware to be more conservative continued to be the case. The two parties in recent years have maintained a vigorous rivalry resulting in a fairly even sharing of governing. Indeed, Delaware is generally considered to have one of the most competitive party systems in the nation.

In recent local elections Democrats have maintained majority control. Of thirteen members of the Wilmington city council in 2008, twelve were Democrats, and the mayor was also a Democrat. Of the seven members of the New Castle County council, five were Democrats and two were Republicans, and the county executive was also a Democrat. However, Democrats held only bare majorities in the Kent County levy court (four to three) and Sussex County council (three to two).

"The state tradition," however, "is for Delawareans to reckon their politics by their governors," wrote Delaware political writer Celia Cohen. "The chief executive is by definition an agenda setter, by necessity a political leader and by custom the very emblem of the state."[11] By such reckoning, since 1949 the Republican and Democratic Parties have operated on a basis of near equality, with first one party and then the other party dominating the state's political life. In the fifty-nine years from 1949 to 2008, the position of governor was held by Democrats for thirty years and by Republicans for twenty-nine. Although Republicans held the governorship from 1977 to 1993, Democrats held that post from 1993 through 2008.

Meanwhile, in the sixty-one years from 1947 through 2006, both houses of the General Assembly were controlled by Democrats for twenty years, and by Republicans for fourteen years.[12] But even more significantly, for twenty-seven years the two parties divided control of the General Assembly, with Democrats controlling the Senate for the period of twenty-three years, from 1985 through 2008, while Republicans controlled the House of Representatives.

Moreover, Democrats held one U.S. Senate seat while Republicans held the other Senate seat from 1973 to 2001, when Democrats claimed both. But Republicans have held Delaware's lone seat in the U.S. House of Representatives since 1967, except for the ten-year period 1983–93 when it was held by a Democrat.

Beginning with the election of President Dwight Eisenhower in 1952, Delawareans voted for the winner in twelve consecutive presidential elections—voting seven times for the Republican candidate and five times for the Democratic candidate—thus earning Delaware the distinction of being a bellwether state. That string appeared to be finally broken in the 2000 election, when Democrat Al Gore trounced Republican George W. Bush (by 13 percent), who became president even though he lost the national popular vote. Delaware's bellwether claim was buried in 2004, when a majority of Delaware voters again supported the Democratic candidate—John Kerry—while Bush was reelected, and this time he won the nation's popular vote as well.

Of the state's 557,736 registered voters in 2006, 44 percent were Democrats, 32 percent were Republicans, and the remaining 24 percent were "declines" (those declaring no preference) and third party members. Of New Castle County's 353,845 registered voters, 47 percent were Democrats, 29 percent were Republicans, and 24 percent others. Of Kent County's 89,821 registered voters, there were 41 percent Democrats, 34 percent Republicans and 25 percent others. Of Sussex County's 114,070 registered voters, Democrats held a bare edge of roughly 600 voters or 39.6 percent over Republicans' 39.2 percent, with 21.2 percent others. Although Democrats counted a sizeable plurality of the state's electorate, Republicans tended to out-hustle the Democrats in all three counties in the 2006 elections. In New Castle County 49 percent of registered Republicans compared with 47 percent of Democrats showed up at the polls. In Kent County 48 percent of Republicans to 44 percent of Democrats voted. And in Sussex County 55 percent of Republicans compared with 51 percent of Democrats actually voted.

POLICY CONVERGENCE

The foregoing statistics demonstrate that both parties have become truly statewide parties, that they have continued to operate on a basis of near equality, and that they remain strongly competitive. In their 1976 book, Dolan and Soles attributed this competitive phenomenon to (1) the large

5. Distribution of Delaware Registered Voters, 1960–2006

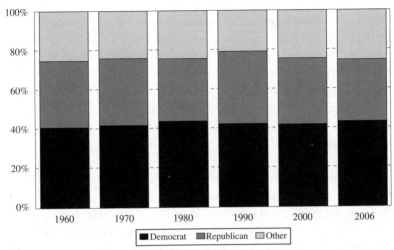

Source: Center for Applied Demography & Survey Research, University of Delaware. Delaware Department of Elections.

number of independent voters in Delaware known as "declines" because they decline to register for a party; (2) the large number of voters who split their tickets; (3) the use by both parties of professional public relations firms in statewide campaigns; and (4) avoidance by both parties of "very liberal or very conservative" candidates, choosing candidates who instead try to appeal to middle-of-the-road voters by emphasizing personalistic—as distinguished from program- or issue-oriented—politics.[13]

The most important reason, however, why Democrats and Republicans have in general maintained parity in Delaware politics since the Second World War is, we believe, the economic ideology they have shared. Party unity and political effectiveness in Delaware arise from political compromise within economic parameters. According to University of Delaware political scientists Janet Johnson and Joseph Pika, "Debate is constrained by the consensual nature of Delaware politics, as well as the consciously cultivated, pro-business climate that is carefully sustained."[14] Since the Second World War, Delaware's two major parties have become ideologically indistinguishable. One could say, if it is good for the economy, it is good for employment and incomes! Accordingly, so far as protecting and supporting Delaware's economic interests, it makes little difference whether one party controls the governorship while the other controls the legislature, or whether each party controls one of the two houses of the General Assembly as has happened since 1985. Simply put, consensus politics in Delaware is not impaired by divided government.

SYSTEMIC SHIFT OF POLITICAL POWER

As we have observed, upstate-downstate rivalries have deep historical roots in Delaware and have persisted from colonial times into the twenty-first century. Shortly after the onset of statehood, assemblymen from Sussex and Kent Counties forced the move of the capital from the town of New Castle, located in northern New Castle County, to Dover in Kent County, where it has since remained. Moreover, regardless of the disproportion between New Castle County's growing population and that of the other two counties, each county retained equal at-large representation in the General Assembly until 1897.

The Constitution of 1897 divided Sussex and Kent Counties into ten representative and five senatorial districts each, and New Castle County into fifteen representative and seven senatorial districts, of which five and two, respectively, were allotted to Wilmington. As we have observed, Wilmington, nevertheless, continued to be underrepresented. Whereas, previously, Wilmington residents dominated New Castle County elections because representatives were then elected at large, the fact that the Constitution of 1897 allotted Wilmington only seven representatives meant they no longer could dominate the county.

No further reapportionment occurred for the next seven decades, even though population gains in Wilmington and New Castle County continued. When the Constitution of 1897 was adopted, Delaware's total population was approximately 175,000, with about 32,000 living in Kent County, 38,000 in Sussex County, and 105,000 in New Castle County (of whom about 70,000 were in Wilmington). By 1960 the state's total population had increased to 446,292, with 65,651 living in Kent County, 73,195 in Sussex County, and 307,446 in New Castle County (of whom only 95,827 lived in Wilmington).

By 1964 Delaware was ranked as having the seventh-worst apportioned state legislature in the nation, with representatives of only 22 percent of the state's total 1960 population constituting a majority of the Senate while only 18.5 percent elected a majority of the House. Accordingly, residents of New Castle County, including those living in the city of Wilmington, were grossly underrepresented in the state legislature. The wealthy New Castle County interests did not in fact "control" the state legislature. Indeed, by virtue of the apportionment ordained by the Constitution of 1897, legislators from Kent and Sussex Counties held majority control for the first two-thirds of the twentieth century. In this respect, crusader Ralph Nader and his associates were in error to have sensationalized Delaware as *The Company*

State, the title given their 1973 book in which they polemicized Delaware as having been dominated by and captive of the DuPont Company and du Pont family of New Castle County.[15]

Finally, seven New Castle County Republicans successfully challenged the constitutionality of the existing apportionment. As we have noted, in 1964 the United States Supreme Court upheld a 1962 federal district court decision declaring the 1897 apportionment unconstitutional on the ground that the Equal Protection Clause of the Fourteenth Amendment of the United States Constitution required that one person is entitled to the same voting power as another person.[16] A new state census of 1967, modified by the 1970 census, formed the basis for a reapportionment law that the courts ultimately found acceptable.[17] Whereas New Castle County was given twenty-nine representatives and fifteen senators, Kent and Sussex Counties each were entitled to only six representatives and three senators. In other words, of the total of sixty-two state legislators, forty-four (over 70 percent) represented New Castle County including the city of Wilmington. And suburban New Castle County alone was to be represented by thirty-five (over 56 percent) of the total.

It is worth reiterating here that one of the most significant developments in the political history of Delaware proved to be the reapportionment forced by U.S. courts. It caused a systemic shift of political power from predominantly rural southern Delaware to New Castle County, including the city of Wilmington.

NEW CASTLE COUNTY'S "BIG FIVE"

The consequences of the reapportionment were that both the Republican and Democratic Parties would be influenced more than ever by the economic interests of northern Delaware and less by the agricultural interests of the southern part of the state, and thereby the two parties would become much more alike than different. Reapportionment also meant that thereafter Republican and Democratic Party tickets for statewide offices had to be balanced with candidates from both upstate and downstate to achieve the political compromise that party unity required. And perhaps most important, the power to select statewide candidates—a major purpose of political parties—would be influenced preponderantly by party leaders in New Castle County, where most of the electorate resided. The most immediate result of reapportionment meant that the "Big Three" of the World War II generation from southern Delaware (Carvel, Boggs, and Williams) would in time give way to the "Big Five" from northern Delaware (Biden, du Pont, Roth, Carper, and Castle).

The first elections subsequent to the reapportionment based on the 1970 census were held in the fall of 1972. That year marked the beginning of an era of New Castle County's Big Five that would last to the end of the twentieth century, when one of the five would be defeated by another of the five, which continued into the next century an era of the Big Four. It was no accident, given the shift of political power, that all five luminaries were residents of New Castle County. All five served in Congress, four were lawyers, and three also were former governors.

The year 1972 marked the election of Democrat Joe Biden to the U.S. Senate, upsetting longtime incumbent Republican Caleb Boggs. Biden still held that seat through 2008, making him the longest serving U.S. senator in Delaware history (thirty-six years). The year 1972 was also the year that Republican Pete du Pont was reelected for his second of three terms to the U.S. House of Representatives, which he followed with the maximum two terms as governor—a total of fourteen years in statewide offices. Both Biden and du Pont would campaign briefly for the U.S. presidency before withdrawing in 1988. Although du Pont held no public office after his service as governor ended in 1985, he continued to wield political influence well into the next century in national and Delaware Republican circles, as a columnist for the *Wall Street Journal*, chairman of the Dallas-based National Center for Policy Analysis, and as a founder and leader of the Delaware Public Policy Institute—the state's only privately sponsored public policy institute.

In the meantime, a third member of Delaware's remarkable Big Five was Republican Bill Roth, who began serving as Delaware's other U.S. senator after his election in 1970, before which he had served two terms as Delaware's lone member in the U.S. House of Representatives. Roth continued to serve in the Senate through the end of the century, when he was defeated by a fourth member of the Big Five—Democrat Tom Carper—in the 2000 election, giving Delaware two Democratic U.S. Senate seats for the first time since 1940. All five members of the group had steadfastly avoided running against each other until the election of 2000, when the aging Roth was defeated by Carper.

Tom Carper is the fourth Big Five member. He has won more statewide elections than anyone else in Delaware's history—two elections as state treasurer (1977–83); five as the state's lone representative in the U.S. House of Representatives (1983–93); two as Governor (1993–2001); and thus far two as U.S. senator (2001–). In all, through 2008, Carper had served a total of thirty-two successive years in statewide offices.

Another of the four undefeated members of the Big Five is Republican Mike Castle, who was reelected in 2008 to serve his ninth successive term in the U.S. House of Representatives, marking his service in the House the longest in Delaware's history. He was first elected to the House in 1992, after serving eight years as Delaware's governor (1985–93), four years as lieutenant governor, and several years in the state's General Assembly. In other words, through 2008 Castle had served twenty-eight successive years in statewide offices.

The years since World War II marked, then, what may be termed "the era of incumbency," distinguished by the prominence of the Big Three of southern Delaware followed by the Big Five of New Castle County. This era was continuing into the first decade of the twenty-first century, signifying that with few exceptions Delaware voters were inclined to continue in office those whose behavior did nothing to embarrass the electorate. One notable exception was Bill Roth's loss in his reelection bid to the U.S. Senate, but it took another member of the Big Five to defeat him and then only after Roth—then seventy-nine and in failing health—had served in Congress for an unprecedented thirty-four years.

A departure from the past, however, was the election in 2000 of Democrat Ruth Ann Minner from Kent County as Delaware's first woman governor. Democrats had chosen Minner to run for lieutenant governor to geographically balance the ticket with Carper, from New Castle County, who was running for governor in 1992. After serving the limit of two terms as lieutenant governor, Democrats chose her to run for governor in 2000. She, in turn, approved state finance secretary John Carney from New Castle County to run for lieutenant governor as her independently elected running mate, again to balance the ticket. Both were reelected in 2004 for second terms. Governor Minner had served in the state Senate from 1982 to 1992, and in the state House of Representatives from 1974 to 1982.

CAMPAIGN CONTRIBUTIONS

Delaware law governing campaign contributions requires candidates for state and local offices, including legislators, to file financial reports thirty days, and again eight days, before the election and also at the end of the calendar year—among the least restrictive disclosure requirements of the fifty states.[18] Campaign contribution limits per election, of $1,200 for statewide candidates and $600 for other candidates, apply equally to individuals, corporations, political action committees (PACs), "and any other organization or institution of any nature"; and contributions in excess of $100 must be reported. The law also limits political party campaign contributions to candidates for governor (a $75,000 limit); other statewide offices, namely lieutenant governor, insurance commissioner, attorney general, treasurer, and auditor ($25,000); state senator ($5,000); and state representative ($3,000). Although political parties are not restricted in expenditures for party ticket-supporting activities, an individual is limited to a $20,000 contribution to any political party "during an election period." Any violation of these provisions constitutes only a misdemeanor.[19] However, no one has ever been found guilty of violating Delaware law governing campaign contributions.

Money from PACs, fundraising arms of special interests, in 2002 made up about 25 percent of Democratic senator Tom Carper's senatorial campaign and 37 percent of Republican congressman Mike Castle's campaign. A major reason Democrat Joe Biden won six successive six-year terms in the U.S. Senate has been his success in attracting campaign finance contributions. According to a Common Cause study of campaign contributions of U.S. senators from 1983 to 1988, Biden relied heavily on PAC contributions while he was a member of the Senate Foreign Relations Committee. Senator Biden later would not accept any PAC contributions, but nevertheless received from other sources $2,260,356 for 1995–96 and $2,726,583 for 2001–2. More than three-fourths raised for his 2002 reelection campaign came from out-of-state contributions, mostly from fundraisers such as $1,000-per-ticket cocktail parties, lunches, or brunches held in hotels, restaurants, or homes.

Biden was the only one among Delaware's three-person congressional delegation in 2002 who took no "soft money" from political action committees, nor did he accept any Democratic Party contributions in 2002.[20] However, after deciding not to run for president in 2004, Biden decided to run for president in 2008, pending substantial financial support. Accordingly, he formed "Unite Our States," a new PAC for that purpose. Although he had been expected to run at the same time for reelection to the Senate yet again in 2008, his bid for the White House remained unaffected by restrictions of the Federal Bipartisan Campaign Reform Act of 2002, which bans national parties from raising and spending "soft money." Indeed, given Biden's past dependency on $1,000-per-ticket fundraisers, he stood to benefit even more from the act's provision raising the limit to $2,000 on individual contributions to House and Senate campaigns.[21] Biden was one of the first aspirants to withdraw from the 2008 presidential campaign.

The most singular consequence of FCDA of 1981 was the phenomenal growth over the following twenty years of MBNA, that became one of the 50 most profitable companies in America, Delaware's largest bank and private employer—surpassing in the state the DuPont Company in local employment—and billing itself "the world's largest independent credit card issuer." Although the DuPont Company continued into the twenty-first century to partner with the state government and the academic and business communities, MBNA emerged as Delaware's and arguably the nation's most active corporate power broker.

It was reported in 2005, according to the Center for Public Integrity, that President George W. Bush received $605,041 over his entire political career from Delaware-based MBNA, more than from any other company. Republican representative Mike Castle, who sat on the House banking committee, also had reportedly received $354,450 in political contributions from MBNA since 1989. But the company announced in March 2004 that in the future it would no longer top the list of the nation's contributors.[22]

MBNA, moreover, had been the top donor to Delaware Senator Biden's campaigns since 1993. Its strategy thereby was to induce lawmakers to toughen laws that would make it more difficult for debtors to declare bankruptcy as a means of avoiding paying off their debts. This proposed legislation was in response to a massive increase in the number of personal bankruptcies during the Clinton years. In Delaware during the period of 1990–2005 personal bankruptcies increased from 1,000 to 3,500 annually.

Senator Biden took "the unusual tack" of inserting the bankruptcy legislation into a foreign relations bill in 2000. Congress passed the bill in December 2000, but President Bill Clinton vetoed it. However, President George W. Bush publicly backed overhaul of the bankruptcy law, and the Republican-controlled Congress ultimately passed the bankruptcy reform in 2005 sought by MBNA and by banks in general. The bill passed the Senate seventy-four to twenty-five with the support of both Delaware senators Joe Biden and Tom Carper. Personal bankruptcy filings dropped sharply after the bill became law.[23] People still went bankrupt, of course, but they no longer had the recourse of filing for bankruptcy to get out of debt in some situations.

In Delaware, MBNA employees were not only the main contributors to the campaigns of all three members of Delaware's congressional delegation (Biden, Carper, and Castle), but the company also played a key role in convincing former president of the state's Chamber of Commerce John Burris to reenter the 2000 governor's race against Ruth Ann Minner, by bankrolling $198,000 for his campaign—to no avail as it turned out because Minner easily won that election. According to the Center for Responsive Politics, MBNA was the top overall political donor nationally within the finance and credit industry between 199 and 2004. However, MBNA's sale to Bank of America, effective in January 2006, ended its role in Delaware and national politics.[24]

In a 1993 book, political scientists Janet Johnson and Joseph Pika described Delaware as having "friends and neighbors politics" in which the combination of its small political elite, low turnover, and preeminent corporate interests "produces a pattern of 'clubby,' old-boy politics operating within consensual constraints." As David Mark observed in his 2006 book, *Going Dirty*, nowhere are negative campaign tactics, a staple of political campaigns in more populous states, shunned more than Delaware. Attributable in major part to Delaware's smallness, according to Johnson and Pika, are "face-to-face," easily accessible, and "highly personalized" political practices, and the fact that—despite general party competitiveness—there is a strong incumbency factor. "Delaware's diminutive size," they wrote, "masks diversity in its socioeconomic base as well as enduring geographic division."[25]

These features account for an unusual degree of bipartisan and consensus politics in this small state, where most principal political actors not only know one another but maintain friendly and cooperative relations across party and sectional lines, which are unlikely if not impossible to develop in larger and more populous states. Several examples, by reference to each member of the Big Five, are illustrative.

Modern bipartisan and consensus politics can be said to have begun with Republican governor Pete du Pont, scion of Delaware's first family. Faced with a severe crisis in state finances and a legislature controlled by Democrats, newly elected Governor du Pont adopted a confrontational style. He acted to freeze all state hiring and construction contracts, provoked legislators to forego a pay raise and cost-of-living increase for state employees, and vetoed the fiscal 1978 budget passed by the legislature, which promptly overrode his veto—the first such override in state history. From this low point, du Pont adopted a conciliatory posture and led an enormously successful bipartisan effort to attract new business by initiating various measures. In 1977 he joined with the leadership of both parties in forming the Delaware Economic and Financial Advisory Council (DEFAC), which from that point forward took the decision as to how much revenue the state would have to spend out of the executive's and legislature's hands. This also heralded a bipartisan financial policy that continues to this day. Governor du Pont also initiated bipartisan income tax cuts and the adoption of the previously discussed Financial Center Development Act of 1981. No other public policy in this small state better illustrates the success of Delaware bipartisan politics, the centrality of economic issues, and the importance of corporate law. Thereafter, bipartisanship, with a consensus style of governing, became institutionalized in Delaware.

Delaware voters were faced in 1992 with finding a new governor to replace popular Republican governor Mike Castle, who was completing his second term and was prevented by the state constitution from running again. The result was that equally popular Democratic congressman Tom Carper simply swapped jobs with Castle, with Carper becoming governor and Castle becoming the state's lone congressman. This exchange of offices became known as "The Swap"—epitomizing the institutionalized consensus politics that rules in Delaware. "Only in Delaware," observed political writer Celia Cohen, "would an entire state join in such an open conspiracy—involving the candidates, their political parties and a majority of the voters."[26]

Another example of Delaware consensus politics concerns its presidential primary. Every four years, Delawareans resented the fact that presidential candidates of both major parties typically shunned campaigning in this small state that has only three electoral votes and a minimum of national convention delegates. To put Delaware on the map, Governor Tom Carper signed a bipartisan measure of the General Assembly scheduling Delaware's first-ever closed presidential primary on February 24, 1996, only four days after the nation's earliest New Hampshire primary. This move upset both national and New Hampshire party leaders, who threatened to punish Delaware for its political "tail-gating." In the end, only wealthy Steve Forbes among leading Republican candidates chose to campaign in Delaware in 1996. He handily won the state's Republican primary but later withdrew from the race. After struggling for more than five years to find still a better way to make little Delaware more prominent in the presidential primary process, which would bring presidential aspirants to campaign in the state, leaders of both major Delaware parties agreed in 2003 to move Delaware voting in 2004 to February 3—a full week after the New Hampshire primary. The trouble was that six other states (Arizona, Missouri, New Mexico, North Dakota, Oklahoma, and South Carolina) also scheduled presidential primaries or caucuses for that day. Once again most candidates bypassed Delaware, with only Reverend Al Sharpton and Senators John Kerry and Joe Lieberman, among the eight remaining Democratic contenders, visiting Delaware prior to its February 3 primary.[27]

Still another example of consensus politics among Delaware's Big Five concerns Republican Mike Castle's tenure as Delaware's lone member of the U.S. House of Representatives, a tenure that seemed assured so long as he wished. Seemingly, he would never fail to win reelections handily, because his record in Congress was calculated to win the continuing support of Delaware's Democrats as well as Republicans. According to the *Congressional Quarterly* listing of Republicans who voted most often against legislation backed by the White House, the independent-minded Castle ranked fifth, voting against President George W. Bush 31 percent of the time in 2003. Among the three Delawareans in Congress, Castle was by far the most independent, ranking third among House members who most often broke ranks with their political party—22.8 percent of the time in 2003, whereas Democratic senator Tom Carper broke ranks with his fellow Democrats 19 percent of the time and Democratic senator Biden bucked his party only about 10 percent of the time. Congressman Castle explained, "I think I reflect Delaware, which is very independent and moderate in politics. . . . Delaware is not a real partisan place."[28] The fact that both Castle and Carper had been recent governors of the state probably had something to do with their behavior. Castle was the only Republican who won election to a statewide office in 2004, when he was reelected to the U.S. House of Representatives once again by a wide margin, with the support of many Democrats.

In Delaware, even a memorial service may have a bipartisan and consensus spin. Former Republican senator Bill Roth died in December 2003 at the age of eighty-two. About five hundred people attended the memorial service, described as "the coming together that is the pride of this small state . . . a mosaic of bipartisanship." Along with Republican stalwarts, many Democratic leaders attended, including Democratic senator Tom Carper, who had ended Roth's long-time congressional tenure, and Joe Biden, who had been Roth's Democratic colleague in Congress for more than a quarter of a century. Indeed, Biden in his eulogy showered accolades on Roth. "Everything about Bill's life was about excellence," Biden was reported as saying. "All of Delaware will miss him."[29]

Delaware has institutionalized bipartisan and consensus politics with a unique celebration known as "Return Day," held every two years on the Thursday after each Tuesday election day at the circle in front of the Sussex County courthouse in Georgetown. Believed to be the only event of its kind in the nation, the ceremony is said to date back to 1792 when Sussex County voters "returned" to the county seat to learn election results. The tradition features a parade around the circle of horse-drawn carriages or antique autos shared by winners and losers in statewide elections. After the parade, Democratic and Republican leaders literally bury a hatchet in a container of sand to signify pushing aside any sour grapes lingering from election campaigns. According to David Mark, "Though losing political candidates across the country often make a perfunctory concession call to the winner on Election Night, only in Delaware do they ride together in a car days after the election."[30]

ASSORTED THIRD PARTIES

As in other states, Delaware also has its assortment of third parties, including the Libertarian, Independent, Natural Law, American Reform, and Green Parties. The main purpose of a political party is to gain control of government by having its candidates elected to public offices. Delaware's so-called third parties, however, do not fit this definition, because none has yet been successful in having any of its candidates elected to a public office, a distinction shared with some other states. Delaware's fledgling Green Party, founded in the late 1990s, came closest when its candidate for state attorney general in 2002 garnered 10 percent of the vote after a spirited campaign. The Green Party of Delaware is affiliated with Green Parties in other states. Crusader Ralph Nader gave the national Green Party prominence as its standard bearer in the 2000 presidential campaign, but he refused to run again as the Green Party candidate in 2004, thus dealing a body blow to that party both in the nation and in Delaware. According to Nader, "the reaction to George W. Bush, has fractured—more than galvanized— the Greens as a Party."[31]

It is fair to say, therefore, that Delaware's third parties exist more as public policy advocacy organizations than as political parties, given their failure to elect candidates to public offices. Accordingly, they resemble Delaware's interest groups that are discussed in chapter 11.

CONCLUSION

In the grand sweep of Delaware history since the Civil War, we have observed that first the Democratic Party controlled Delaware government and politics until 1888, followed by dominance of the Republican Party until 1936, after which the two parties operated on a basis of near equality, with first one party and then the other dominating the state's political life.

Meanwhile, the two parties evolved into highly competitive statewide parties while so-called third parties have proven politically inconsequential. The old sectionalism has been greatly modified. No longer is the strength of Democrats confined to the south below the canal and that of Republicans evidenced only above the canal. Court-ordered one-person-one-vote reapportionment in the 1960s has proven one of the most significant developments in the state's political history. Political power shifted once and for all to above the canal.

Shared governance, divided government, business-friendly parameters, consensus politics, bipartisanship, long-time incumbency, political compromise—these are some of the defining characteristics that accurately describe contemporary Delaware government and politics.

CHAPTER SIX

The Governor and Administration

The governor is arguably the most powerful government official in Delaware.[1] But this was a late developing phenomenon in the state's history. This chapter provides an overview of the governor and administration of the state government, especially analysis of the governor's role in terms of constitutional powers and constraints, administrative impediments, and activism or leadership.

CONSTITUTIONAL POWERS

Throughout the nineteenth century, Delaware's state government was dominated by the legislature, since the governor lacked any veto power. As we have already discussed, the legislature at that time was organized with equal representation among the counties. Thus, it was dominated by the two sparsely populated agricultural counties in the south. Social and economic changes set the stage for the constitutional convention of 1897 to address the question of whether the political power of the two southern counties would permit placing more power in a governor who would be elected in effect by the more populous and industrial northern county. Since Kent and Sussex Counties controlled the legislature, the more populous New Castle County stood to gain should the power of the popularly elected governor be strengthened with respect to the legislature's power. Still, the two rural southern counties would continue to control the state government if the powers of the popularly elected governor could be sufficiently constrained.[2]

Reference has already been made in chapter 4 to the greater powers of the governor in article 3 of the Constitution of 1897, notably expanding the governor's term of office from three years to a maximum of two four-year terms, consecutive or otherwise, providing for the governor's use of the power to veto legislation and to veto line items of appropriation bills, and for the governor to be "the supreme executive." Article 3 defined the scope of gubernatorial power in the broadest terms, by vesting "the supreme executive powers of the State" in the governor, and directing that the governor "shall take care that the laws be faithfully executed."

CONSTITUTIONAL CONSTRAINTS

At the behest of Kent and Sussex County delegates to the 1897 convention, the legislature was given the power to override a governor's veto by a three-fifths vote. Moreover, the southern delegates successfully pushed for restricting the governor's appointment power by requiring Senate confirmation of the governor's appointments. Neither of these constraints would be seen as controversial even today. However, the establishment of five other separate elective state constitutional officers—lieutenant governor, treasurer, attorney general, auditor, and insurance commissioner—did further reduce the power of the governor at least in specific areas. Although article 3 of the constitution is entitled "Executive" and creates and empowers the office of governor, it also creates the five elective row offices. One could reasonably conclude that the intention of the framers was to diversify and spread the exercise of executive power as a constraint on the governor.[3] An alternative view would be that these row offices are relatively specialized and relieve the governor of duties with less policy focus. While it is not unusual to find such elective offices in most other states, it is somewhat unusual to find them detailed in the state constitution. Of course, the governor and legislature control the budgets of these offices.

The most important function of the lieutenant governor is to succeed the governor in case of that officer's resignation, death, or disability, but the former also presides over the Senate and may cast the deciding vote in case of a tie. Section 19 stipulates that the lieutenant governor be "chosen at the same time, in the same manner, for the same term" as the governor—a provision held by the state supreme court as meaning that the governor and lieutenant governor are separately elected.[4] Since the lieutenant governor is elected separately from the governor, the two have sometimes been of different parties, as occurred in the elections of 1912, 1916, 1972, 1976, and 1984. Even if the governor and lieutenant governor are of the same party, that fact does not necessarily guarantee that party discipline or loyalty will ensure their harmonious relationship. They may each have their own power base given the fact that they were elected independently. This holds equally true for the other row officers as well. And, in fact, those contesting these offices may not even tie their campaigns to the gubernatorial candidates of their parties. In 1992 Delaware voters elected Democrats for governor and lieutenant governor while electing Republicans for all four remaining constitutional offices.

Since all of the five other constitutional row officers also have statewide constituencies, they may use their offices as springboards for higher elective offices. In recent years, lieutenant governors were elected governors— Democratic lieutenant governor Sherman Tribbitt was elected governor in 1968, Republican lieutenant governor Mike Castle became governor in 1984, and Democratic lieutenant governor Ruth Ann Minner was elected Delaware's first female governor in 2000. Before being elected governor in 1992, Democrat Tom Carper had served as Delaware's lone congressman for five terms, and before that he served as state treasurer for two terms. Republican Jane Brady was elected Delaware's first female attorney general in 1994, and reelected in 1998 and 2002; during her tenure she was widely considered a possible candidate for governor.

Even the insurance commissioner, one of the five elective row officers, may seek to be governor. It was well known that Democratic insurance commissioner David Levinson, elected in 1984 and reelected in 1988, aspired to be governor. After the state Democratic Party backed Tom Carper for governor, thus thwarting Levinson's gubernatorial aspirations in 1991, the latter talked to Republicans about running against Carper on the Republicans' 1992 ticket. Spurned by the Republicans, Levinson then formed his own breakaway and short-lived third party—"A Delaware Party"—but lacking adequate support he failed to launch his campaign.[5]

Regardless of the constitutional mandate that the governor be the "supreme executive" of the state government, two other administrative impediments to the exercise of the governor's powers persisted through most of the twentieth century. Within the executive branch of the state government was the prominence of a patronage system governing state employment, and the pervasiveness of boards and commissions within the executive branch. Patronage was marked by political (party and locality) favoritism rather than by proficiency of job performance. Boards and commissions were marked by dispersed authority rather than by accountability, which limited the governor's authority and commensurate responsibility "to take care that the laws be faithfully executed" as ordained by section 13 of article 3 of the Constitution of 1897.

THE PATRONAGE SYSTEM

Both the federal government and the state of New York adopted merit systems in 1883, followed by Massachusetts in 1884. Neighboring New Jersey became in 1908 the fifth state to join the movement. By the mid-twentieth century most states and most local governments of fifty thousand people or more had merit systems.[6] But this was not the case in Delaware's state or local governments, where patronage continued to prevail. Wilmington's city government 1964 charter included a merit system, and New Castle County government adopted a merit system in mid-1966 covering only 46 percent of county employees. A quasi-merit system was also begun in Kent County in 1967 and in Sussex County in 1969.[7] In February 1967 New Castle County's first director of personnel under the new merit system complained: "Patronage has been a way of life in New Castle County from time immemorial and with it all the personnel problems that one could expect. . . . We have people on the County payroll who are not working at all, others completely incompetent, some competent but who won't work, some physically unable to perform any duty and I believe others with severe mental and emotional problems. A considerable number of our employees are so old that senility is apparent from their actions."[8]

Similar conditions prevailed in the state government, in which patronage had long been regarded, especially by legislators, as the best way to recruit state employees. Each state agency had handled personnel matters separately and variably, except for the few that were required by the federal government to have a merit system in order to receive federal funds. All other state agencies had patronage systems marked by hiring through political parties and county leaders, widespread turnover after elections (even of engineers of the highway department), purchase of political dinner tickets by state employees, and contributions by state employees to party funds and political campaigns.

Among the reasons for continuation of the "spoils" system (viz., to the victors belong the spoils!), according to Dolan in his 1956 book, included "intense countyism" (each county shared appointments), "intense departmentalism," "interdepartmental job raiding," and "public apathy."[9]

Soon after taking office in January 1966, Democratic governor Charles L. Terry appointed a bipartisan study committee that concluded: "State employees must have assurance that they will not be swept out of their job each time change in political leadership occurs, or will not have their job position, pay or progress dependent upon their response to political pressure." The committee drafted a bill that the legislature enacted, and Delaware belatedly adopted a merit system for state employees.[10]

Today, most but not all state employees are covered by the merit system. There is a classification of "exempt" employees who serve "at the pleasure" of an executive officer. Most serve in high level executive positions, but there are other agencies that have other employees who are exempt. For example, the Department of Technology and Information was created from the Office of Information Systems to address the problems of attracting and keeping technology workers. The flexibility needed was hampered by the merit system. Moreover, the Delaware Economic Development Office (DEDO) is entirely within the Executive Department. Its role is policy sensitive and also requires a flexibility to change direction that would be made difficult by the merit system. Nevertheless, even those who are exempt are entitled to file grievances if they have been improperly terminated.

BOARDS AND COMMISSIONS

Historically, the board or commission form of administrative organization was predominant in Delaware's state government. By 1917 there were 117 boards and commissions making up the state's administrative system, whose members were appointed by the governor, drawn more or less equally from the three counties following the make-up of the legislature. This meant that members from Kent and Sussex Counties generally dominated the commissions, which a 1918 study characterized as a "hydra-headed administrative structure" and "a chaotic jumble of anachronisms."[11]

The 1966 law authorizing establishment of a merit system provided that it would be "implemented" by the next administration. Accordingly, it fell to Republican governor Russell Peterson, who had defeated Democrat Terry in Terry's 1968 bid for reelection, to put the merit system into effect. The trouble was that the law had expressly exempted from merit system coverage all members of boards and commissions, who totaled over 1,000 members according to Peterson's task force on reorganization of the state's executive branch. Peterson was later to recall that there were approximately 1,400 Delawareans involved in 140-some agencies in the commission form of government, and though the governor appointed the commission members, they "could tell the governor to go to hell" if they wanted. Each commission hired its own chairman and executive director who had "a little fiefdom of their own," Peterson noted.[12]

Shortly after assuming office in 1969, Governor Peterson announced plans to replace the many boards and commissions with a cabinet system of government comprising administrative departments headed by secretaries appointed by and directly responsible to the governor. Division heads of each department were to be appointed and removable by their respective secretaries with the consent of the governor. The bulk of other state employees would be covered by the merit system. By the end of 1970, ten new departments and the

Executive Office of the Governor were established. The departments were Health and Social Services, Natural Resources and Environmental Control, Agriculture, Public Safety, Finance, Highways and Transportation (renamed the Department of Transportation in 1976), Labor, Community Affairs and Economic Development, Administrative Services, and State.[13]

Reporter Joe Distelheim of the *Wilmington News Journal*, observing at the time that Kent and Sussex Counties "traditionally have had more politicians per square foot than perhaps any place this side of Chicago's City Hall," concluded that "Peterson and his new-fangled Cabinet government have decimated the last bastion of power south of the canal, and the resentment is fierce."[14] In his memoir, Peterson attributed his failure to win reelection to his success in abolishing most boards and commissions. He explained that Delaware citizens south of the canal constituted only 30 percent of the state population but had occupied 70 percent of positions on the state commissions. "Nearly everyone in Kent and Sussex Counties had a relative or friend who once served on a commission, a prestigious position in most circles. They did not like losing that prestige. This was probably the most significant factor in my getting clobbered downstate when I ran for reelection."[15]

Curiously, since 1996 there have existed more boards and commissions than ever before in Delaware state government, but almost all of their members serve as unsalaried volunteers, and in the aggregate their powers have been greatly diminished. Most governmental functions by far are performed by the cabinet departments. In fiscal year 2006, the principal executive branch departments, together with their full-time equivalent General Fund positions, were the following:

Executive (327.8)

Technology and Information (213.0)

State (290.1)

Finance (243.0)

Health and Social Services (3,738.1)

Children, Youth and Their Families (1,030.2)

Correction (2,622.7)

Natural Resources and Environmental Control (396.9)

Safety and Homeland Security (949.0)

Transportation (1,836.0)

Labor (38.9)

Agriculture (92.3)

Elections (49.0)

Education (12,970.6)

Although Delaware was late among the states to adopt merit-based public employment, well over 90 percent of state employees were under a merit system in 2006.

GOVERNORS IN ACTION

As noted in the last chapter, the Republican and Democratic parties since 1949 have shared political power in the state almost equally, resulting in Delaware having one of the most competitive party systems in the nation. A list of the elected governors in recent years best illustrates this phenomenon:

ELECTED GOVERNORS SINCE 1949

Elbert N. Carvel (D) 1949–53
J. Caleb Boggs (R) 1953–60
Elbert N. Carvel (D) 1961–65
Charles L. Terry Jr. (D) 1965–69
Russell W. Peterson Jr. (R) 1969–73
Sherman W. Tribbitt (D) 1973–77
Pierre S. du Pont IV (R) 1977–85
Michael N. Castle (R) 1985–93
Thomas R. Carper (D) 1993–2001
Ruth Ann Minner (D) 2001–9

The fact that Democrats and Republicans have held the governorship almost equally since the mid-twentieth century has given rise to a lively competition for the state's top post and hence the advent of the activist governor in Delaware government and politics.

While Democratic governor Charles Terry (1965–69) will always be most known for ordering National Guard troops to patrol the streets of Wilmington to restore order in the wake of the assassination of Reverend Martin Luther King Jr. on April 4, 1968, he also instituted several major changes that reshaped the governmental landscape in Delaware. As noted, he initiated legislation to replace the patronage system with a merit system for state government employment. In addition, he led a badly needed reform of the magistrate system that affected the overall criminal justice system. While the true effects of these changes would not be felt until the next administration, Governor Terry began the process.[16]

Republican Russell Peterson (1969–73), a Phi Beta Kappa PhD chemist from Wisconsin who had headed a DuPont Company research division while becoming a civic activist, was Terry's successor and destined also to serve only one term. In a wide range of public policy, Peterson's activism as governor far surpassed that of Terry. After initiating change to a cabinet system from the existing commission form of government, he spearheaded major election reform: first by discarding the "Big Lever" that made straight-party voting easy; and second by requiring a primary election for a party nomination whenever a candidate failed to win nomination by a vote of more than two-thirds of the party's convention delegates. Other Peterson initiatives included the end of debtors' prisons; efforts to cut juvenile crime; reforming juvenile corrections and the family court; appointing the first female judge, Roxanna Arsht, as a Family Court judge; plans for a new state prison; eliminating the nation's only remaining whipping post, last used in 1952 ("one of the things of which I am most proud," Peterson later claimed); pushing welfare reform and equal rights for women and minorities; desegregating the state police; and expanding state health services.[17]

Foremost among Peterson's initiatives, especially in retrospect, was his move to preserve Delaware's coastal zone from further industrial development. His perseverance and boldness not only brought opposition from the federal government prior to enactment of Delaware's landmark Coastal Zone Law, but federal authorities—as discussed in chapter 3—also attempted in vain to gut the law well after its enactment. Peterson's initiative was kindled by Shell Oil Company's proposal to build an oil refinery south of the canal almost adjacent to a wildlife refuge. Whether Peterson ever declared "To hell with Shell!" may be questioned, but there is no disputing the fact that he publicly cast his self-styled image as a *Rebel with a Conscience*—the title of his 1999 memoir.

Democrat Sherman Tribbitt defeated incumbent governor Peterson by almost eight thousand votes in the 1972 election. Various reasons have been given, but Peterson's conversion to the cabinet form of government, and his difficulty in understanding certain fiscal and political issues, were certainly central. Governor Tribbitt also was destined to serve a single term—given shaky fiscal conditions, an emerging international energy crisis, and a resulting recession.[18] The actions taken by Tribbitt to resolve the fiscal problems, that is, raising the personal income tax to the highest marginal tax rate in the country and struggling to gain control over government expenditures and bonded indebtedness, set the stage for the next governor to initiate major reforms in financial administration.[19]

Whereas Peterson may be credited with beginning the role of governor as an activist in Delaware public policy, Tribbitt's successor—Republican governor Pierre "Pete" du Pont—may be credited with institutionalizing the governor as activist leader. Subsequent to du Pont's two terms, each of his successors in turn used the powers of the office to wrest control from the legislature to mobilize the state government and the populace for improvements in Delaware's quality of life.

Prior to du Pont's tenure as governor (1977–85), each of his three predecessors—Democrat Terry, Republican Peterson, and Democrat Tribbitt—failed reelection to a second term. Meanwhile, two related changes in Delaware's governmental system served to augment the influence and power of the governor. The first was the change from the commission system to the cabinet system. This change enhanced the governor's control over the executive branch. The second was the court-induced reapportionment ordaining the "one-person, one-vote" rule that shifted political power in the legislature from downstate to upstate and also augmented the power of the governor. It also appeared that the reorientation of the composition of the legislature affected the selection of candidates for governor. It was no accident that five successive governors—three Republicans and two Democrats—were all residents of New Castle County: Peterson, Tribbitt, du Pont, Castle, and Carper. This pattern was to be broken by a resident of Kent County—Democratic governor Ruth Ann Minner (2001–9).

These institutional changes combined to bring about a new relationship between the governor and the legislature, since both were elected by a properly proportioned population, which paved the way for greater cooperation. However, when Republican governor Pete du Pont took office, he was confronted with both houses of the legislature controlled by Democratic majorities—twenty-six to fifteen in the House of Representatives, and thirteen to eight in the Senate. Moreover, as we have noted, he started off on the wrong foot. Although he had defeated Tribbitt for governor by garnering 57 percent of the vote, one of the greatest margins in state history, he inherited a financial mess—expenditures were not in line with revenue, debt service was eating up much of the budget, and the unemployment rate was higher than the national average. Governor du Pont flatly declared the state was bankrupt. Although it wasn't quite bankrupt, major bond-rating agencies continued a pattern begun in 1975 of lowering Delaware's bond ratings.

When the Democratic-controlled legislature overrode du Pont's veto of the budget bill, du Pont knew that he had to replace confrontation with cooperation with the legislature. He reversed course and ushered in the era of bipartisanship and consensus politics that has since dominated the state. Revenue estimates were placed in the hands of an independent body; expenditures were limited to 98 percent of revenues without a 60 percent vote; borrowing was limited to 75 percent of the bonds retired during the previous year; and 5 percent of revenues were excluded from the appropriation process to serve as a rainy-day fund. The result was a watershed in fiscal responsibility which was accepted in a bipartisan fashion by the executive and the legislature.

Pete du Pont had institutionalized bipartisanship and had crafted a consensus style of leadership that effectively ended political warfare between the legislative and executive branches. For example, the Democratic-controlled legislature had acceded to du Pont's choices of able cabinet officers and thereby suspended its longtime opposition to top political appointees from out of state.[20]

Each of Pete du Pont's successors followed his lead by combining bipartisan and consensus politics with strong leadership and policy initiatives. His handpicked lieutenant governor for his second term, New Castle County's Mike Castle, was his immediate successor. Beginning with Castle's election to the General Assembly in 1966, he was never to lose an election. Pete du Pont's legacy was enough to decisively propel Castle into the governor's office, making the Republicans' win of the governorship the first party since World War II to do so in three successive elections.

While electing Castle in 1984 to be governor, Delaware voters appeared almost fickle by splitting their votes seemingly every which way. They elected Democrat S. B. Woo, a University of Delaware professor, to be lieutenant governor, who thus became the nation's highest-ranking politician of Chinese descent to be elected a statewide officer. They contributed to Republican Ronald Reagan's landslide victory to the nation's presidency. At the same time, they reelected to Congress by wide margins Democrats Senator Joe Biden and Representative Tom Carper. They elected Democrat David Levinson to be insurance commissioner, the first time they had ousted a statewide incumbent in fourteen years. And perhaps most significant for the future of Delaware politics, Delaware voters replaced the Democratic majority in the state House of Representatives with a Republican majority of twenty-two to nineteen, while retaining a Democratic majority of thirteen to eight in the state Senate.

Regardless of Delaware voters' propensity to split their votes, chaos did not result, principally because du Pont's legacy of bipartisan and consensus politics, together with a shared desire for a good business climate, would continue to efface party differences. Besides initiating more tax cuts, Castle introduced so-called quality-of-life legislation aimed at controlling land development, now that Delaware had become a predominantly suburban state. The Transportation Trust Fund was created for the funding of roads and transportation facilities; counties were required to adopt comprehensive development plans; and the Delaware Agricultural Lands Preservation Act was passed. Castle also put the issue of health care high on the state's agenda, and moved to initiate business-led reform of the state's public education system. In 1988 Castle was reelected for a second term by a resounding 71 percent of the vote.

Since Republican governor Mike Castle was constitutionally limited to two terms, Democratic congressman Tom Carper had his eye on succeeding Castle as governor. But first Carper needed to gain effective control of the leadership of the Democratic Party in New Castle County, then under the tight control of political boss Gene Reed, who was also office manager for political maverick David Levinson, the state insurance commissioner. Fifty-five percent of the state's population lived in suburban New Castle County, and whoever controlled the Democratic Party there could wield preponderant statewide power. As Reed faced reelection in 1989 to the chairmanship of the New Castle County Democratic Committee, Congressman Carper successfully mobilized his supporters to wrest that post from Reed.

Tom Carper's takeover of the county organization, and thus the state Democratic Party, effectively ended Insurance Commissioner David Levinson's aspiration, as we have noted, to become governor himself.[21] Instead, Carper became the Democratic Party's nominee and was elected governor in 1992. Meanwhile, Republican Mike Castle was elected to replace Carper in the Congress. They had simply exchanged jobs, as we have already noted, which became known as "the Swap"—another testament to the consensus politics and to voting for incumbents that had come to prevail in Delaware.

As governor, Tom Carper continued the activist leadership of his predecessors that Delaware had come to expect of its governors. Carper's two terms were highlighted by his continuation of Castle's initiative of business-led reform of the state's public education system. Perhaps most important was Carper's leadership in reforming the state's welfare system, as discussed in chapter 3, which became the model for national welfare reform. His campaign for reelection emphasized his twice cutting personal income taxes, securing the highest bond rating in the state's history, achieving Delaware's ranking as one of the ten best financially managed states, and creating thirty thousand new jobs. In 1996 Carper won reelection by an overwhelming 69.5 percent of the vote. During his second term, income taxes were again cut three successive years, and the state's booming economy produced surpluses of $430 million in 1998 and more than $300 million in 1999.

After Carper's lieutenant governor, Ruth Ann Minner, was elected governor in 2000, she continued to support most of Carper's policy initiatives, but the national economic bubble of the 1990s had burst and she was beset with belt-tightening necessities and job losses. However, Delaware fared much better than other states that had incurred deep deficits and huge budget shortfalls occasioned by the post-9/11 recession (see chapter 10). Moreover, Minner was the state's first Delaware governor who had to face homeland security demands wrought by the war on terrorism. Nevertheless, she boldly initiated the nation's toughest indoor smoking ban against the wishes of casino owners and some bar owners.

CONCLUSION

In sum, it appears that activist governors in Delaware are here to stay. Delaware voters have demonstrated they would vote to reelect incumbent governors of both parties, and that they like a leadership style from their governors that encourages consensus politics and bipartisanship. To be sure, party competition is likely to remain spirited. The legislature might continue to be divided. But so long as business interests remain protected, Delawareans expect their governors to be strong leaders who will initiate the major policy thrusts of the state. There is no longer any doubt that political power of the state government has shifted from a poorly apportioned legislature to the chief executive and a legislature that mirrors the population of Delaware. But—lest political warfare of the past between the two branches resurface—it is still necessary for governors to maintain good relations with the General Assembly, and to assuage powerful interests, as discussed in our next chapter.

CHAPTER SEVEN

The General Assembly

The primary legislative body in Delaware is known as the General Assembly. It is in a very real sense a creature of the counties. Both the counties and the precursor of the General Assembly predate the creation of the State of Delaware by many decades. The counties were first asked to provide representatives to an assembly in 1682, joining three Pennsylvania counties. Together they constituted the proprietorship of William Penn. However, leaders in the three "Lower Counties" were not particularly interested in continuing that joint venture and formed the Assembly of the Lower Counties in 1704. While the assembly was ostensibly under the direction of a deputy governor from Pennsylvania and the Crown, it was able to control its own affairs much of the time.

The equality of the counties and the streak of independence from higher authority (e.g., a king, a governor, or the federal government) have influenced the General Assembly since its formation over three hundred years ago. It is not difficult to detect these characteristics even today.[1] In this chapter, the personality of the institution is explored primarily through its actions, or lack thereof.

ROOTS

An early indication of how the General Assembly would develop was the Constitution of 1776, which was completed in September of that year. In view of the fact that Delaware is a state formed from three preexisting counties that had essentially run their own affairs for some time, it was hardly surprising that the counties in the state's first constitution were equally represented in both the assembly's so-called House of Assembly and the Legislative Council. In addition, the General Assembly's president was to be chosen by the joint vote of these two legislative bodies that were also given the task of choosing the state's U.S. congressional delegation. Finally, Delaware's first constitution could only be changed by a vote of five-sevenths of the House of Assembly and seven-ninths of the Legislative Council. In short, Delaware was going to be run by the General Assembly, and that body itself was to be organized by the counties.

As noted in chapter 4, a second Delaware constitution was adopted in 1792, three years after the U.S. Constitution was written and adopted. The structure of Delaware's General Assembly remained the same, although the names of its two houses were changed to the House of Representatives and the Senate to follow the U.S. model. Notably, each county still retained an equal number of representatives. (As noted before, the three counties had similar population totals until 1820, after which New Castle County's population became substantially larger than that of the other two counties.) A popularly elected governor replaced the president, which theretofore had been chosen by the General Assembly. With the advent of the U.S. Constitution, the General Assembly lost its ability to choose Delaware's sole U.S. representative to Congress but did retain its role, as did the other states, in selecting its two U.S. senators.

The General Assembly retained its role in amending the state's constitution, although the governor's approval and a two-thirds vote in both houses were required, with the proposed amendments to be published three to six months prior to the next election. If three-fourths of both houses concurred on an amendment after the election, it would become part of the constitution. While provisions were made for calling a constitutional convention, no direct vote by the electorate on amendments was ever thereafter to be provided. The power of impeachment was granted to the General Assembly in 1792 as well. The General Assembly still retained supreme control of public affairs.

The next Delaware constitution was drafted in 1831 by a constitutional convention provided for in the constitution of 1792. Changes were minor for the most part and certainly did nothing to change the dominant role of the General Assembly, and it did make it more difficult to call for a constitutional convention.

In 1852 a second constitutional convention was called after a majority of those voting favored the convention. Although the number of voters approving the calling of a convention was far short of the required "majority of eligible voters," the General Assembly called the convention anyway and even submitted the newly drafted constitution to the voters for approval. However, it is important to reiterate here that the voters, by rejecting this new draft constitution, became thereby the first and only Delaware voters to ever vote on changes to a Delaware constitution.

A STREAK OF INDEPENDENCE

The General Assembly ratified the Bill of Rights to the U.S. Constitution in 1790. One might have expected therefore that article 1 of Delaware's 1792 constitution, entitled "Bill of Rights," would simply have incorporated or repeated those ratified in 1790, but this was not the case. Most, not all, of those rights were incorporated in different language, but freedom of speech was missing. Many other items, moreover, were included in Delaware's list of nineteen rights.

As amendments were made through the years to the U.S. Constitution, the General Assembly was asked to ratify each. Its record is somewhat spotty, however, which probably reflects a streak of independence, together with the conservatism emanating from the equal representation of the counties regardless of their fundamentally different characteristics. Accordingly, the General Assembly, joined by Connecticut and Massachusetts, rejected in 1804 the Twelfth Amendment, which created the Electoral College.

Although Delaware was a slave state, it was also a fierce defender of the Union and states' rights.[2] The Delaware Constitution of 1776 and all subsequent versions banned the entry of new slaves; by 1860 less than 10 percent of all blacks in Delaware were classified as slaves. Nevertheless, all efforts in the General Assembly to ban slavery prior to the Civil War failed, because slaves were considered private property. Had the General Assembly been apportioned in accordance with the population, instead of the equal representation of the counties, it is likely that slavery would have been banned much earlier.

The so-called Reconstruction Amendments to the U.S. Constitution—comprising the Thirteenth, which ended slavery; the Fourteenth, which provided for equal protection and due process; and the Fifteenth, which guaranteed the right to vote to black males—were all rejected by Delaware's General Assembly in 1865, 1867, and 1869, respectively.[3] All three were finally ratified in 1901, after the state's political balance of power changed. The rejection of all three amendments was driven by two main arguments: violation of the reserved powers of the states in the U.S. Constitution; and the shift in national political power toward Republicans, with the addition of newly minted black male voters.

As discussed in chapter 4, Delaware's current constitution, adopted in 1897, gives the governor the veto power over any bill emerging from the General Assembly, but it excludes the governor from approving constitutional amendments. We have also noted that, by the Constitution of 1897, black males were permitted to vote, and the number of representatives in both chambers of the General Assembly was divided equally between New Castle County (outside Wilmington) and each of the other two counties.

The General Assembly chose neither to vote on the Sixteenth Amendment, providing the income tax, nor the Seventeenth Amendment, providing for direct election of U.S. senators. The latter ended vote-buying opportunities of wealthy Delaware aspirants to U.S. Senate seats, which had generated negative publicity nationally (see chapter 5).[4]

The General Assembly did not hesitate in 1919 to ratify the Eighteenth Amendment, prohibiting the manufacture and sale of alcoholic beverages, although it failed to ratify (as the thirty-sixth required state) the Nineteenth Amendment guaranteeing women the right to vote in 1920, but belatedly did so in 1923.[5]

By 1960, 69 percent of Delaware's population resided in New Castle County, but the General Assembly still only allocated one-third of the state's representatives (outside Wilmington) to its most populous county. In 1962 the U.S. Supreme Court intervened with a decision that affected many states, including Delaware. As we have recounted before, the court essentially rejected the equal representation of counties as acceptable and ordered reapportionment by population for the 1964 elections. Predictably, the General Assembly put its own stamp on a plan that was invalidated by the court in 1967. Finally, a bipartisan plan was passed minutes before the court's deadline in 1968.[6]

Although this court-induced acquiescence finally shifted the state's political power to New Castle County residents, it by no means ended the independence of the General Assembly or its struggles with the courts, as is apparent by the subsequent discussion of other classic cases.

COMPOSITION

Although the General Assembly has lost its dominant position, its vital role in terms of the politics and government of Delaware—the thrust of this book—remains indisputably important. To understand the legislature's proper place, we must consider its composition and actual functioning.

Like the small state it represents, the General Assembly is also small. It consists of only sixty-two members—forty-one in the House of Representatives and twenty-one in the Senate—making it the smallest bicameral legislature among the fifty states and second only to the forty-nine members of Nebraska's unicameral legislature. Since 1959 the legislature has met annually instead of every two years as before. House members are elected to two-year terms, whereas Senate members serve staggered four-year terms.

By virtue of the court-ordered "one-person-one-vote" reapportionment of the 1960s, forty-four (twenty-nine representatives and fifteen senators)—or over 70 percent—of the sixty-two legislators in 2000 represented the population of New Castle County, while Kent and Sussex Counties each had only six representatives and three senators.

Base salaries of legislators in 2004 were $35,000, with leaders receiving more (legislators acted in 2005 to increase their salaries by 9 percent and in 2006 by another 5.5 percent). In addition, all members received $6,600 for expenses, and each had an allotment of $300,000 (reduced to $250,000 in 2005) of the suburban street program designated for street repairs within the legislator's district, typically for paving and curbing, fixing runoff drainage problems, installing speed bumps, sidewalks, and traffic signs, and planting trees. The street money is held in an account by the state Department of Transportation (DelDOT) for allocation by legislators, who have passionately fended off repeated DelDOT attempts to eliminate or cut the program. "It's anything but good government," said one civic leader.[7]

As a result of the elections in 2006, Democrats held thirteen of the Senate seats, while Republicans held the remaining eight seats. In the House, Republicans held a majority of twenty-three seats to eighteen held by Democrats. Delaware's ticket-splitting voters had opted for divided government since 1984, when they chose a Republican House and a Democratic Senate, marking the advent of what journalist Celia Cohen has labeled "the age of incumbency." Cohen explained, "As long as officeholders embarrassed neither the state nor themselves, the voters generally were content to leave them where they were."[8] As many as half are usually reelected without opposition. By redistricting after every census, the majority party in each house makes sure it retains control.[9] Few members, therefore, fail to be reelected. Generally, newcomers defeat incumbents less than 10 percent of the time in any election year. Accordingly, a Republican majority in the House and a Democratic majority in the Senate remained unchanged, given the assurance of longtime incumbencies, a circumstance that appeared to become permanent until the 2006 election when voters once again chose to continue a divided General Assembly.

Almost all legislators have other jobs. Over half are either employed by—or retirees of—other state-funded organizations, most notably public education institutions. Article 2, section 14 of the Delaware Constitution forbids "any person holding any office under this State" from also serving as a senator or representative. Moreover, the Delaware Supreme Court ruled in 1968 that "state office" in this section involves the exercise of "some part of the sovereign power of the State either in making, administering, or executing its laws." This ruling does not necessarily mean that no state employee can serve in the General Assembly. It does imply, however, that there are probably some positions that would be inconsistent with the constitution. Private sector employees constitute only a minority in the General Assembly.[10] Among them were five farmers and four lawyers in 2000.

Although African Americans constituted 20.7 percent and females were roughly 51.5 percent of Delaware's population in 2006, only three African-Americans were members of the General Assembly—one senator and two representatives, each from Wilmington—and just slightly over one-third of all members were women. Of the sixty-two members of the General Assembly, twenty-one were women—the second highest percentage of female legislators in the nation (Maryland ranked in first place with women filling 34 percent of its members). Governor Ruth Ann Minner (2001–9) was the nation's oldest governor in 2005, at the age of seventy, and the most prominent woman in the state's political history, having served seventeen prior years in the General Assembly—seven in the House and ten in the Senate.

HOW THE GENERAL ASSEMBLY FUNCTIONS

Delaware's part-time legislature "works" through close interpersonal contact, marked by informal collegiality among its members and by intimacy with lobbyists and constituents. Small-town and neighborly Dover, the state capital, is located in the middle of the state, easily accessible within forty-five miles of the farthest reaches of the state. Beginning the second Tuesday in January, the General Assembly meets in session at Dover's Legislative Hall—in the afternoons of Tuesdays, Wednesdays, and Thursdays—for most of the first six months of each year, except for three breaks of six weeks beginning in early February (when hearings on the proposed budget are held by the joint finance committee); two weeks over Easter; and one week in late May or early June (for budget writing). Budget makers, however, forego taking breaks because they sit on the most important committees, comprising legislators from both houses—the joint finance committee and the joint bond-bill committee. The session frequently concludes in a frenzy of activity on June 30, often after midnight.

The General Assembly in the early twenty-first century is organized along political party lines regardless of bipartisan cooperation on crucial issues. The majority party caucus in each house makes the major decisions, with the House Republican caucus and the Senate Democratic caucus choosing the leadership that controls the committees and legislative process. However, the twenty-three committees in the larger House with forty-one members loom more important than those in the smaller Senate. With only twenty-one members, the thirteen Senate Democrats and eight Republicans can easily meet as a committee of the whole or in separate party caucuses to obviate the necessity for meetings of the Senate's twenty-one standing committees which, in fact, seldom meet.

The House of Representatives is the more open body, whose rules require that all bills be sent to a committee in which each committee member has a vote, often after holding public hearings in a large meeting room of Legislative Hall. A key difference in the Senate is that the committee chair can simply hold a bill and no vote will ever take place. This cannot happen in the House. In both bodies the majority party has the majority of votes in each committee. If the majority party's caucus is unified, the bill will either pass or be filed according to the wishes of the caucus. In the Senate a bill must have the affirmative vote of the committee chairs as well.

Not only are committee meetings and party caucuses frequently held behind closed doors, but it is also not uncommon for key legislators to gather privately late in each session to make final decisions without any open debate or public input. Although the joint finance committee and joint bond bill committee do hold public hearings, final budget and bond-bill decisions are made in closed-door sessions. Regardless of the stipulation in Delaware's 1977 Freedom of Information Act (FOIA) that all "public bodies," unless specifically excluded, must conduct their business in public, FOIA does not apply to the General Assembly or to the courts. Annual efforts to include the legislature within FOIA have failed in the absence of public pressure to change the law.[11]

Article 2, section 4, of the Constitution of 1897 as amended stipulates that "each session shall not extend beyond the last day of June unless the session is recalled by the Governor or the mutual call of the presiding officers of both Houses." This time constraint is responsible for a flurry of activity as the session is running to a close. Normally, the procedures and rules of the General Assembly allow for adequate public and departmental input and review. However, during the last days and hours of the session both houses typically suspend their rules, which permit the General Assembly to do whatever it wants—without hearings, review or deliberation—including the passage of three omnibus money bills, namely the budget bill, the bond bill, and the grants-in-aid bill, each of which will have been more or less finalized already by the respective powerful joint committees of the legislature. Suspension of the rules by the presiding officers of both houses also permits extending the session past midnight of June 30, if necessary, which usually happens.

The budget bill lists each line item with an associated dollar amount. However, the way this money is to be used is contained in the so-called "epilogue language" of the bill, in which the General Assembly directs administrative agencies how to spend the money in a general way, thus delegating administrative spending discretion within epilogue standards and parameters. Programs can be created and laws amended in this epilogue language without public comment or input. The procedure for the bond bill is similar to the already passed budget bill. The language in the bond bill may modify the budget bill, amend laws, authorize agencies to carry out programs, and/or spend money.

The grants-in-aid bill, usually passed last, may also contain language modifying the budget bill or even creating new programs. Thus, the fiscal year 2008 grants-in-aid bill, totaling over $47 million, was introduced after midnight July 1, passed the House at 12:19:07 AM, passed the Senate at 1:47:25 AM, and was signed by the governor the same day.

A scathing editorial in the July 2005 issue of Delaware's leading newspaper protested "sneaky and deceitful lawmaking" by the General Assembly for inserting pork-barrel legislation and favorite projects in the "epilogue" of the operating budget "to avoid public ridicule and open hearings." The editorial deplored "legislative hijinks" as "deceitful and dishonest" and a clear violation of the state constitution. "The practice has become so common today there is even an informal group of legislative leaders and budget officers known as the 'Big Head Committee' who . . . quietly pass legislation with last-minute bills that elude scrutiny in the final days of the session. . . . We have to wonder if among the 62 members of both chambers there are any honest ethically minded legislators who would stand up for the rights of the voters who put them in office."[12]

It is understandable that journalists and newspapers champion open government, but to contend that Delaware's "epilogue lawmaking" is unconstitutional is at least an overstatement, given the right of the General Assembly to suspend its rules and of its presiding officers to extend the session. It is true that new legislation is passed from start to finish at the end of the session without any meaningful comment, but it is also true that it is, if anything, an expedient and very effective process. Moreover, the process would not "work" without bipartisan support of the Senate controlled in 2008 by Democrats and the House by Republicans. And, finally, nothing of consequence would happen without the acquiescence, approval, or participation of the governor, who signs the bills into law.

Two Democrats dominated the Senate leadership as president pro tempore for twenty-five years, from 1977 until 2002—Richard S. Cordrey, an agricultural businessman from Millsboro in Sussex County, and Thomas B. Sharp, a building construction foreman from New Castle County. Cordrey served as Senate president for nineteen years, from 1977 to 1996—the longest in both Delaware's and the nation's history—and was known for his "quiet leadership," whereas his outspoken successor Sharp, who served from 1996 until 2002, was very intimidating and it was said that colleagues "crossed him at great peril." Sharp retired in 2002, succeeded by a gentler Senate president Thurman Adams, an agricultural businessman from small-town Bridgeville in Sussex County, who had served thirty years in the Senate. As Governor Ruth Ann Minner began her second term in January 2005, she surprisingly nominated seventy-one-year-old Cordrey to be her secretary of finance and sixty-four-year-old Sharp to be her secretary of labor. Although nomination of the two long-time Senate politicians "left a trail of disbelief in its wake," both were easily confirmed by the Senate, dominated by a majority of fellow Democrats.[13]

Senators Cordrey, Sharp, and Adams had exercised great power over the Senate, achieving their leadership through seniority. Republican senator Steven Amick estimated in 2002 that the eight Senate Republicans on average were ten years younger and had much less seniority than the thirteen Senate Democrats, a circumstance that contributed to some partisan chafing. Moreover, the combined power of the tightly-knit cadre of Senate Democrats allowed them to greatly influence the General Assembly as a whole.[14]

Given such a concentration of legislative power in the hands of a few senators, the Senate remains a collegial body. In Cordrey's and Sharp's time, according to one observer, "at the end of each day's session all members as well as lobbyists and other guests were invited to an open house in the president pro tempore's office to intermingle and have a drink, alcoholic or otherwise."[15]

THE 2006 SESSION

Although each annual legislative session is unique, commonalities persist over time. Nothing new in 2006 was added to the basic characteristics of Delaware public affairs. Among recurring themes that have distinguished the government and politics of Delaware is the prime importance of business and employment, and this was certainly true in 2006 and thereafter (see epilogue).

When the 143rd General Assembly convened its session in January 2006, its members were faced with pressing problems, including fallout from the unexpected buyout effective January 1 of the state's largest employer, credit-card behemoth MBNA, by Bank of America, and an impending 59 percent increase in electric rates caused by legislation passed seven years previously.

Lawmakers promptly acted to increase the probability that MBNA's charter—and most of its tax dollars and jobs—remained in Delaware. They improved Delaware's ability to compete with other states by approving an overhaul of the state's bank franchise tax by establishing a two-tiered system by which banks may choose how they are taxed, making Delaware the only state having such a dual system. (This dual system reduced revenues by as much as $25 million in fiscal year 2008.) As a result of this new law, two banks by the end of the session reportedly were considering to locate in Delaware. It was likely, however, that Bank of America (BofA) would not take over all the roles that MBNA had played both in Delaware politics and with respect to other community activities.

As a huge entity, BofA's interests were national and less confined to Delaware. Indeed, it was impossible to know whether BofA remained Delaware's top employer. BofA does not release employment figures by state, regardless of the claim by the *Wilmington News Journal* in March 2007 that 3,100 jobs were cut when BofA took over MBNA in 2006. Jobs lost, of course, mean less revenue for the state. With the addition of projected closings of Chrysler and Avon plants in Newark and possible major cuts in AstraZeneca employees in Wilmington, the future budget picture for the state looked grim.

With regard to the mammoth increase in electric rates that consumers would have to pay effective May 1, 2006, lawmakers did nothing to prevent the seven-year expiration of rate caps they had put in place when they deregulated the electric power industry in 1999. The increase had threatened to mobilize some irate voters to oust incumbent legislators in the forthcoming November 2006 elections, but few changes would actually be made by the electorate.

Although the General Assembly failed to enact, during its 2006 session, business-supported bills to reform the state's expensive workers' compensation insurance program, and to further cut the gross receipts tax, both measures were held over to be considered again in 2007. Delaware's business-driven political culture—an "individualistic political culture" to use Elazar's parlance—remained alive and well. Indeed, the most defining characteristic of Delaware governance was its business-supportive components and policies, largely intended to promote employment.

Another recurring theme of the government and politics of Delaware was the historic persistence of sectionalism, notably between the more populous and industrial area north of the canal and the larger less populous and more rural area to the south. Sectional politics played a role with still other business interests that also had their way with the legislature in 2006. Farmers backed by developers, especially in southern Delaware, were successful in opposing Governor Ruth Ann Minner's year-old attempt to limit development on nearly 435,000 rural acres statewide, thus thwarting implementation of her Sprawl Prevention Act designed to steer growth away from rural areas and to restrict community septic systems.

Another bill introduced in 2006 also had sectional overtones. In 2000 the General Assembly had removed the Public Service Commission's authority to limit the size of rate hikes charged existing customers by for-profit water companies to pay for subsidizing expansion of water service to new customers. The 2006 bill would have restored the PSC's authority to limit such hikes. For example, Artesian Water Company, which served mostly customers in populous New Castle County, would thus be limited in how much it could charge such customers to pay for equipment needed to serve new customers in fast-growing Sussex County. But that bill was killed by the end of the session because it was never released for a vote by the assembly's Democratic Senate Energy and Transit Committee chair, who had written the 2000 law that prevented the PSC from limiting such rate hikes. The demise of the 2006 bill, accordingly, not only continued to pit New Castle County water customers against Sussex County's new residents, but it also illustrated the power of committee chairpersons in the Democratic Party–controlled Senate to resort to a "desk-drawer veto" by simply preventing bills they opposed from being brought out for a hearing or vote, thus hindering public debate and consideration of proposed legislation. The bill's demise, moreover, related to the politics of Delaware, which traditionally rises to a crescendo of frenzied activity as the annual six-month session of the legislature comes to a close.

At the end of June 2006 Delaware's 143rd General Assembly once again was criticized by good government groups and the media for making important decisions behind closed doors. Having exempted itself from the state's Freedom of Information Act, the legislature's so-called "Big Head Committee"—consisting of eight leaders drawn from both chambers— shaped the state's three largest spending bills, including the $3.11 billion operating budget, in the waning days and hours of the session. It was business as usual in the General Assembly.

The Joint Finance Committee (JFC) hearings early in the 2006 session were as usual open to the public. The governor's budget, which the JFC reviewed, was based on DEFAC's revenue estimates of the previous September. However, DEFAC's increased estimates late during the session gave the Big Head Committee together with the governor's office more discretion in finalizing the budget. Thus, appropriation bills were not accessible to lawmakers or the public until the last three days of the session. Simply put, the Big Head Committee, a creation of the General Assembly, has been empowered to act in the assembly's stead to finalize these bills. As a result, it wielded more financial power than any public body in the state.

Lawmakers in 2006 likewise failed to pass any of eight reform bills introduced to deal with scandalous 2005 revelations in the state's prison health care system that prompted an ongoing federal investigation of that system. The chair of the Democratic-controlled Senate Judiciary Committee let the bills die by refusing to let his committee consider them. Losers of course were prison inmates whose welfare in any event was not likely to rise to a high-profile issue during an election year.

Among other measures that failed passage were a mandate for statewide curbside recycling, authority for Wilmington to annex adjoining land, solution to the $2.7 billion gap between needed road construction through 2008 and money to pay for it, and annual payment of $750 per student of charter schools for capital needs. The legislators did approve a bill providing for all-day kindergarten to apply throughout the state, and a bill establishing a needle-exchange program in Wilmington aimed at stemming the spread of HIV/AIDS—thus leaving neighboring New Jersey as the only state failing to enact such legislation. Also, the part-time legislators had no trouble in approving a 5.5 percent pay raise for themselves, just one year after they had enacted a whopping 9 percent increase.

LEGISLATIVE RESEARCH

The General Assembly, as already noted, is a part-time operation. In addition, it is largely a reactive body. While there undoubtedly are major pieces of legislation on occasion that originate solely as a brainchild of particular legislators, the General Assembly is usually responsive to the following: the governor's legislative agenda, the needs of the various cabinet agencies, individual counties and municipalities, and scores of individual constituents and lobbyists. In addition, the legislature responds to a multiplicity of task forces established by the governor and/or the General Assembly to identify areas where legislation may help address particular problems.

For the most part, the General Assembly rarely begins the legislative process with a blank piece of paper. As noted in other chapters, it is not unusual in Delaware for laws to be drafted by external or nongovernmental sources and then often passed by the General Assembly with little or no review or change. It is largely the responsibility of the individual caucus and its at-torney to make sure that proposed legislation is appropriate.

Similarly, individual state government agencies often draft legislation to address pressing problems or federal mandates, and in these cases a sponsor among legislators is identified to introduce the bill. Each cabinet depart-ment has at least one legislative liaison who walks the halls of the General Assembly and monitors bills that affect the department. Agency representa-tives and experts frequently respond to inquiries or requests from legislators for information. Legislation proposed by a department or the governor's office is usually reviewed by interested bureaucrats and, if appropriate, by a deputy attorney general. The department liaison pays particular attention to bills that affect the department and those that have not emanated from the department itself. Legislative liaisons make sure that their department experts appear before committee hearings or confer informally with appro-priate legislators. In other instances, usually involving major initiatives, the Legislative Council's staff is requested to undertake appropriate research and/or to draft legislation.

On some occasions, the lack of in-depth research needed to produce ef-fective legislation is a major problem. Carol Hoffecker has observed that members of Delaware's permanent legislative staff "are capable but few." Accordingly, to provide research assistance individual legislators and legis-lative committees must sometimes depend on the staffs of national legisla-tive organizations, particularly the National Council of State Governments (NCSG) and the National Conference of State Legislatures (NCSL). "Where in larger states legislators typically depend on in-house staff to research and draft bills," Hoffecker noted, "Delaware legislators are more likely to make their own inquiries at NCSG."[16] Of particular interest is model legislation adopted in other states.

Legislative staff constitutes the cornerstone of state legislatures. "One of the most frequent recommendations to enhance opportunities for individual members and increase the effectiveness of the legislature is to create or aug-ment professional staff," according to Alan Rosenthal. And there is "virtual unanimity among reformers and substantial consensus among practitioners" that staff "will provide the information necessary for the legislature to do its job."[17]

The practicality of providing more full-time staff to Delaware's part-time legislature—which usually focuses on local issues rather than major legis-lation—is open to question. Carol Hoffecker has attributed great importance to the Legislative Fellows Program introduced in 1982, comprising tempo-rary part-time University of Delaware graduate and undergraduate students.

"Incredibly, these college students serve as . . . staff for House committees," she notes, "and have become indispensable for the functioning of Delaware's modern General Assembly."[18]

Traditionally, incumbent legislators of both houses had been able to draw their own election district lines to give themselves "safe" seats that assured their reelection. In this manner, longtime incumbency became the rule rather than the exception in the General Assembly, where Democrats in the Senate and Republicans in the House were able to retain their comfortable majorities since the 1980s. So institutionalized had this "gerrymandering" or "safe-seat" practice become that upward to one-half of all legislators were reelected without any opposition, making a mockery of sorts of democracy, while newcomers defeated incumbents less than 10 percent of the time.

The United States Census of 2000 became the occasion once again for redistricting by the General Assembly. The new redistricting map needed to reflect the state's 17 percent population growth, from 666,168 in 1990 to 783,600 in 2000. Population shifts toward the south, whereby southern New Castle County and Sussex County registered the greatest relative population gains while Wilmington had the greatest relative losses, evoked vexing redistricting choices for the General Assembly, which had agreed to approve redistricting maps by June 30, 2001. But that deadline passed and the dispute remained unresolved for over a year. The redistricting process called for the majority in each house to develop its own map. The two maps then would be combined into one bill that had to be approved by both houses and signed by the governor.

The impasse was reached when House Republicans proposed an increase from forty-one to forty-five House districts, which Senate Democrats rejected. Opposing each other were the majority party leaders of the two houses, notably longtime House speaker Republican Terry Spence against Senator Pro Tempore Democrat Thomas Sharp. Spence proposed to reduce the demand to expand the House from forty-one to forty-five seats if the Senate Democrats would let the House grow by only two seats. The new House proposal could have still eliminated four Democratic incumbents, whereby two would face sitting Republicans in redrawn districts and the other two would have to run in districts that already had Democratic incumbents. Were Republicans to win all four of these House districts, they would increase their previous twenty-six to fifteen majority to a seemingly insurmountable thirty to eleven majority. Spence lamented, "If the leadership in the Senate will agree to compromise with us, this will all be done and we can go home."[19] But Sharp refused to budge, showing he would go to the wall.

Meanwhile, in January 2002 activist Independent Party chairman Frank Sims filed suit in Delaware's Superior Court, where a three-judge panel ordered legislators to adopt new maps by April 19 to continue the Senate at twenty-one seats and the House at forty-one seats, and failing to do so the redistricting would become the responsibility of the Chancery Court, which threatened to enlist the help of University of Delaware demographer Edward C. Ratledge to draw a redistricting map. That did it! Lawmakers beat the court-ordered deadline and passed a compromise map that Senator Sharp described as "shameful . . . a disgrace," and "one of the most partisan maps I have ever seen." An African American Democrat in the House called the map "racist" and in violation of the federal Voting Rights Act, because—in a state where 20 percent of the population was African Americans—it placed two of only four African American lawmakers in the same district. Nevertheless, Democratic governor Ruth Ann Minner promptly signed the redistricting bill into law.[20]

In the November 2002 elections, with the new redistricting in place, Republicans gained three seats, thus increasing their twenty-six to fifteen control of the House to a twenty-nine to twelve majority, the largest such margin in the state's history, while Democrats continued to maintain their thirteen to eight majority in the Senate. Of the forty-one winning candidates in the House, eighteen were unopposed (44 percent), whereas nine of twenty-one Senate winners had no opponent (43 percent). Third-party chair Sims complained, "Redistricting is intended to adjust for population shifts and equalize the number of people represented by each legislator. Instead it has become a power-grab to pack political opponents into as few districts as possible."[21]

TURNING THE CLOCK BACK?

There were no public schools in Delaware until the General Assembly passed its first school law in 1829, which provided only for the education of white children. Although article 10 of the Delaware Constitution of 1897 directed the General Assembly to establish and maintain "a general and efficient system of free public schools," it stipulated that "separate schools for white and colored children shall be maintained."

In the early years of the twentieth century, Delaware reportedly "sank to last place in the rank order of the states in . . . the education of its young people."[22] Until 1920 almost all public education remained under county boards, and state aid made no provision for high schools. No standards existed for school buildings or for the certification of teachers. Racially segregated public schools persisted, and Delaware was the only state that required that local taxes to support segregated schools for black children be levied on the property of black citizens.

Although efforts had been made from the 1920s through the 1940s under the leadership and money of Pierre S. du Pont to establish a modern state-controlled public school system, at midcentury schools, restaurants, and theaters remained segregated throughout the state. The ensuing process of desegregation of public education in Delaware was to stretch over the next four decades.

Delaware's desegregation process actually began in higher education, when Vice Chancellor Collins J. Seitz of the Delaware Chancery Court ruled in 1948 that the state of Delaware, through its then all-white University of Delaware and the black Delaware State College, was not providing equal education to black college students, and thus ordered the university to admit black undergraduate students. Soon after Seitz was elevated to chancellor, he became the first judge in the nation—in an April 1951 landmark decision—to order black children be admitted to white public schools, finding that black schools were clearly inferior to white schools in Delaware.[23] This case was to become part of the U.S. Supreme Court's momentous 1954 decision in Brown v. Board of Education, which ordered the ending of segregation in the nation's public schools with "all deliberate speed."[24]

Following "white flight" from Wilmington to the northern New Castle County suburbs, the General Assembly passed the 1968 Educational Advancement Act, allowing the Delaware State Board of Education to consolidate and reorganize the state's school districts, except for the Wilmington School District, which had the effect of keeping blacks in the city district while northern New Castle County suburban districts remained almost entirely white. In 1975 the federal district court declared this 1968 act unconstitutional on the ground that the General Assembly had perpetuated one system for white children in the suburbs and another inferior system for Wilmington's black children.[25]

What followed were attempts to achieve racially balanced public schools within northern New Castle County. The year 1978 marked the advent of court-ordered busing in the county. Federal District Court Judge Murray M. Schwartz ordered suburban students be assigned to Wilmington schools for three successive years and city students be assigned to northern New Castle County suburban schools for nine of the twelve post-kindergarten years. The General Assembly acted in 1981 to divide northern New Castle County into four districts with each of the four districts comprising a section of

Wilmington and a larger suburban part of the county. Both the Schwartz and General Assembly models required reliance on busing to achieve racial balance.

Finally, in 1995, another federal district court judge declared that the four districts had achieved desegregation, thereby ending federal supervision of the desegregation process. This meant that northern New Castle County schools would no longer have to obtain prior approval from a federal court before proceeding with new policies. The General Assembly wasted little time in introducing two new educational initiatives authorizing state school districts to establish, with approval of the State Board of Education, publicly funded charter and choice schools that enabled selected qualified children from one district to attend such schools in another district. By the end of the century, however, the four districts in northern New Castle County continued to function as before, and busing was alive and well.

This then was the background for the ongoing attempt to create "neighborhood schools"—a movement that aroused much controversy in long-troubled northern New Castle County. In an attempt to end more than twenty years of busing, Republican House majority leader Wayne Smith introduced in the year 2000 a little-debated bill to reinstitute neighborhood schools in northern New Castle County, which passed by a comfortable majority in both houses of the General Assembly and was promptly signed into law by Governor Tom Carper, who was campaigning for a U.S. Senate seat.

The Neighborhood Schools Act required each of the four northern New Castle County school districts to submit a plan "that assigns every student within the district to the grade-appropriate school closest to the student's residence." The law directed that a "Wilmington Neighborhood Schools Committee" be constituted to submit a plan for Wilmington schools to the General Assembly by March 15, 2001. In the context of the Wilmington plan, each of the four suburban school districts was directed to submit its plan by November 15, 2001, to the State Board of Education for its approval. Once each district's plan was approved, the district would receive $1.25 million for its "costs incurred by the district in implementing the plan." Failure to submit an approved plan would result in the attorney general's office bringing a court action to compel compliance.[26]

The ease with which the measure passed does not indicate that it had overwhelming public support. A local columnist characterized "Smith's folly" as "based on myths about 'the good old days' of neighborhood schools before the court forced the . . . people of Delaware to desegregate their public schools."[27] The *Wilmington News Journal* editorialized that the law "was an ill conceived and irresponsible effort on the part of legislators to pander to the lingering anti-busing faction in the state. The law, if enforced strictly, would re-segregate schools in the City of Wilmington and is therefore unconstitutional."[28] University of Delaware professor Jeffrey Raffel agreed, pointing out that the law was similar to the 1968 state law that isolated Wilmington from surrounding districts, leading to federal court action. "We have an act," Raffel said, "that clear on its face is going to segregate kids in the city of Wilmington."[29]

The research of Leland Ware, the Louis L. Redding Professor of Law and Public Policy at the University of Delaware, showed that Wilmington had the highest levels of residential segregation in the state, and that therefore enforcement of the law would likely mean a return to resegregation of public schools in Wilmington.[30] But another prominent University of Delaware professor disagreed. Raymond Wolters, the Thomas Muncy Keith Professor of History, declared he was pleased to be a member of the National Association for Neighborhood Schools. "This organization," said Wolters, "has worked long and hard opposing the idea that students should be assigned to school on the basis of race."[31]

More than six years had passed since passage of the Neighborhood Schools Law. The law was still on the books, and the debate continued. But not much had changed. Busing continued as before.

CO-EQUAL BRANCHES OF GOVERNMENT?

The foregoing examples clearly demonstrate the subordinate positions of the legislative and executive branches of Delaware state government, with the judiciary seemingly holding most of the cards and attempting to give specific advice to the legislature. Occasionally, however, the tables are turned, whereby the General Assembly seeks to assert political power over the judiciary. Such a confrontation produced a messy sequence of events in late 2004 and early 2005, constituting the appearance of an historic contest for power between the two branches.

The events leading up to this conflict began in 1982 when a Delaware jury convicted Ward T. Evans of rape and sentenced him to life in prison with the possibility of parole. The state Board of Parole in 1993, 1996, and 1999 denied Evans's repeated requests for parole. In January 2004 Evans filed a motion with Delaware's Superior Court, claiming that under the state's conditional release statute he was entitled to conditional release as if his life sentence were a forty-five-year term. The Superior Court denied Evan's motion without analysis or opinion. On appeal, Delaware's Supreme Court held in November 2004 that Evans was entitled under relevant statutes to have his conditional release date "accelerated by whatever good time credits he has earned or may earn in the future." Accordingly, the Supreme Court reversed the Superior Court's refusal to modify Evan's sentence and remanded the case to it for determination whether Evans "has earned any good time or merit credits, and for an appropriate adjustment of his 'maximum release date.'"[32]

The decision evoked press coverage of public fears that many other life-term felons might similarly be released from prison. In mid-December 2004 the Delaware Supreme Court denied the state attorney general's motion for re-argument.

Confrontation by the General Assembly had to wait the convening of its 2005 session. On January 25 House majority leader Wayne Smith promptly introduced House Bill 31 on behalf of himself as primary sponsor plus twenty-eight other representatives and ten senators, composing a substantial and bipartisan majority of the General Assembly's sixty-two members. The bill passed unanimously by the House the same day, by the Senate the next day, and was signed by Governor Ruth Ann Minner three days later.

HB31 declared the Supreme Court's decision in the Evans case "null and void" because the court misconstrued two sections of the Delaware statutes, contrary to legislative intent, which "will result in nearly 200 Delaware prisoners who have committed serious and heinous crimes . . . being released from prison." Under Delaware's Constitution, according to HB31, the General Assembly has "sole authority for lawmaking" and "asserts its right to be the ultimate arbiter of the intent, meaning, and construction of its laws and to vigorously defend them." Then, throwing down the gauntlet, HB31 added: "Delaware judicial officers may not create or amend statutes, nor second-guess the soundness of public policy or wisdom of the General Assembly in passing statutes, nor may they interpret or construe statutes and other Delaware law when the text is clear and unambiguous."[33]

Although Governor Minner had signed the bill on February 1, 2005, she stated in a letter to the Supreme Court, "I question the constitutionality and enforceability of several provisions of the bill." On February 3 the court granted a motion to reconsider the Evans decision, asserting that "no judgment entered in this matter shall be deemed to be final." On April 11 the Supreme Court concluded that its previous opinion "must be withdrawn" and that "the judgment of the Superior Court must be affirmed," thereby deciding that "unless he is granted parole, Evans is not eligible for release from incarceration prior to his death."

This seemingly disposed of the possibility that two hundred life-termers could be granted earlier release. But what made its opinion extraordinary was the court's retaliation against the General Assembly by declaring HB31 "unconstitutional in its entirety." In so doing, the court reviewed a litany of authorities to the effect that the separation of powers prohibits "legislative interference with the judgments of American courts in specific cases." To support its reasoning, the court went to great lengths by citing a number of authorities, including Aristotle, Montesquieu, John Locke, James Madison, Alexander Hamilton, Thomas Jefferson, John Marshall, John Dickinson, and a host of federal and state court decisions.[34]

Thus, a historic contest had ended for political power between Delaware's state legislature and judiciary. Given the result of this confrontation, the two branches might not be considered co-equal for the reason that the judicial branch came out on top. On the other hand, one could conclude that the General Assembly's aggressiveness forced the Supreme Court in essence to reverse itself. This is to say that HB31 caused the court finally to rule against Evans by withdrawing its original decision, which had appeared to pave the way for a politically untenable consequence—the early release of Evans and possibly two hundred other life-term felons.

CONCLUSION

In sum, Delaware's more than three centuries old General Assembly has been transformed from its uncontested paramountcy to a position of balance at best with the advent of activist governors who have seized major policy initiatives, and with the gradual strengthening of the judiciary. Among the factors that potentially contributed to the General Assembly's position have been its relative conservatism, tendency toward incremental change, dependence on outside expertise, and focus on short-term and local problems. Nevertheless, the General Assembly's vital role vis-à-vis the politics and government of the state remains indisputable.

CHAPTER EIGHT

Courts, Judges, and Lawyers

The judiciary, as in other states, is the third branch of Delaware's state government. However, the influence of Delaware's judicial branch extends far beyond the boundaries of this small state, which cannot be said of its other two branches. Delaware's corporate law is preeminent in the nation, and its judicial system's role in administering that law, elevates its judiciary to be one of the most important in the country. This chapter discusses the path by which the state's judicial system has achieved this position; how courts, judges and lawyers have handled this awesome responsibility; and how the legal profession has played a significant role in the public's business outside the courtroom.

AN EVOLVING COURT SYSTEM

Like the rest of Delaware's governmental structure, the court system was heavily influenced by the colonial experience. After Pennsylvania's three lower counties split from Pennsylvania to form Delaware, the Delaware Constitution of 1776 made English common law the foundation of law in Delaware. Provisions were made for a "supreme court" (which was really a court of general jurisdiction, not an appeals court), for a court of common pleas in each county to hear civil cases, and for justices of the peace to hear minor civil and criminal cases. Appeals were to be heard by a court consisting of six persons appointed by a legislative council and the state's president. These courts were clearly considered capable of dealing with both matters of law and equity. Combining law and equity jurisdiction, as in the courts of most states at the time, was short-lived in Delaware. Significantly, Delaware's Constitution of 1792 separated equity jurisdiction from the common pleas courts in the counties, and vested it in the Chancery Court, headed by a chancellor. In addition, the appeals court was abolished and a Court of Errors and Appeals was provided, consisting of the chancellor and the judges of the Supreme Court and the common pleas courts. In other words, the appeals court no longer had its own judges.

Delaware's Constitution of 1831 abolished the common pleas courts and assigned the duties of the Supreme Court to the so-called Superior Court. The Court of Errors and Appeals was further defined but still consisted of judges drawn from other courts. Then the Constitution of 1897 assigned the duties of the appellate Court of Errors and Appeals to a new Supreme Court whose judges, however, were still drawn from other courts—namely the Court of Chancery and the Superior Court—who were not involved in the original litigation, or so-called "left over" judges. This unique and untenable situation—of not having a supreme appellate court with its own independent judges—was not resolved until a 1951 amendment to the 1897 Constitution provided for a chief justice and two associate justices.[1]

The final structural changes of the judiciary came with the reemergence of courts of common pleas in the three counties—New Castle in 1917, Kent in 1931, and Sussex in 1953—which in turn were unified into a single state-wide court with jurisdiction over some civil cases and criminal misdemeanors. The Family Court of Delaware, which evolved from juvenile courts in the three counties, was fully formed in 1971.

Throughout the period since 1792, while Delaware's other courts were undergoing sometimes convoluted change, the Court of Chancery remained largely untouched, with its jurisdiction solidified and its staff expanded. In fact, Chancery gained importance as the processes of incorporation and general corporate law were streamlined, whereby this court developed a national reputation of specializing in corporate law.

EVOLUTION OF JUDICIAL APPOINTMENTS

Throughout the nation, several issues arise with respect to judicial appointments. Are judges to be elected or appointed? If appointed, who appoints them, and what roles if any do the executive and the legislature play? How long are their terms? If not for life, how are they retained? Choices made with respect to each of these issues are supportable by persuasive arguments.

Delaware since the 1776 constitution has avoided elections as a means of choosing judges. Initially, judges were jointly chosen by the President of the Delaware State and the General Assembly (which also chose the weak president), to continue in office during "good behavior." Justices of the peace were nominated by the General Assembly and appointed by the president for terms of seven years if "they behave themselves well."

Sixteen years later, with the Constitution of 1792, the system changed, with the popularly elected governor appointing all judges to continue in office during good behavior, with the caveat that the governor could remove judges with the consent of two-thirds of the General Assembly. Nomination of justices of the peace by the General Assembly was abolished. The 1831 constitution continued these changes.

The Constitution of 1897, still in effect today, made several important changes in the process. First, judges now served a fixed term of twelve years. Second, all judicial appointments required confirmation by a majority of the Senate. Third, terms for the justices of the peace were reduced from seven years to four years, and their appointments required Senate confirmation.[2] These changes still remain.

Unique features of Delaware's judicial appointment scheme were added to the constitution when the Supreme Court was fully restored and staffed in 1951. There are now three conditions required for new appointments. First, the make-up of the Supreme Court must be bipartisan—three of its five justices shall be of one major political party and two must be of the other major political party. Second, no more than a bare majority (assuming an odd number) of the judges of the Superior Court can be of the same major political party, with the remainder being from the other major political party. Third, no more than a bare majority (assuming an odd number) of the justices of the Supreme Court, the judges of the Superior Court, and the chancellor and vice-chancellors of the Chancery Court can be from the same major political party, while the balance must come from the other major political party.[3]

In 1977 Governor Pierre S. du Pont IV issued an executive order creating a judicial nominating commission to supply him with qualified nominees from which he could fill judicial vacancies. This process has been continued by Governors Castle, Carper, and Minner. The commission's nine members include an appointee of the president of the Delaware State Bar Association (with consent of the governor), four members of the Bar of the Supreme Court of Delaware, and four members "who are not members of the bar in any state." The same political balance required of the judiciary is also required of the nominating committee—only a bare majority of one political party is permitted among the nine members. Judges who have completed their twelve-year terms are free to reapply to the commission. Unless two-thirds of the members of the commission agree not to submit a judge's name to the governor, the incumbent will be nominated for another term. Thus, there is no absolute guarantee that a sitting judge will be nominated by the commission or selected by the governor for another term.[4]

This chronology leads to the conclusion that Delaware has gone to extraordinary lengths to keep politics out of the judiciary, far more than have other states. No judges are elected in Delaware. The appointment term has been reduced from life to twelve years. The governor has moved from a largely unfettered appointment power to one constrained by the Senate. The requirement of political balance on the courts tends to ensure that balanced decisions may be more likely. The addition of the judicial nominating commission reinforces political balance among the nominees and sends a message to sitting judges that their work during their tenure will undergo bipartisan scrutiny if they seek reappointment. Whereas judges in many other states must typically face reelection to be retained, Delaware's judges must face a bipartisan (or nonpartisan) gauntlet. Moreover, the fact that constitutional amendments in Delaware require a two-thirds agreement of members of the General Assembly, in each of two successive sessions with an intervening election, without being submitted to the electorate for approval as in other states, tends to remove that process further from excessive political partisanship and thus to mitigate any but incremental changes in the judiciary.

THE COURTS TODAY

At the base of Delaware's court system are fifty-six justices of the peace courts in which 493,666 cases were filed in fiscal year 2007, mostly consisting of motor vehicle and civil cases involving money not exceeding $15,000; those in excess of $15,000 are handled by the Court of Common Pleas. Appeals from the justices of the peace courts are referred to the Court of Common Pleas.

The Court of Common Pleas has original jurisdiction over all misdemeanor cases (unless another court has original or concurrent jurisdiction). In fiscal year 2007, 110,765 filings were handled by the court. It also handles cases not within the jurisdiction of justices of the peace courts or when a defendant wants the case transferred. The Court of Common Pleas also conducts preliminary hearings in felony cases (if requested) to determine probable cause. Finally, it has concurrent jurisdiction with the Supreme Court in civil matters up to $50,000 (10,413 filings in fiscal year 2007). There are nine judges in the Court of Common Pleas who hold court in each of the three counties. The court also has three commissioners, one in each county, who have authority to take pleas, conduct hearings, and perform other specific duties.

The Family Court has jurisdiction over juvenile delinquency and domestic relations in general. Within the court's purview are actions such as child neglect, child abuse, adult misdemeanor crimes against juveniles, child and spousal support, custody and visitation of children, adoptions, terminations of parental rights, divorces and annulments, and orders of protection from abuse and intrafamily misdemeanor crimes. The Family Court does not have jurisdiction over juveniles charged with first- and second-degree murder, rape, or kidnapping. Seventeen judges are currently on the bench in the Family Court that operates in each of the three counties. Sixteen commissioners also hear a broad range of cases but are subject to review by Family Court judges.

The Superior Court is Delaware's court of general jurisdiction handling all criminal and civil cases except equity and domestic relations cases. It also handles appeals from the Court of Common Pleas, Family Court, and other administrative agencies that render adjudicative decisions. The Superior Court has locations in all three counties. There are nineteen judges and five commissioners currently serving on the court. Decisions of the Superior Court may be appealed to the Supreme Court of Delaware. The court handled 23,075 filings in fiscal year 2007.

The Court of Chancery has general equity jurisdiction in Delaware. Litigation in the Court of Chancery consists largely of corporate matters, trusts, estates, and other fiduciary matters; disputes involving the purchase and sale of land; questions of title to real estate; and commercial and contractual matters in general. When the rare need for a jury trial arises, the Court of Chancery may order such a trial before the Superior Court, since the Chancery Court does not conduct jury trials. The Court of Chancery currently consists of one chancellor and four vice-chancellors. The court handled 4,142 filings in fiscal year 2007.

As has been noted, Delaware's Supreme Court, the state's highest court of appeals, was not created as a separate and independent court until a constitutional amendment in 1951. The current Supreme Court consists of five justices—a chief justice and four associate justices. Together, Delaware's Court of Chancery and its appellate Supreme Court serve as the chief arbiters of the nation's corporate law, and it is within their ambit that the interdependence of Delaware's bench and bar is most salient. The court handled 666 filings in fiscal year 2007.

POLITICS OF JUDICIAL APPOINTMENTS

Regardless of Delaware's extraordinary efforts to keep politics out of the judiciary, political considerations play an integral role in the nomination and approval of all Delaware judges. As we have noted, Delaware's constitution requires that all judges—except for justices of the peace, who have four-year terms—be appointed for twelve-year terms by the governor with the consent of the Senate, and with a political party balance in the judiciary.

For example, Democratic governor Ruth Ann Minner had to fill a vacancy on the Supreme Court in 2004 when Chief Justice E. Norman Veasey retired. There were then three Democrats on the court, so the new justice was required to be a Republican. Governor Minner selected sitting Associate Justice Myron Steele, a Democrat, to replace Veasey as chief justice, and then she named Henry du Pont Ridgely, a Republican, to fill the associate justice vacancy.

While the prior example is straightforward, some others are not as simple. In 1921 Republican chancellor Charles M. Curtis wanted to be reappointed to a second twelve-year term. However, he had displeased some Republican comrades in a particular court decision. Meanwhile, Delaware's U.S. senator Josiah O. Wolcott, a Democrat, wished to become chancellor. Republican governor William D. Denny decided to appoint Wolcott to the bench, which created an unexpired vacancy in the U.S. Senate that Denny could fill. At that time, the U.S. Senate was controlled by Republicans, who favored appointment of another Republican. Accordingly, Republican Coleman T. du Pont became a U.S. senator, and Republican Curtis lost his chancellor's job to Democrat Wolcott.[5]

A much more contentious example is the 1994 controversy surrounding the reappointment of Associate Justice of the Delaware Supreme Court Andrew G. T. Moore II. Governor Pete du Pont had appointed Moore to the Delaware Supreme Court in 1982 because of his expertise in business law. Studies conducted in 1992 and 1993 had indicated gender bias in Delaware's legal system—that women attorneys were overrepresented in the lowest-level positions of Delaware's court system and underrepresented in the highest-level positions.[6] Although a cause-and-effect relationship of these studies cannot with certainty be connected to subsequent events, they did serve as a backdrop to the Justice Moore saga.

During his twelve years on the bench, Justice Moore had joined his fellow justices in hearing appeals from Delaware's Chancery Court that dealt with corporate law issues. Such Delaware Supreme Court decisions, like those in the Chancery Court, affected businesses throughout the United States. However, Justice Moore had undertaken with vigor to "police" lawyers appearing before him, thus incurring the wrath of some members of Delaware's bar. He had also developed a reputation as a "pro-shareholder" (as distinguished from a "pro-management") justice that also evoked criticism.

Justice Moore applied in 1994 for appointment to a second twelve-year term. At the time, the nine-member judicial nominating commission consisted of five male lawyers and four female "public members" who were not lawyers. Heading the commission was James H. Gilliam Jr., senior vice president and corporate counsel of the Beneficial Corporation and a former cabinet secretary in the Pete du Pont administration. Following the procedure of Governors du Pont and Castle, Governor Carper issued Executive Order No. 3 soon after his election in 1992, which created a judicial nominating commission to submit nominees from whom the governor could appoint subject to Senate confirmation. The commission reportedly blocked Moore's reappointment by a vote of six to three because he lacked requisite "judicial temperament" and "civility" for the bench (a two-thirds vote was required by Carper's executive order to omit an incumbent's name from the nominating list).

Although a list of three qualified people willing to fill a vacancy would normally be submitted to the governor, the commission in this instance submitted only one name—Vice-Chancellor Carolyn Berger—which was allowed by the executive order in view of the fact that the governor could have requested a supplemental list but chose not to do so. Accordingly, Berger was appointed by Governor Carper and confirmed by the Senate. Justice Moore was obviously not pleased, and in a letter to Governor Carper he asked that the confidentiality of the commission's process be waived. The issue of the confidentiality of its deliberations was subsequently litigated and executive privilege was upheld.[7]

Moore thus became the first justice in the Supreme Court's history not to be reappointed, and Berger became the first woman Supreme Court justice. Amidst the controversy, Berger said that both her 1984 appointment to the Chancery Court and her 1994 appointment to the Supreme Court "sent a signal of opportunity to women, that doors are open to them." With regard to Moore's ouster, Berger added: "It has occurred to me that some of this talk has very little to do with Justice Moore and much to do with the fact that I am a woman."[8] Just as Republican governor William D. Denny wanted a Republican in the U.S. Senate, for which he was willing to forego the reappointment of Republican chancellor Curtis, Governor Carper may have wanted to appoint a woman to the Delaware Supreme Court.

Twelve-year terms, as distinguished from life terms, permits responses to changing times. In Delaware, judges who seek reappointment are held accountable by a process involving a nominating commission, the governor, and the state Senate, just as politicians who seek reelection are held accountable by the electorate. The fact that reappointment of judges is not automatic requires a sitting judge to stand on a record of individual decisions and behavior, much as politicians who want to run for another term.

The nomination process is heavily influenced by members of the Delaware bar, from which many Delaware judges are drawn. Interaction among Delaware's elite law firms and the judicial system is more apparent in the higher courts than in the lower courts. A majority of judges in Delaware's higher courts have long been drawn from these prestigious law firms, invariably with the approval of the Delaware State Bar Association. For example, most judges of the Court of Chancery and Supreme Court in 2004 had served as members of prominent Delaware law firms—a fact that enhances the influence of those firms. Given the importance of corporate law in both the Chancery Court and the Supreme Court, it is not surprising that the judiciary springs from those that practice that art.

DELAWARE CORPORATE LAW

The Constitution of 1792 set the initial foundation for corporate law in Delaware by explicitly stating that "corporate bodies shall remain as if the constitution of this state had not been altered." Following earlier English law, corporations could only transfer or sell shares or take corporate action by special act of the legislature. While there were some changes in the process of obtaining these special acts in the 1831 Constitution, the key item was a requirement that any special act of incorporation required the approval of two-thirds of each house of the General Assembly.

In 1875 and 1893 limited versions of general corporate laws were passed, but their scope was limited to corporate organizations covered by the Constitution of 1831. For this reason these laws had little impact except to spur further action when the 1897 constitution was drafted.

In 1896 New Jersey had adopted a corporation law credited with attracting the incorporation of the old Standard Oil Company and other trusts or holding companies in that state. Not to be outdone by its neighbor, Delaware's 1897 constitution, as noted previously, authorized incorporation by a general incorporation law. Most importantly, the requirement of approval by two-thirds of both houses of the General Assembly for any change in the general corporation law was continued as it had been for special acts of incorporation. A specific provision was also included to require all existing corporations incorporated previously to formally accept the provisions of the new constitution when they renewed or amended their current charters with the secretary of state. While it took several years for all corporations to fall under the same set of laws, the super majority required for changing the laws ensured a very stable foundation for Delaware corporate law. The Constitution of 1897 also set in place the importance of the secretary of state (a constitutional office since 1776) in dealing with incorporation activities in Delaware.

Pursuant to the Constitution of 1897, the Delaware legislature adopted an 1899 law copied largely from the New Jersey act, providing a general incorporation process as an exclusive method of incorporation that ended special acts by the General Assembly. Then in 1913, at newly elected Governor Woodrow Wilson's insistence, New Jersey greatly tightened its corporation law, which left it open for Delaware's less restrictive 1915 law to enable Delaware to take the lead among the states to attract the lucrative incorporation business—a lead that Delaware was never to surrender.

THE MOST BUSINESS-FRIENDLY STATE?

It may be questioned why other states have not simply adopted Delaware's general incorporation law and thus reduce the attractiveness of incorporating in Delaware. Some states, such as Nevada, have indeed sought to duplicate Delaware's corporate code and common law decisions, and several other states have created business courts modeled after Delaware's Court of Chancery, namely Maryland, New York, North Carolina, Michigan, and Florida. But Delaware nevertheless has retained its lead for several reasons:

First, Delaware's secretary of state and Division of Corporations conduct an extraordinarily efficient operation with twenty-four-hour turnaround, if desired.

Second, the Chancery Court allows a corporation to do its business in a single place, whereas other states allow multiple courts to have equity jurisdiction.

Third, because of this centralized operation, Delaware judges are specialists in corporate law, deal with many cases, and have a rich history of decisions to guide them.

Fourth, a major characteristic of the Chancery Court is its unique flexibility. Two prominent Delaware attorneys, in their history of Delaware's Chancery Court, observed: "Equitable judging still requires an individual craftsman to analyze the facts, apply the ancient principles, carve a specific remedy and communicate the result. The product is human art; it cannot be scientifically produced."[9]

Fifth, the Delaware bar is rich with corporate law talent to practice in the forums specialized in business law, and on a continuing basis to identify and frame measures for changing or upgrading Delaware law for referral to the General Assembly.

Sixth, "Delaware's unique advantages as a legal home for corporations" have made the Federal District Court of Delaware "a national focal point for the resolution of disputes concerning corporations, securities, and patents."[10]

The influence of Delaware attorneys is recognized by Rule 83.5(d) of this court, entitled "Association with Local Counsel Required," which stipulates: "An attorney not admitted to practice by the Supreme Court of Delaware may not be admitted . . . in this Court unless associated with an attorney . . . who maintains an office in . . . Delaware."

However, with all of Delaware's attributes, not every observer considers the state an appropriate center for business law and incorporation. In a classic 1974 article of the *Yale Law Journal*, Columbia University Law professor William L. Cary described this phenomenon as "the race for the bottom," which Delaware has continued to win, as follows: "It [Delaware] likes to be number one. With some justification Delaware corporate counsel take pride in their role and enjoy the fees that flow from it. The system 'engenders a volume of business for the bar which tends to be regarded as a vested interest, so that any attempt to retrace steps would encounter opposition in powerful quarters.' Most important, the raison d'etre behind the whole system has been achieved—revenue for the state of Delaware."[11]

In 1992 Norman Veasey became chief justice of Delaware's Supreme Court. Veasey claimed Delaware's court system was "largely responsible for a very significant contribution to the Delaware economy." He added that Delaware's "glittering" national reputation in business law "is driven by the national respect for our Court of Chancery and Supreme Court, as well as the historic and current initiatives of the General Assembly and the Governor in providing modern statutes and outstanding service to Delaware corporations."[12]

Veasey was not by implication referring primarily to the revenue accrued from corporation franchise taxes, which otherwise would have to be offset by other taxes paid by individuals and businesses. Rather, he was referring to the scale and productivity of the entire legal industry in Delaware—the employment generated, wages paid, and services consumed—that contribute mightily to Delaware's overall economy. Upon his retirement in 2004, the *Wilmington News Journal* lauded Veasey for having "worked diligently to cooperate with the legislative and executive branches of state government," and for the fact that "Delaware courts were ranked the best in the nation by the U.S. Chamber of Commerce for excellence in civil litigation."[13] That ranking was repeated in 2005.

In his 1974 article Professor Cary had called for federal standards of corporate responsibility to overcome the lack of uniformity among the states in their governance of corporations. "The first step," according to Cary, "is to escape from the present predicament in which a pygmy among the 50 states prescribes, interprets, and indeed denigrates national corporate policy as an incentive to encourage incorporation within its borders, thereby increasing its revenue."[14]

Thirty years later, in the wake of corporate scandals, calls for increased federal regulation presented an ominous challenge to the First State. A local editorial in 2004 warned:

> The current threat to Delaware's status as the corporate capital of the world comes from the federal government. As Chief Justice Myron Steele noted . . . , Securities and Exchange Commissioner Harvey Goldschmidt promotes the idea of "a new national system with one set of rules to promote certainty, clarity of oversight of a national process, all under   the supervision and control of the SEC."
>
> Federal oversight of corporate legal governance wouldn't result in precision but in a cacophony of conflicting decisions in each federal court district. Delaware's excellent century-old corporate legal tradition not only provides an extraordinary service to Delaware corporations but to the country.[15]

A COMMON LAW STATE

Political proclivities explain only part of the power exercised by Delaware's legal profession. On the whole, its power may also be considered to derive from the fact that Delaware is a common law state. In this sense, a strong case can be made that the power of Delaware's judiciary—by virtue of its adherence to the common law—may exceed, or at least is on a par with, the power of Delaware's legislature.

The common law was originally developed in England from judicial decisions based on tradition, custom, and precedent. From this developed the system of equity administered in English courts of chancery, as distinguished from law courts.[16]

The common law of England as it existed before the American Revolution became the law of Delaware in its first constitution, adopted in 1776; the importance of the common law remains undiminished in Delaware. Whereas in England courts of law and equity were combined by the Judicature Acts of 1873 and 1875, with equity remaining supreme in case of conflict, other jurisdictions also combined law and equity during the nineteenth century. Even in England, therefore, the distinction between law and equity has eroded, but not in Delaware.

Unlike virtually all other states, Delaware maintains the distinction between law and equity in a separate equity court—the Court of Chancery established by article 6, section 14 of the Constitution of 1792. Delaware's Court of Chancery thus acquired all general equity jurisdiction of the High Court of Chancery of Great Britain that had existed prior to the American Revolution.[17] Richard Kiger, Master of Delaware's Court of Chancery, has commented: "More English than the English, we adhere to old ways. The late Professor Morgan of Harvard Law School is said to have described Delaware as a 'museum of the Common Law' and the preservation of a separate court of equity has more than antiquarian charm or curiosity value. Chancery, exercising a highly flexible jurisdiction, has evolved into the premier court of corporate law in the country."[18]

The 1897 Constitution continued the long tradition of the rights of the people originating from the English common law. The 1897 convention delegates passed the 1792 bill of rights, which derived from the common law, with "scarcely a dot from the *i* or a cross from the *t* being omitted."[19] Indeed, according to Paul Dolan, Delaware is one of few states that retained almost completely the common law inherited from colonial days.[20]

Today, common law is generally thought as applying only to civil disputes from which the system of "equity" has developed. In the federal courts, there is no separation between law and equity. But Delaware has long maintained separate courts of law and equity (as does Tennessee and Mississippi). Thus, the Constitution of 1897 continued the Court of Chancery essentially unchanged in structure and jurisdiction. Most states had abolished separate equity jurisdiction, and even England abolished its High Court of Chancery in 1875. "Courts of chancery, with the concomitant denial of trial by jury," according to Walsh and Fitzpatrick, "were viewed in many parts of the United States as vestiges of royal government and centralized authority, ill-suited to an egalitarian society. . . . It has been suggested that Delaware's Court of Chancery endured in a time of court reform because the state continued to reflect a basic conservatism and strong mercantile interests."[21]

Accordingly, Delaware is very much a "common-law state" in which some judges accord greater authority to unwritten common law than to statutory law or even to the Delaware Constitution of 1897 as amended.

CONCLUSION

Key to understanding the flexibility Delaware judges enjoy is their disposition to accord greater authority to the common law than that accorded to statutes, accounting for the broader discretion they thereby possess.

Legislatures enact statutes that have the force of law, but even these are subject to the common law principle followed consistently in Delaware that any statute in derogation of the common law shall be strictly construed. It is this principle that ensures broad judicial discretion. These circumstances combine to motivate hundreds of thousands of corporations to incorporate in Delaware. By choosing Delaware, company directors know that they will be able to function within a framework of corporate law that is highly predictable, where expert judges tailor equity decisions, and the legislature must have a super majority to change the law.

CHAPTER NINE

State-Local Relations

Delaware is so small in area and population that the economy-of-scale princi-ple ordains that Delaware's state government administer many public services that are functions of local governments in other states. The consequences for state-local relations in Delaware are profound. The trend in other states is for state governments to devolve increasing authority to their local governments.[1] The trend in Delaware by and large is the opposite. Delaware's local govern-ments willingly and increasingly give up functions to their state government, even though they could possibly claim some functions by amending their charters. Except perhaps for Wilmington's city government, Delaware local governments do not want or seek more authority; they do seek state funding. The thrust of this chapter is to analyze these phenomena.

OVERVIEW OF MUNICIPALITIES

Delaware has few local political jurisdictions compared with most states—only 3 counties, 57 municipalities, 19 school districts, and 201 special (mostly utility) districts. The borders of the three counties—Sussex, Kent, and New Castle—have remained virtually unchanged since colonial times. In the south is mainly rural Sussex County, with a U.S. Census Bureau es-timate of 184,291 residents in 2007, and home to the state's beach resorts. In the center is small-town oriented Kent County, the state's most rapidly growing county, with a 2007 population of 152,255, where the state capital city of Dover is located. And in the north is mostly urbanized New Castle County with 528,218 residents, or almost 61 percent of the state's total esti-mated population in 2007 of 864,764.[2]

Each of the fifty-seven municipalities listed by the Delaware League of Local Governments has been incorporated under a charter granted by the

General Assembly. Three are major cities. The largest city is Wilmington, with a nearly stable population estimated to be 72,868 in 2007, followed by growing populations in Dover with 35,811 and Newark with 29,992. Major reasons Wilmington's population is growing very slowly are its falling household size as well as legislation requiring its annexations be approved by New Castle County's council and executive, whereas Dover and Newark have successfully expanded their borders through annexation. Some smaller municipalities, such as south-of-the-canal Middletown and Townsend in New Castle County, have also annexed contiguous land for residential development. Wilmington, however, is the only Delaware municipality with a wage tax; thus suburbanites who currently live and work outside the city are less than enthusiastic about Wilmington annexations.

Except for Wilmington, elections for municipal officials are nonpartisan, meaning that candidates campaign without political party designations. Again with the exception of Wilmington, all municipalities over five thousand in population (Dover, Newark, Middletown, Milford, Smyrna, Elsmere, Georgetown, and Seaford) have a city manager system under an elected council and mayor.

No standard nomenclature differentiates Delaware's municipalities. Unlike other states, Delaware does not classify its municipalities by population. Those incorporated municipalities with fewer than five thousand residents are commonly known as small towns, although three designate themselves as "villages." There are twenty-four small towns in Sussex County, seventeen in Kent County, and only ten in New Castle County, where most of its people live in unincorporated suburban developments.

Many Delaware localities, housing developments, communities, and neighborhoods are not incorporated. Their only governing bodies are their county governments. Less than one-third of Delawareans live in incorporated municipalities. Hundreds of housing developments have organized civic or neighborhood associations to deal with common concerns of their residents, and these in turn have pooled their resources to form larger umbrella civic organizations to lobby or interact with state, county, and municipal governments. The more influential of these organizations sometimes act like governing bodies themselves, in league with politicians, builders, and others.

A 2005 survey asked Delawareans the question "Where would you like to live?" Only 5.7 percent responded they preferred to live in a city and 8 percent preferred a rural development, whereas 36 percent chose the "country," 21 percent chose a suburban development, while 17.3 percent chose a "small town."[3]

6. Respondents to "Where would you most like to live?" 1995–2005

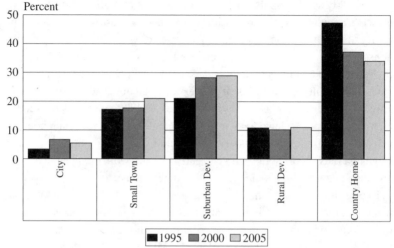

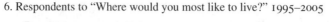

Source: Center for Applied Demography & Survey Research, University of Delaware.

An implication is that these responses reflect a longtime trend of Delawareans' continuing search for living in a less dense environment, which explains the phenomenon of urban sprawl (discussed in chapter 12) that reduces open spaces and hence opportunities to live in the country. If a person does not choose to live in a suburban development and cannot find an appropriate "country" habitat, the survey suggests that the next preferable option is a "small town."

Although all Delaware municipal governments have the power to regulate land use, state law now mandates that such regulations "shall be made in accordance with a comprehensive plan."[4] Most small towns, however, have yet to formulate a plan, and some do not even have a budget. Delaware's small town governments by definition have limited tax bases (e.g., property taxes, user fees, and perhaps fines) to fund improvements. Although the state government may provide various grants and undertake some projects for small towns, most state legislators represent urbanized northern New Castle County and few have much empathy for the small towns of Kent and Sussex Counties.

FICTION OF "HOME RULE"

The state charters granted by the General Assembly that have incorporated Delaware's fifty-seven municipalities have enabled them to elect their own governing bodies and to exercise the powers granted to them under their charters. Each municipality can assume any of the powers in the state constitution that are not specifically reserved nor prohibited by existing statutes, but such powers must be explicitly stated in its charter and approved by the General Assembly. One may be astonished to learn that the U.S. Constitution makes no mention of municipalities or other local jurisdictions, and neither does Delaware's constitution.

As in other states, Delaware's local governments are subdivisions of the state government, which determines their existence and powers. In 1923 the U.S. Supreme Court ruled: "In the absence of state constitutional provisions safeguarding it to them, municipalities have no inherent right to self-government which is beyond the legislative control of the state. A municipality is merely a department of the state, and the state may withhold, grant or withdraw powers and privileges as it sees fit. However great or small its sphere of action, it remains the creature of the state exercising and holding powers and privileges subject to the sovereign will."[5]

Delaware's constitution makes little mention of local government, the intention being that the General Assembly is the supreme legislative authority. Since the municipal charter is granted by the state and its contents must always be consonant with the state constitution and existing statutes, the state can always alter the powers it has granted without municipal approval.[6]

While neither home rule nor municipalities are mentioned in the state constitution, Delaware's General Assembly has enacted detailed legislation over the years on the subject of municipalities, comprising title 22 of the *Delaware Code Annotated*. Chapter 8 of title 22, enacted in 1953, is entitled "Home Rule." This chapter authorizes all municipal corporations in Delaware having a population of at least one thousand persons to amend their charters to "assume all powers which . . . it would be competent for the General Assembly to grant by specific enumeration and which are not denied by statute." Either of two methods are available for such charter revision: passage by the General Assembly acting on its own or by request of the local government; or a referendum in which a majority of voters favor charter revision, proposed by the local legislature, or by an elected seven-member charter commission that the General Assembly may negate by a two-thirds vote in both houses.[7]

On their face, these home rule statutory provisions seem to give broad discretionary authority to local governments. Citing these provisions in a 2001 study, four University of Delaware professors extolled the virtues of home rule in Delaware by declaring that Delaware "has few restrictions on local government," that indeed it is "the fourth least restrictive state," and that "Delaware has broad functional rather than limited home rule."[8] A 1990 study revealed that only twelve municipalities with populations over one thousand had assumed so-called "home rule" status by amending and filing their charters.[9] As of fiscal year 2007 only fourteen of twenty-six qualified municipalities had taken advantage of this option.

Some municipalities may not wish to assume any of the broader powers currently enumerated in their charters. Although they are not required to adopt such powers that are beyond their capability, they may not have the tax bases to assume some powers. Many municipalities may consider home rule status unnecessary for conducting their affairs. The most plausible explanation is that, unlike in other states, there does not appear to be any general movement for Delaware local governments to assume more power. The bottom line is that almost all important functions of government in Delaware are administered by the state government, not by local governments, which—compared with local governments in other states—are generally smaller and thus lack critical expertise and tax bases to reach for or exercise more authority.

Home rule in Delaware, therefore, is not fully developed. Compared with other state governments, the executive and legislative branches of Delaware's state government are extraordinarily concerned with "local" matters, prompting one University of Delaware professor to observe that the state government is the biggest local government in Delaware.

SHIFTING LOCAL FUNCTIONS TO THE STATE

Recently, government spending in Delaware has been growing. Part of this rise can be attributed to the consequences of inflation, part to Delaware's population growth causing, for example, increasing state-supported public school and day care enrollments, prison populations, and Medicaid rolls, and part to federal government mandates. Another factor, of course, is the gradual shifting of governmental functions over the past few decades from Delaware's local governments to its state government, largely because of constitutional changes, economies of scale, and inadequate funding sources at the local level.

It is indisputable that Delaware's state government accounts for most governmental expenditures and public employees in Delaware. In 2005 Delaware ranked fifth in the nation in state expenditures per capita and forty-first in local government expenditures per capita. Delaware state government ranked third in the number of employees per ten thousand population; only Hawaii and Alaska had higher rates among the states. In the 1930s Delaware's state government began to take over county and municipal functions, a process largely complete by the 1970s.

The Great Depression motivated the state government to begin a *welfare system* whereby the state established an old-age pension system in 1931, followed by its opening of a state home and hospital for the indigent—the State Welfare Home—at Smyrna in Kent County in 1933. In 1935 and 1936 a special income tax was levied in New Castle County for relief of the poor. In 1967 Delaware counties gave up all welfare functions, formerly financed by local taxes, to the state government. In fiscal year 2007, the state was spending $928 million on public assistance and $442 million on Medicaid (health care for the poor), which were never county functions.

Since 1935 the state government has had responsibility for the construction and maintenance of most *roads* in the state; the balance was within municipalities. In 2003 Delaware's state department of transportation (DelDOT) had jurisdiction over 96 percent of all of Delaware's public roads and streets—the highest percentage of public roads under state DOTs in the nation and well above the national average of only 20 percent. Accordingly, DelDOT's clout is far greater than that of transportation departments in most states.

Regardless of article 10 of the Delaware Constitution of 1897 that enjoins the General Assembly to maintain a "general and efficient system of free public schools," *public education* remained almost completely dependent on the vagaries of county governments for decades. But through the years this circumstance has undergone drastic change, whereby public education has become essentially a state function in which Delaware's counties and municipalities do not participate. By 2007 about one-third of the state budget went to public education; the state government funded roughly 70 percent of public education, from teachers to books to buildings. Whereas variations in local property tax rates and yields account for wide differences in public school funding from state to state and within other states, this is not true in Delaware. Instead, Delaware's complicated "unit" funding system is generally viewed as one of the most equitable state systems of school finance in the nation. This reputation derives from Delaware's state government providing a base foundation level of approximately 70 percent of education resources to all nineteen public school districts (including one countywide vocational school district for each of the three counties). Funding is weighted to adjust for differences in student needs and in the sixteen regular school districts' ability to raise their local share of school funds—so-called "equalization funding." Thus, the state allocates funds based on the number of pupils but also reserves about 7 percent of the total funds in any given year for equalization purposes.[10]

The *justice system* in Delaware is under the state government, not local governments. The vast majority of the *courts* in the state are state courts, with only six alderman/mayor courts in cities that added that power to their charters; Wilmington's municipal court was transferred to the state government in the 1990s. All *judges* are named by the governor with confirmation by the Senate (the six aldermen are selected by the local city councils).

Likewise, all *corrections facilities* are state facilities. Until 1955 each of Delaware's three counties administered a criminal detention facility, while state institutions for juvenile and female offenders were maintained separately. In 1956 the state established a statewide correctional system having jurisdiction over all adult prisoners confined to county jails. In 1967 the counties gave up all prison functions to the state. The antiquated New Castle County Workhouse that had served as the state's central prison was replaced by the opening in 1971 of the Delaware Correctional Center near Smyrna in Kent County.

Although the governments of New Castle County, Newark, Wilmington, and Dover maintain their own police forces, the state police provide *law enforcement* within Kent and Sussex Counties, whose county governments maintain no police forces of their own. The state police also has concurrent jurisdiction with all police forces existing within New Castle County, while many small towns throughout the state maintain modest police forces.

Similarly, all *public health services* are now provided by Delaware's state government—none by local governments. By 2002 the state government provided all adult and juvenile *public social services*, about 60 percent of county *paramedic funding*, and half of *public library construction funding*. In 1995 the government of New Castle County transferred its *airport* to the Delaware River and Bay Authority, an intergovernmental agency of Delaware and New Jersey. Also in 1995 the *Port of Wilmington* was sold by the city to the state for $4.5 million, removing about 110 jobs from the city's payroll and wiping out millions of dollars in accumulated port debt. Meanwhile, county administration of *elections* and several Wilmington and New Castle County *parks* have been transferred to the state.

The trend to transfer even more local functions to the state government was likely to slowly continue. In 1998 Republican state legislators proposed that the state fully fund all public schools, thus eliminating the remaining 30 percent of school funding from local school district property taxes. Moreover, the question remains whether the state would take over the *property assessments* function to eliminate inequities arising from the failure of county governments to conduct periodic and fairly contemporary assessments—Sussex County last reassessed in 1974, New Castle County in 1983, and Kent County in 1987.

Delaware's local governments are becoming more dependent on, and co-ordinated with, the state government's *planning and environmental activities* to deal with sprawl, land-use planning, and air and water pollution—state government activities that were decidedly on the increase during the first decade of the twenty-first century.

THE THREE COUNTIES

The "Lower Counties on the Delaware" have been in existence since 1682, when they provided representatives to the proprietorship of William Penn. Together they formed in 1704 a separate British colony with representatives meeting in their own assembly. By the mid-1700s their current boundaries were fixed, although not undisputed at the time. Each county had courts, justices of the peace, and a levy court for taxation. A sheriff and coroner were also in evidence. In 1776 the three counties formed the Delaware State, and the Delaware Constitution of 1776 recognized each county as a place of residence for representation in the Delaware Assembly. However, no specific powers of the counties were defined in any of Delaware's constitutions, from the first (1776) through the last (1897). Over time, the levy court assumed various administrative functions and organized charitable arrangements to deal with some welfare issues. The counties did not have the power to pass ordinances on their own. In general, they collected taxes and founded agencies with duties specified by the General Assembly.

An example of state-county relationships was that of transportation. Prior to 1935, the state government maintained all roads it had constructed. As housing developments were created and new suburban roads were built, usually by developers, the question arose who should maintain such roads. While ostensibly the county levy courts had the responsibility, they did not have the resources. Accordingly, in 1935 the state government took over responsibility for all public roads in the state. Thereafter, so long as roads in suburban developments were available for public use, the state was responsible, not the levy courts.

When the state government reorganized in 1967, the limited patchwork of welfare services provided by the levy courts became part of a state welfare system. The state addresses the powers delegated to the counties in title 9 of the Delaware Code.

Currently, the counties play an important role in comprehensive planning, zoning, building codes, and sewer services. All of these issues have become far more crucial with the rapid expansion of population. The three county governments are not only local governments but also regional governments as well. Many quality-of-life problems, abetted by population growth, transcend contemporary county government capabilities and resources, but are within their purview and designated powers—such as urban sprawl, loss of farmland and open space, inappropriate zoning, and obsolescent infrastructure. Yet municipalities within the counties may be even less capable of addressing such problems. A basic challenge for the three counties, therefore, is not only to serve as local governments for their people residing outside their municipalities but also to serve as pivotal regional governments that provide cooperation and coordination among their constituents and communities. Although the three counties share these commonalities, they are yet distinctly different from one another, as the following discussion demonstrates.

Sussex County

State legislation replaced Sussex County's levy court government in 1970 with a modern structure. Since 1970 Sussex County's government has consisted of an elective council of five members representing five council districts, and a county administrator who is appointed by the council and serves at its pleasure, while coordinating much but not all county administration. Sussex County has the largest land area and a rapidly growing population. According to the U.S. Census, Sussex County's population jumped 38 percent from 113,000 people in 1990 to about 156,000 in 2000. Meanwhile, housing units in the county increased from 74,253 to 93,070. Over 60 percent of the population is in the eastern part of the county, yet the five-member county council continues to be overrepresented by members of the rural area in the western part. Eastern residents want the state to add more council seats, but efforts to redistrict have been successfully thwarted by western residents.[11]

Effective land-use and growth management problems loom as the county government's greatest challenge as it wrestles with the framing of comprehensive planning approved by the state government. These problems are aggravated by sharp contrasts and conflicts between its eastern tourism-dominated beach area and the rest of the county, which is dominated by agribusiness. Of Delaware's fifty-seven municipal corporations, the twenty-five in Sussex County are members of the Sussex County Association of Towns (SCAT), which attempts to influence both county and state governments to serve municipal needs. Meanwhile, the county government has sought to keep county services and property taxes at a minimum, by counting on the state government to provide needed services.

Annexations of farmland to incorporated small towns in eastern Sussex

County account for the construction of thousands of new homes and commensurate population growth in the county, together with a myriad of attendant infrastructure problems challenging county government. Indeed, most of the county council meetings are devoted to considering such problems. Thus, its meeting agenda for September 18, 2007, called for considering wastewater facilities, sanitary sewers, proposed zoning ordinances, and subdivision issues.[12]

Average prices of Sussex County property and homes were reported to have grown 250 percent between 1995 and 2005. "There's a 'wow' factor to it. These towns are really growing," observed a staff member of the Delaware Office of State Planning Coordination. For example, adjacent to tiny Millville—an easy drive to the beach area—developers were proposing a ten-year plan in 2004 to annex 678 acres calling for construction of upward of 2,700 new homes that would increase the town's population from 259 to 3,500 residents. Real estate in Millville, selling for an average of $101,000 in the mid-1990s, was reported to have increased to more than $716,000 by the mid-2000s—about a 609 percent increase. Yet Millville still did not have its own police department or a sewer system; the town sought to contract with the Delaware State Police for police protection, while the county government intended to extend sewer service by 2006 in the proposed annexed area. Meanwhile, nearby Millsboro, with a population of about 2,300, had already annexed 371 acres proposed for 2,400 homes and a golf course; its average property sales had reportedly jumped about 381 percent during the same period, from $107,000 to $515,000. Likewise, in the town of Milton, with a 2000 population of 1,657, a local development group proposed building thousands of homes in a planned community that would include a sewer system serving the development area and the existing town.[13]

One complicating factor is that these development plans must accommodate both part-year and full-year residents. Nearly half of the housing units in Sussex County are occupied only part of the year. Moreover, there are many proposals for new development that are all competing with one another to attract people. Just because a development is proposed does not mean that it will be built in the immediate future. In fact, several proposed developments with more than a thousand housing units were canceled in 2007.

New housing developments mean, of course, the prospect of more property tax revenue for the government of Sussex County to provide needed services. However, the county council has shown little inclination in recent years to increase county taxes—the lowest among the three counties. The council went so far in 1993 to sell its own county courthouse and engineering building to the state government for $4.3 million. It has refused to establish a county department of parks and recreation, preferring instead to continue to depend on the state government to administer these functions exclusively. Moreover, the county government does not have a police department, but instead relies entirely on the Delaware State Police and the municipal police departments in the county. Sussex County officials and residents do not appear the least concerned that residents of New Castle County pay for their own county police while, at the same time, also pay state taxes supporting the activities of the Delaware State Police in Sussex County. Writing about this "subsidization of southern Delaware," opinion columnist Al Mascitti observed: "For years, downstaters—especially those in Sussex County— have been pulling a fast one on upstaters, who help pay for everything from law enforcement to farmland preservation."[14] This contention is probably overstated, since many New Castle County residents also have houses in Sussex County. In addition, it was far more efficient to introduce a New Castle County police force when the large majority of the state's population increases occurred in New Castle County, whose residents should bear the burden of their support. Furthermore, the state police have concurrent jurisdiction and have a strong presence in New Castle County.

Internal politics in Sussex County revolve around conflicts between the eastern resort areas near the ocean and bays represented by a lone county council member, and the largely rural interior of farms, agribusiness, and small towns represented by the remaining four council members. Sussex politics is rife with land-use conflicts between developers and their agents on the one hand, whose development proposals are pitched to a receptive council majority, and coastal residents and their oft outvoted council member on the other hand. For example, the council voted four to one for a 2004 ordinance to allow "cluster houses" on smaller lots without a zoning change. The lone councilman from the coastal area, who voted against the ordinance, cautioned: "What we're going to be getting is sprawl countywide. We are directing development . . . outside the development districts. There's no hope with this change."[15] A decade earlier, the executive secretary of the nearby Angola-area civic association, the Friends of Herring Creek, had complained: "These developments are approved by people who live nowhere near here, and don't know what we go through."[16]

Kent County

Kent County shares many of the same problems experienced by Sussex County, and both counties form what is sometimes termed as "slower, lower

Delaware." Given the burgeoning population and growth problems of the two lower counties, however, referring to them as "slower" has become less appropriate. Small towns dot the landscape of both counties, and some are growing rapidly through annexations.

Delaware's state government is most accessible to Kent County residents because the state capital is located in the midcounty city of Dover (population of 34,735 in 2006)—site of the city and county governments as well. About ten miles north of Dover is Kent County's second largest city of Smyrna (population 7,837 in 2006), very close to the southern border of New Castle County and rapidly expanding.

In 2006 Smyrna was one of the state's fastest-growing communities, second only to Middletown in southern New Castle County, which registered a growth of nearly 64 percent between 2000 and 2006. Smyrna's population grew about 35 percent between 2000 and 2006. In 2003 Smyrna annexed five hundred acres of southern New Castle County land over the objections of state and New Castle County governments. Indeed, because of Smyrna's defiance of state regulations controlling growth and its willingness to exercise the home rule power given to it in its charter by the General Assembly, the state government's Cabinet Committee on Planning Issues decided to withhold $2.9 million in state aid slated for water main connections, a new water storage tank, and other upgrades. Among various development projects, another annexation in 2004 southwest of town portended construction of 2,500 new housing units. Smyrna's planning director bragged: "We're not in a hot area of development. We're on fire. We're at meltdown." Smyrna's mayor Mark Schaeffer added that "every piece of developable land between Smyrna and Dover [about ten miles apart] is being actively pursued—every square inch of it," and he predicted that housing would soon appear as one long corridor up and down the state.[17]

Three circumstances had combined to spur development in northern Kent County, namely the effects of Delaware Highway 1, Governor Ruth Ann Minner's "Livable Delaware" policies, and New Castle County's recently adopted Unified Development Code (UDC). Highway 1, a new controlled-access, divided, high-speed toll road, runs parallel to the old Dupont Highway 13, extending from northern New Castle County southward through Kent County to the beach areas of Sussex County. Although constructed mainly to serve tourists' access to the beaches, it provides quicker commutes south to Dover or north to Wilmington and Philadelphia for nearby residents of new housing developments in northern Kent County and southern New Castle County.[18] Meanwhile, "Livable Delaware" called for concentrating development near towns and areas where infrastructure—such as roads, schools, sewers, and police protection—is already in place (see chapter 12). And finally, Smyrna and northern Kent County have become more attractive to developers because New Castle County's UDC contains stricter open space and environmental regulations for unincorporated land that make it more difficult to build homes in southern New Castle County, where land prices are cheaper.

A unique characteristic of Kent County is retention of its levy court governing body, which comprises seven elected commissioners who enact ordinances and lead administrative departments. Accordingly, no real separation of powers and checks and balances exist in Kent County's government as in Sussex and New Castle Counties. This fusion of legislative and administrative powers has meant that Kent's system has not been as open or "public" as the other two counties' systems. For over three decades, efforts to modernize Kent County's governmental system have failed. There is no question that the state's General Assembly has the power to reshape also Kent's governmental system, but so far it has not intervened.

New Castle County

Contrasted with Sussex and Kent County governments is the upstate government of populous New Castle County—Delaware's second largest government—with about 1,500 full-time employees in 2004 and an elected county executive reputed to be the state's second most powerful public official. The General Assembly replaced the county's three-member levy court in 1965 with a seven-member elective council—which exercised taxing, ordinance, planning, and zoning powers—and a county executive with budget, appointive, and item-veto powers.

Through the late twentieth century, New Castle County government's most important function had been to control land-use development through planning and zoning functions. The basic problem was that real estate developers had seldom failed to obtain what they wanted from the county council. Indeed, developers became so influential in the 1990s that public confidence in the county council was eroding. Unfettered urban sprawl and a series of scandals involving the council's land-use decision-making led to federal corruption investigations. At least six public officials went to jail in the 1990s for soliciting bribes. The county executive, of course, could have acted to curtail sprawl by vetoing council decisions too favorable to developers. But county executive Dennis Greenhouse left office at the end of 1996, after serving the maximum of two four-year terms, without becoming directly involved in planning and zoning—a "deliberate decision," according to a local journalist, that "may be part of the underlying cause for the current furor over greed and growth."[19]

Various reform efforts had failed. Developers dominated New Castle County politics, and the county council's "rezoning-on-demand" approach to suburban housing and commercial development appeared unabated. One reform proposal in the 1990s, however, did have life. Local newspaper editor John Taylor proposed in 1991 that the seven-member county council be doubled in size, arguing that a larger council would provide a wider range of views, including those responsive to civic groups and others, which would thwart the influence of developers and their business allies. A 1996 editorial proposed raising council members to thirteen to dissolve "old associations between council members and development interests, nurtured by campaign contributions, proximity and strenuous lobbying." These arguments, together with the contention that existing council members represented election districts nearly twice the population as represented by state senatorial election districts, moved the General Assembly to pass a bill in the final hours of its 1996 session to expand the New Castle County council from seven to thirteen members. But it was not until the elections in November 2006 that the additional six seats were actually filled, and as of this writing it is too early to tell whether developers would thereby lose clout or that expanding the council would lead to any positive changes.[20]

Meanwhile, election in 1996 of a reform-minded New Castle County chief of police, Democrat Tom Gordon, to the post of county executive marked a departure of sorts from the past. Together with his chief deputy, Sherry Freebery, the Gordon-Freebery administration served for the maximum eight tumultuous years through the end of 2004. Freebery sought to succeed Gordon as the Democratic candidate for county executive, but she was soundly defeated in the September 2004 Democratic primary of that year. Contributing to her defeat were federal indictments by Republican U.S. attorney Colm Connolly of Democrats Gordon and Freebery in May 2004 on charges of racketeering, mail fraud, and wire fraud, which tended to obscure what some believed were significant accomplishments during their tenure. Litigation ended in 2007, however, when their felony charges were dropped and they pleaded guilty to misdemeanors only.

Initially faced in 1997 with an alleged "projected $100 million deficit," Gordon had claimed in 2004 a combined financial surplus of $242 million, with no tax rate increases in the eight years of his administration, making New Castle County one of only twenty-one counties of the nation's three thousand counties to have been awarded an AAA bond rating. Although Delaware's Chancery Court was to rule in February 2005 that New

Castle County's $242 million surplus had been accumulated illegally, Gordon boasted in his "swan-song" budget address that the New Castle's surplus was the highest, and its property tax the lowest, of any of the nation's twenty-one triple-A counties. "Ladies and gentlemen—we have earned our bragging rights! We are number one!" Had Gordon explained how this "miracle" was accomplished, he would have had to point to the thousands of new homes constructed during his administration in southern New Castle County—most south of the Chesapeake and Delaware Canal—whose new owners had paid property taxes at existing rates, together with the explosion of property-transfer tax revenue, to add to the county coffers. Completion of new state Highway 1 had paved much of the way for this phenomenon. Gordon did not refer to these new circumstances in his budget address. But he did refer to what could prove in time to be a turnaround legacy of his administration: adoption of the Unified Development Code, which brought a measure of order to real estate development and zoning to New Castle County.[21]

Better understanding of the county's true financial situation emerged during the succeeding administration of County Executive Chris Coons who sought a 17.5 percent increase in the county's real estate tax to offset an approximate 30 percent drop in property-transfer tax revenue spurred by a housing market collapse. Moreover, county employee wage commitments were eating up the surplus carried over from the Gordon-Freebery administration. Nevertheless, Gordon unsuccessfully sought to replace Coons in 2008 with the promise once again not to raise taxes.

WILMINGTON'S UNIQUENESS

No other local government in Delaware has had the problems with which Wilmington, the state's largest city, has been forced to contend. Whereas the populations of the three counties and many municipalities have been growing, Wilmington continued to experience a slow decline in its population, from a high of 110,168 in 1920 to 72,664 in 2000 and stability through 2007. Between 1940 and 1980, New Castle County's population quadrupled, while Wilmington's population plummeted 38 percent. Among reasons given for the city's elongated decline were projects such as urban renewal in the 1960s and 1970s that cleared many blocks of housing, and the construction of Interstate 95, which cut a swath through some of Wilmington's most stable neighborhoods. Then, too, the growth of minority populations during school desegregation doubtlessly contributed to "white flight" that augmented suburban New Castle County's population. The 2000 census showed a racial makeup of nearly 36 percent white (the lowest of any jurisdiction in the state), 57 percent African American (the highest in the state), and 10 percent Hispanic or Latino of any race. Wilmington joined many other eastern cities in experiencing a population decline.

While Wilmington's number of households was continuing to decline, the city's industrial and commercial growth burgeoned, creating many jobs, most of which were filled by outsiders who commuted to Wilmington from their bedroom communities in the county and beyond. On workdays, Wilmington's population swelled to roughly 123,000, which strained city government services (parking, traffic, police, fire, water, sewer, etc.). For example, Wilmington not only maintains a sizeable police force but is the only Delaware local government that does not have a volunteer fire department, but rather has a full-time salaried fire department.

The city's property tax base was affected by the relatively slow residential growth. Property tax exemptions for new businesses were common. In the mid-1990s there were more than three hundred tax-exempt properties in the city (government-owned property, churches, hospitals, nonprofit service organizations, and exempted businesses) occupying 46 percent of the city's land. These exemptions further exacerbated the productivity of the city's tax base. And the city was in effect forbidden by the General Assembly to annex adjoining land. Moreover, the city's wage tax of 1.25 percent, levied on all wage earners in the city, was as high as the state legislature would permit and the only wage tax in the state. Since the employment base was not growing, the revenue potential was limited and at times volatile. The city government's greatest problem, therefore, was to find additional revenue to fund needed services for workers from outside and for many low-income residents.

In 2002 Wilmington mayor James Baker warned, "The city is going out of business—unless its revenue sources are expanded." He feared that increasing property and wage taxes would drive residents and employers from the city. Only the state government could provide answers. Governor Minner responded by establishing a state task force to recommend new money sources. Of the task force's seven recommendations, only three were approved by the General Assembly—a mere stop-gap allowing city officials to create a $2.50 per ticket entertainment tax, a 2 percent tax on natural gas providers, and a 3 percent surcharge on the lodging tax. Together these measures were projected to yield only $1.4 million, not enough to eliminate a $4.9 million projected budget shortfall by June 2004, and far below a possible $12 million shortfall in four years. Mayor Baker said, "We need a large infusion of money for the long term." A task force member responded,

"Getting money for Wilmington has always been a battle in Dover. The lawmakers bought in this time. But all the credibility we've built up is shot if the city doesn't keep cutting expenses."[22]

Beginning in 2005, a turnaround occurred when the state provided a form of revenue sharing—a recurring $10 million to the city as payouts in lieu of property taxes. In addition, the city actually achieved a $22 million surplus from a substantial increase in wage-tax revenue resulting from the transfer of MBNA to Bank of America, accompanied by a large total of MBNA payouts of bonuses. The city's surplus enabled it to give New Castle County $317,000 in 2007 for libraries and parks—seemingly a mere pittance compared to the $16 million previously given by the county to the city to help it weather its financial slump. Accordingly, a paradox of sorts had occurred whereby the county government's surplus had evaporated while the city government enjoyed a newly found surplus.

City-county give-and-take interdependencies were bound to continue for some time to come, leading some observers to project an eventual county-wide metropolitan government. For example, the city announced in July 2007 that it wanted an additional $8.5 million a year by 2012 to dispose of the county's sewage in its regional wastewater plant—a whopping 55 percent hike over five years from the county that was contributing at least 70 percent of the sewage treated there. County administrators considered the proposal two or three times higher than reasonable.

CONCLUSION

The foregoing discussion demonstrates that the subject of state-local relations in Delaware is filled with political overtones. If we define politics as dealing with power in society, and define power as the capacity to allocate resources, then our discussion reveals continuing political or power conflicts between Delaware's state and local governments as well as conflicts between and within county and municipal governments.

We have observed that Delaware's state government has assumed many of the functions formerly carried on by local governments in Delaware, and that home rule is not aggressively implemented by local governments. Yet, counties and municipalities retain vital land-use planning and zoning functions. It is for this reason that analysis of state-local relations in Delaware must highlight land-use conflicts.

In chapter 12 we will analyze a few selected policy problems, including the vexing problem of sprawl. Suffice it to note here that the state government is attempting to contain sprawl by influencing local governments to restrict growth to locales that already possess needed infrastructure. Several local governments have been disposed nevertheless to annex land for new housing developments where such infrastructure does not exist. Such growth activity not only pits local governments against the state government, but also produces conflicts between local governments and county governments, as well as generating sectional conflicts between local governments and residential areas within the same county. For example, county officials know that to the extent that municipal governments administer their services to embrace residents from former unincorporated locales, the property taxes paid to the county government are thereby lessened. And, as conflicts within Sussex County illustrate, beach area residents feel they are underrepresented in a county government disposed to defer to creeping development and rural interests.

In short, the political conflicts in state-local relations in little Delaware are complex, multifaceted, and seemingly beyond the capacity of orderly growth and comprehensive planning.

CHAPTER TEN

Public Finance

Previous chapters have shed some light on the status of public finance in Delaware. We have learned, for example, that Delaware deserves plaudits for its "triple-A" bond rating, that public schools are funded largely by the state government, and that businesses that incorporate in Delaware are willing in the aggregate to pay handsomely to have access to Delaware courts.

There are other facets of Delaware public finance that also merit analysis in this chapter. But first we explore salient historical antecedents that contributed to the state's fiscal woes through the 1970s. We then turn our attention to what has been done to correct them. And, finally, we attempt to evaluate contemporary public finance in the state, by reference to charges, countercharges, and major components of the state's financial system.

OVERCOMING EARLY PROBLEMS

As noted previously, the Constitution of 1897 sought to strengthen governors by increasing executive control over state government, notably by giving the governor an item veto of state appropriations. In 1920, however, a state study commission concluded that "by far the most important problem confronting the people of Delaware was the methods involving the raising of public revenue and the appropriation and expenditure of public funds." The commission's recommendation—that the governor be given strong budgetary powers over the agencies—resulted in the Delaware budget law of 1921. Nevertheless, Delaware governors were "loath to . . . stretch their influence over the agencies in this manner."[1] Persistence of the old commission system, before the one-person-one-vote reform in the 1960s, guaranteed that the governor—-with or without new budgetary powers—-would not have been able to exert much more control over state agencies so long as the predominantly rural southern two counties controlled the General Assembly.

Among persistent fiscal problems were executive-legislative discord, differences among county delegations in deciding what programs should be funded, unbalanced budgets, and failure to obtain all available federal funding. Moreover, as the cabinet form of government took hold, and service delivery was more focused at the state level, financial cracks occurred. Indeed, between 1972 and 1977, Delaware's state government had budget shortfalls four times, and taxes were increased twenty-two separate times. Delaware's top income tax bracket of 19.8 percent was the nation's highest at that time, and its unemployment rate was consistently higher than the national average.[2]

Republican Governor Pete du Pont (1977–85), who inherited this financial mess, institutionalized lasting fiscal reforms supported by the Democratic-controlled legislature. A cabinet form of government and court-induced "one-person-one-vote" reapportionment in the 1960s, which gave New Castle County forty-four of the sixty-two seats in the General Assembly, had shifted the center of political power and reduced the disproportionate power of the southern counties. After a shaky start with the Democratic-controlled legislature, Governor du Pont shifted to a consensus-style bipartisanship that paved the way for overcoming revenue-expenditure imbalances (hence executive-legislative discord), ending deficit financing, balancing the budget, controlling indebtedness, managing investment of state funds, and acquiring available federal grants.

Specifically, Governor du Pont supported an 8.8 percent cut in personal income tax revenues in 1979 and reducing the top rate to 16.5 percent, actions initiated by leaders of the legislature and business community, which became precedents for more tax cuts during the administrations of his successors. He also supported two 1980 statutes that drastically reduced the risk of having a budget deficit at the end of a fiscal year by requiring either increased taxes and/or increased borrowing. One statute restricted annual appropriations to 98 percent of estimated revenue by a simple majority vote or 100 percent by a three-fifths vote, and established a Budget Reserve Account, commonly called the rainy day fund, by setting aside 5 percent of estimated revenue. The other statute required a three-fifths vote of each house of the General Assembly to adopt any new tax or tax increase. A limitation in new bonded debt was also introduced. As a result, the cost of debt service as a percentage of gross General Fund receipts was cut in half from 16.8 percent in 1977 to 8.4 percent in 1989, helping state bond ratings to soar and freeing money from paying debt service for other uses. Furthermore,

Governor du Pont obtained all available new federal block grants at the earliest date allowed by federal law.[3]

In retrospect, perhaps the most important fiscal control put in place during Governor du Pont's tenure, and one contributing to the emerging dominant role of governors in the state's public finance, was his 1977 executive order creating the Delaware Economic and Financial Advisory Council (DEFAC), conceived to advise the governor on the state's overall financial condition, tax policy, debt management issues, and national and local economic trends affecting Delaware and the state's revenue. Comprising representatives of Delaware's academic and business communities, as well as the state's General Assembly and executive branch, DEFAC was charged with providing nonpartisan and objective revenue and expenditure estimates used to determine the following year's fiscal budget. Specifically, DEFAC's estimates became accepted as authoritative by all public officials, and the basis for the amount of general obligation debt the state may issue, the funding level required for the state's rainy day fund, and estimated revenues and cash carryover that determine the maximum size of the operating budget.[4]

The General Assembly's joint finance and bond bill committees have ensured bipartisan cooperation, fostered by the decades-long majority control of the Senate by Democrats and House by Republicans. And acceptance of DEFAC's authoritative role has reduced executive-legislative fiscal conflicts. Some observers believe that DEFAC could well serve as a model for other states and for the federal government as well.

THE "ROGUE STATE" CHARGE

On the cover of an August 2002 issue of the *New Republic* magazine was a colorful cartoon showing a driver looking at a billboard proclaiming "Delaware: The Worst State—not the First State!" Inside was an article by senior editor Jonathan Chait entitled "Rogue State: The Case against Delaware." Chait charged that "The organizing principle of Delaware government is to subsidize its people at the rest of the country's expense . . . a rapacious parasite state with a long history of disloyalty and avarice." His polemics spoke of Delaware's political tradition of "self-serving venality," and of Delaware's greatest specialty as "finding ways to siphon money out of nonresidents." Chait ended his indictment by concluding: "To hell with the national interest. Delaware is looking out for number one."[5]

Apparently Chait was driven to write his tirade after experiencing a two-mile backup at Delaware's I-95 toll plaza near the Maryland line. He based his diatribe mainly on two points. First, Delaware's I-95 toll of two dollars amounts to an "exorbitant" eighteen cents per mile (compared to less than five cents motorists pay per mile in New Jersey and four cents in Maryland) that, together with a three dollar fare for the Delaware Memorial Bridge, constitutes 6 percent of Delaware's budget. And second, Delaware has an "appallingly lax" of regulation of banks and corporations. Thus, by "eviscerating its usury laws," Delaware has enabled its credit-card banks to provide thousands of jobs that in turn produce enough tax revenue to allow the state to "slash" its other taxes. Moreover, unlike banks actually located in Delaware, all that the hundreds of thousands (mostly nonresident) corporations incorporated in Delaware have to do is for each to pay an annual fee, as low as fifty dollars, that collectively adds up to almost one-fifth of total state revenue, making it possible for the state to do without a sales tax. Referring to "Delaware's sycophantic approach to corporate regulation," Chait asked: "Who needs the Cayman Islands when there's a tiny, secretive corporate haven on U.S. soil?" And, finally, Chait made the point that no sales tax enables Delaware merchants to lure many out-of-staters to shop in Delaware—"yet another way for Delaware to suck money from its neighbors."[6]

Without explicitly referring to Chait's article, the February 2003 issue of the authoritative nonpartisan *Governing* magazine seemingly answered his charges against Delaware. Published by the Washington-based *Congressional Quarterly*, the magazine concluded after a year-long study that no other state handled taxes better than Delaware.

The *Governing* magazine study appeared at the time the National Conference of State Legislatures released its own study showing all fifty states struggling with the most serious budget crisis since World War II. Indeed, the crisis prompted *The Kiplinger Letter* of February 2003 to predict "all states will raise taxes" and to note their "rainy-day funds . . . are long since gone."[7]

Governing magazine rated all the states in three areas: adequacy of revenue, fairness to taxpayers, and management of the system. For each of these three categories, the study gave each state from one to four stars. Delaware was the only state receiving four stars in two of the three categories—in adequacy and management; it was given three stars in fairness. Only nine other states received as much as one rating of four stars. In its commentary about Delaware, the magazine acknowledged that the state "is sometimes portrayed as a buccaneer on the high seas of state finance," and that its laws "help firms evade taxation in other states," but the magazine gave high marks to its "predictability" for corporations and to DEFAC—"one of the country's best revenue-estimating systems." The commentary concluded:

"All in all, this is a carefully managed fiscal enterprise. From a distance, Delaware may look like it's wearing a pirate's hat, but from the inside, the headgear bears a closer resemblance to a green eyeshade."[8]

Democratic Governor Ruth Ann Minner successfully campaigned in 2004 for election to a second term. Without raising income taxes or using the state's rainy day fund, she was able to steer Delaware through the post-9/11 recession with minimal pain. The state's leading newspaper—in endorsing her for a second term—commented, "While governors in surrounding states worried how they could avoid raising taxes and cutting programs, Delaware functioned well during the economic downturn."[9] The corporate franchise tax was raised substantially, and a hiring freeze on state government employment was implemented. Neither the editorial nor any other commentator, however, attributed at least some of Delaware's success in weathering that storm to bipartisan fiscal reforms put in place a generation before, during Republican Pete du Pont's administration.

REVENUE SOURCES

As do most other states, Delaware makes an effort to shift the tax burden away from individual households. Delaware is fortunate to have two revenue sources—the corporate franchise tax ($540.4 million yield in 2007) and abandoned property ($364.9 million)—that derive almost exclusively from out-of-state businesses. To these can be added corporate fees ($65.4 million) and limited liability corporations ($91.9 million). Thus, a total of $1,066.6 million, or 32.3 percent of all 2007 revenue of Delaware's state government came from businesses that for the most part were not doing business in Delaware.

Meanwhile, Delaware businesses paid the corporate income tax ($140.3 million), gross receipts tax ($157.3 million), bank franchise tax ($175.2 million)—which is really a business income tax—public utility tax ($46.2 million), and insurance taxes ($88.3 million). Together these Delaware business levies yielded $607.3 million, or 18.5 percent of all state revenues.

The Delaware video lottery yielded $218.8 million, of which 60 percent came from nonresidents, or 7 percent of the revenue base. The Delaware personal income tax is deductible on the federal income tax, thus accounting for roughly $181 million (a shift from $1,008 million), or 6 percent of state revenues. In other words, about 63 percent of all Delaware taxes in 2007 was shifted to out-of-state.[10] Figure 7 depicts by category the state's recent General Fund revenue.

Borrowing, of course, is another way for the state to acquire revenue

7. Delaware General Fund Revenues, FY2007

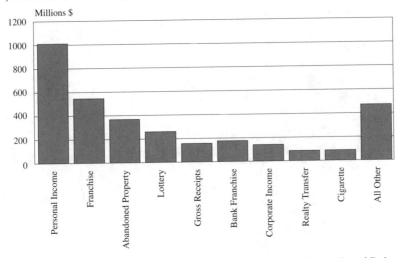

Source: Center for Applied Demography & Survey Research, University of Delaware. Delaware Department of Finance.

for state government activities. The cost of incurring debt, moreover, has decreased as Delaware's bond ratings have increased, from a low of Baaa-1 in 1977 to the highest possible rating in 2007 of AAA. Accordingly, the cost of debt service, as a percentage of General Fund receipts, has dropped from 11.2 percent in fiscal year 1984 to 5.1 percent in 2007. And although the per capita state debt during the same period increased from $921 to $1,517, the real debt per capita (controlled for inflation) decreased from $1,271 to $1,044, while debt as a percent of personal income plummeted from 6.22 to 3.80 percent.

Delaware has adopted a debt limit that restricts the principal amount of new "tax-supported obligations of the State" authorized in any one fiscal year to 5 percent of estimated net budgetary general fund revenue for that fiscal year and has established certain tests to be met at the time of issuance. Regardless of the debt incurred, Delaware law also requires a "balanced budget" whereby total appropriations may not exceed the state revenue from all sources estimated in the budget. Republican congressman and former governor Mike Castle has commented, "Before Delaware passed a balanced budget amendment, Delaware was an economic disaster."[11]

We may conclude, therefore, that Delaware law does not permit the state to incur deficits, and that the state's indebtedness is carefully managed. The governor must immediately begin cutting expenditures when DEFAC revenue estimates fall below the planned expenditures. There has yet to be any case when the budget was not balanced at the end of a fiscal year.

8. Delaware General Fund Expenditures, FY2007

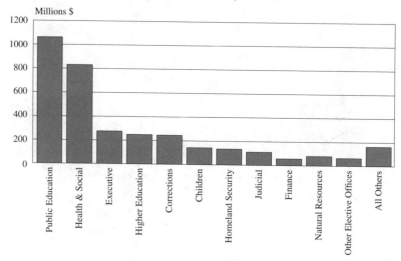

Source: Center for Applied Demography & Survey Research, University of Delaware. Delaware Department of Finance.

Finally, the federal government's fiscal year 2005 expenditures in Delaware totaled $5.5 billion (forty-eighth among the states) including nearly $2.1 billion for social security (about 106,000 Delawareans were on social security of Delaware's total population of 836,000). Also included within this total was $1.24 billion in federal grants and payments to Delaware state and local governments—the least among the fifty states—most of this largess was in grants that went to fund state government functions that are done locally in other states.

With a per capita basis in fiscal year 2005 at about $6,537, Delaware ranked thirty-ninth among the states for federal expenditures, somewhat lower than the national average of $7,583. In fiscal year 2006, Delaware's per capita contribution to federal internal revenue gross collections, personal and corporate, was $20,196, ranking Delaware first among the states in per capita contribution to the federal treasury. Delaware is a net contributor to the federal government since it receives only seventy-seven cents for every dollar it contributes.[12]

EXPENDITURE CATEGORIES

Delaware's real general fund expenditures increased approximately 3.0 percent annually over the thirty-two years between fiscal year 1974 and 2006, as the state government became more service oriented, as new federal mandates such as Medicaid were added, and as the population increased on average at 1.2 percent per year. Whereas total general fund expenditures were $342.0 million in fiscal year 1974, they were almost ten times greater in 2007, at $3,389.9 million—the largest categories of which were 32.1 percent for public education, 25.2 percent for health and social services, 7.5 percent for higher education, 7.4 percent for corrections, and 3.8 percent for public safety. The chart at figure 8 depicts the state's recent general fund expenditures by category.

Two decades earlier, in fiscal year 1987, the largest expenditure category was also public education at 33.3 percent, but the second largest was health and social services at 18.8 percent. It is also interesting to note that the 1987 figure for corrections was 5.2 percent, indicating a much faster growth than the budget as a whole. Notably, higher education's share fell to 7.5 percent in 2007 from 11.4 percent in 1987.

OTHER PROMINENT FEATURES

Not included in the above analysis of state government revenue and expenditures are so-called "earmarked" funds that are designated for certain purposes. Sources for such funds include fees charged for certain permits that are issued by, and help support, the state's Department of Natural Resources and Environmental Control (DNREC); child-support collections that pay for part of the state's Department of Children, Youth and Their Families (DCYTF); the Housing Trust Fund; and Medicaid, which funds the medical program for the poor in the state's Department of Health and Social Services (DHSS).[13]

Prominent among designated funds is the Transportation Trust Fund (TTF), established during fiscal year 1988 for maintenance and construction of the state's major transportation infrastructure, and to alleviate pressure on the General Assembly's so-called joint bond bill committee, whose bond bill funds other capital projects such as construction of schools. The state collects certain taxes (e.g., motor fuel tax), fees (e.g., motor vehicle sale and registration fees), and toll road revenues (from I-95 and Route 1) that fund operations and administration of TTF as well as the Delaware Department of Transportation (DelDOT). Taxes and fees totaled $395.3 million for TTF in fiscal year 2007. Added for TTF were $104.4 million in federal funding and $183.6 million from the state's bond bill, making a grand total of $683.3 million. Approximately 10.7 percent of combined revenues were earmarked for the TTF.

In general, Delaware earmarks far less of its revenues than many other states, and the revenues earmarked are related to the recipient, as for example motor fuel tax revenue is designated to the transportation trust fund.

Built into Delaware's governmental system is an extraordinary amount of redundancy for ensuring that expenditures comply with the law. Delaware is one of only twenty-two states that has an independently elected state *auditor*, who is empowered to audit all state and school district financial transactions. Another independently elected constitutional officer is the state *treasurer*, who has custody of all state money and invests the same (except pension funds) until required to make authorized disbursements. The state department of finance, headed by the cabinet *secretary of finance*, is directed by statute to "audit, inspect, and examine the accounts, affairs and records of any agency of the State" and to administer all revenue laws. The *controller general*, appointed by the legislative council, has "complete access to all the records" of all state agencies and authority to perform "management and program reviews." And, finally, the state *budget director*, who serves at the pleasure of the governor and prepares the governor's budget, also has extensive authority to audit agency accounts and to prescribe "accounting records and procedures as shall be adequate for the control of the fiscal affairs of the State."[14]

That these five state officers have avoided turf battles and squabbles, given their overlapping jurisdictions, is a reflection of Delaware's nonpartisan attitude toward financial affairs and the consequent ease with which cooperative relationships among them are maintained.

POLITICS OF STATE FINANCE

Throughout the late twentieth century, Democrats and Republicans vied with each other to propose the biggest tax cuts. Successive governors understood the political efficacy of tax cuts in Delaware. The issue was not whether to cut taxes, but by how much. From the nation's highest personal income tax of a top rate of 19.8 percent during the term of Democratic governor Sherman Tribbitt (1973–77), who became known as "One-Term Sherm," two-term Republican governors Pete du Pont (1977–85) and Mike Castle (1985–93) cut the income tax two times and three times, respectively.

In 1996, with robust DEFAC estimates in hand, Democratic governor Tom Carper (1993–2001) offered his second personal income tax cut, the seventh since 1979, dropping the top rate to 6.9 percent, and placing Delaware below the top tax rates of fourteen other states. On November 5, 1996, Carper was easily reelected to a second term by 69.5 percent of the vote, his ninth successive statewide election, thus becoming the most winning politician in Delaware history—first as treasurer, next as congressman, and then as governor. His campaign for reelection emphasized his cutting income taxes twice, securing the highest bond rating in Delaware history, and achieving the state's ranking as one of the ten best financially managed states in the nation.[15]

No one of influence was heard against income tax cuts. Republicans, Democrats, and business leaders approved. No argument was made that Delaware, as one of the nation's wealthiest states, could afford to raise income taxes to pay for more spending on Delaware's social problems. Throwing money at a problem, however, was not viewed favorably in Delaware. With a poverty rate, uninsured rate, and unemployment rate near the lowest in the country, Delawareans were generally satisfied. Delaware's mid-2007 per capita income at $40,608 ranked twelfth among the states and well above the nation's per capita income of $38,611.

Moreover, rare proposals to raise franchise taxes were quickly stilled (except in times of severe financial stress, such as 2003). For example, Governor Carper in 1996 rejected a proposal of the Wilmington Interfaith Network for a 10 percent surcharge on the state's corporate franchise tax to establish a $30 million fund to support youth programs aimed at reducing city crime. Carper responded, "We have to be very careful about sending a message that we're interested in raising the corporate franchise tax and unwillingly push 250,000 corporations into the waiting hands of other states." And a 1996 proposal by the Delaware Association of Nonprofit Agencies that newly incorporated companies pay a surcharge to fund expansion by tax-exempt agencies evoked a similar response by a Wilmington councilman who cautioned, "There's this issue of killing the goose that laid the golden egg."[16] Such proposals were judged inappropriate earmarks and were doomed so long as rival states, Nevada among them, had no franchise tax. In addition, the franchise tax was increased in 1991, just prior to Carper taking office, and again in 2003 to offset reductions in franchise tax receipts after the 2001 market debacle.

The state's booming economy continued to produce sizeable state surpluses—$430 million in 1998 and over $300 million in 1999, for example. Accordingly, the scenario of cutting income taxes was repeated in 1997, 1998, and 1999. This last cut fixed the top income tax rate at 5.9 percent, helping to pave the way for Tom Carper to win election to the U.S. Senate in 2000 and for Lieutenant Governor Ruth Ann Minner to win the governorship—both by large margins.

Democratic governor Minner became the first governor in twenty-five years not to cut personal income taxes. Her first term was challenged by the post-9/11 recession, which caused most state governments to reduce state payrolls and the number of state employees, to raise taxes, to spend their rainy day funds, and to cut programs. Instead, Minner was able to weather the storm in Delaware without cutting programs, raising income taxes, or dipping into the state's rainy day fund, and by freezing state jobs and payrolls. As the recession abated, Governor Minner narrowly won reelection in 2004 with 51 percent of the vote over former judge Bill Lee, who won his native Sussex County as well as Kent County but failed to win populous New Castle County. It was the closest gubernatorial election in more than thirty years, with incumbent Minner becoming the fourth successive governor to win a second term—two Republicans (du Pont and Castle) followed by two Democrats (Carper and Minner).[17]

The politics of finance have played no significant role in the campaigns for the governorship since Pete du Pont won reelection in 1979. When it came to projecting and raising revenue and to agreeing on expenditures, basic conflicts between the two major parties were avoided. Instead consensus politics ruled. There were a number of reasons for this phenomenon: responsibility for taking the lead in fiscal policy was posited in the governor, whose success depended on engineering consent of major political actors of both political parties; fiscal controls in place ensured keeping order in fiscal policy decision-making within agreed parameters; all fiscal policy participants deferred to nonpartisan DEFAC's analyses and projections; continuing Republican majorities in the House of Representatives and Democratic majorities in the Senate ensured that bipartisan agreement was required for fiscal policy to become law; and, perhaps most significantly, deliberations of the General Assembly's bipartisan joint finance and bond bill committees crafted consensus budget legislation that ensured passage at the very end of each annual session of the legislature, thus precluding partisan discord.[18]

Regardless of bipartisanship governing state financial policy, consensus politics appeared to be challenged in late 2004 by some Republican leaders calling for reduction or repeal of the gross receipts tax. Instead of relying on a retail sales tax, Delaware instead had a broad-based tax on gross receipts, although it did not apply to very small businesses. The gross receipts tax rate was very low, but it yielded $157.3 million in fiscal year 2007, or 4.8 percent of the state general fund even after that tax was cut. The gross receipts tax was not inherently volatile, unlike other revenue sources, such as abandoned property, the corporate income tax, and—for that matter—revenue from slot machines given the prospect of competition by 2007 from slots in neighboring states (Pennsylvania authorized slots in 2004). William Remington, former director of Delaware's Division of Revenue, arguing that the gross receipts tax should remain undisturbed, reasoned: "Because the gross receipts tax is so broadly based, it is in general not subject to erosion as the economy shifts to modes of trade and production. For this very reason, the gross receipts tax is one of the state's most stable sources of revenue. We should therefore be cautious about decreasing the gross receipts tax because the stability of the gross receipts tax is part of the reason Delaware has been able to weather past economic storms."[19]

Nevertheless, Republican leaders in the General Assembly announced in 2005 a goal of cutting the state's gross receipts tax. During the flurry of last-minute legislation, with support of Democrats, they were successful. As the 2005 session ended, the General Assembly approved a 20 percent cut in the gross receipts tax for all taxpayer categories, except for a 25 percent cut for automobile manufacturers (see epilogue).

CONCLUSION

A dramatic story is how this small state emerged from bankruptcy to become the strongest state fiscally. Solvency was reached within a span of only three decades, while income taxes were cut and services were expanded. Leadership by governors during this period was essential. But the effort could not have been successful without a great measure of bipartisanship. Both major political parties proved dedicated to establishing and maintaining fiscal responsibility in the state government.

CHAPTER ELEVEN

Nongovernmental Influence
and Participation

Nongovernmental involvement in public affairs in the United States is so pervasive that it resists attempts toward simplification, orderly classification, or even public-private differentiation. Our purpose in this chapter is to isolate and illustrate selectively the character of nongovernmental influence and participation in the governance process of Delaware. Accordingly, we emphasize two dimensions of nongovernmental interaction with public affairs in the state: lobbying with particular reference to the cancer and tobacco issue, and the politics of nonprofits that perform contracted public services and/or receive government grants. We conclude the chapter with an overview of the nongovernmental media in this small state.

LOBBYING

A 1989 study completed by a University of Delaware graduate student depicted Delaware lobbyists on the whole as "hard-working and dedicated representatives of larger organizations," and that "much, but not all, hard-ball lobbying takes place between corporate executives and high-ranking officials" of the executive branch of the state government rather than in the legislative branch. Besides money, their effectiveness with legislators depended on "friendliness, and social skills like golf and small talk." Moreover, the study conjectured that buying tickets to the legislators' reelection fundraisers was the most common method for a Delaware lobbyist to gain access. "For a twenty-five dollar ticket a measure of contact can be bought." To the legislator, on the other hand, "the lobbyist's main value . . . is a source of information."[1]

Political scientists Janet Johnson and Joseph Pika called their 1993 study of lobbying "Delaware: Friends and Neighbors Politics"—an apt title considering the closeness of lobbyists and politicians in this little state. "The small political elite, low turn-over among legislators and lobbyists, and commanding presence of corporate interests," according to Johnson and Pika, "produce a pattern of 'clubby,' old-boy politics operating within consensual constraints." The authors emphasized three features for understanding interest-group politics in Delaware: the small size of the state; a small number of media outlets; and a part-time state legislature.[2]

We are told by Johnson and Pika that the fact that Delaware politics is highly personalized can be attributed to the smallness of the state, to the longevity of state legislators, and to the most influential as well as long-time lobbyists including former Delaware legislators and administrators. Also, according to Johnson and Pika, only two newspapers (*Wilmington News Journal* and *Delaware State News* in Dover) constitute such a small universe as to account for much less investigative reporting compared with newspapers in more populous states. The authors quoted one observer of the close relations between lobbyists and legislators as saying, "The real influence that lobbyists have is camaraderie. It's such a small state and they're all friends." And they quoted another unnamed observer of the sixty-two-member legislature as follows: "Because our legislature is there part-time and essentially the whole operation is part-time—they have very little staff—on any sophisticated issue they're going to rely heavily on lobbyists and outsiders to provide information to them . . . They're being fed information, background justifications for legislation from competing sides, along with the wine and steak dinners and . . . whatever else." Johnson and Pika emphasized that lobbying in Delaware is not only conducted in a weak regulatory framework, but no penalties had ever been assessed for the failures of lobbyists to file required reports of their expenditures on legislators.[3]

Johnson and Pika named the Delaware State Chamber of Commerce, the Delaware State Education Association, and the Delaware Trial Lawyers Association as "particularly important interest-group organizations," while public-interest and social-issue groups are "particularly weak and inactive." Their study found that three-fourths of surveyed legislators acknowledged receiving financial contributions from lobbyists or interest groups during their campaigns.[4]

In his 1995 memoir, former Delaware state senator Roger Martin characterized lobbying as a part of "our democratic heritage" and that lobbyists are responsible people. "The most unfavorable time to be a lobbyist," according to Martin, "is during an election year when all legislators seem to have fund raisers primarily at local watering holes in Dover. Woe to the lobbyist who declines purchasing any tickets for these affairs!" Martin distinguished four other types of lobbyists: members of "organized good government" groups; "big time lawyers with great influence and stature"; constituents interested in particular legislation; and employees of the state.[5]

Delaware's lobbying community has three other features: it is a fairly large community for such a small state; it exhibits considerable stability reflected by the low turnover of its most active members; and many lobbyists have accrued experience and expertise in public affairs that equal or surpass those of many state officials and legislators; indeed, some influential lobbyists are former state legislators. The Delaware State Public Integrity Commission, which oversees implementation of the state's ethics laws, in 2007 listed 268 registered lobbyists, representing 607 employers. Each of a total of 206 lobbyists represented a single client, whereas each of the remaining 62 lobbyists represented multiple employers. Those representing the most employers were Robert L. Byrd (38), W. Laird Stabler III (33), David S. Swayze (26), Chistine P. Schiltz (22), and William T. Wood, Jr. (21). Byrd, a former Delaware legislator, remained a close associate of Ruth Ann Minner after she was elected governor in 2000, while he also chaired the important Delaware Economic and Financial Advisory Council (DEFAC—see chapter 10), which raised questions about a potential conflict of interest.[6] It is also interesting to note that Stabler, who formed his government relations business in 2000, was legal counsel to Republican Mike Castle when he was governor, and that Swayze was chief-of-staff for former Republican governor Pete du Pont.

Delaware's enforcement of lobbying and campaign finance regulations suggests that Delaware permits wide latitude for interest group influence. But this is not the same as saying that powerful interests have always prevailed in the affairs of the state. The following case study is illustrative; it concerns interconnections during the administration of Governor Ruth Ann Minner between the incidence of cancer and lobbying by big tobacco companies and casinos.

The Cancer-tobacco-Slots Nexus

Delaware has long had one of the higher lung cancer rates in the United States (see chapter 12). Delaware's lung cancer death rates have remained above national rates (a 2007 rate of 65.8 per 100,000 in Delaware compared to 53.3 in the U.S.). In 1999 Delaware's rate was 68.2, 3.5 percent above the national rate of 55.4. Both Republican governor Mike Castle (1985–93) and Democratic governor Tom Carper (1993–2001) approached the problem by appointing advisory councils to study cancer and to make recommendations. And both studies concluded that lifestyle choices, particularly smoking, were the major causes of cancer in Delaware. Smoking declined in Delaware from 25.4 percent of the population in 1999 to 24.4 percent in 2004 and 18.9 percent in 2007. To the extent mortality rates may be correlated with smoking rates, some reduction was to be expected. This has not been the case, however, perhaps partly because of other air quality problems. Mobile sources in Delaware, such as car emissions, and fixed sources, such as industrial sites and public power plants inside and outside Delaware, are known to contribute substantially to the hazardous air pollutants that increase the risk of cancer.[7]

In 2007 Delaware ranked sixteenth among the states in prevalence of smoking, down from thirty-ninth in 1990 (see chapter 12). Overall, the rate of smoking in the state is continuing to decline. The state government has been operating a so-called telephone "Quitline" and has spent substantial sums on public service announcements. How effective such stop-smoking activities would become had yet to be determined.

In August 2007 Delaware increased its tax on each pack of cigarettes from 55 cents to $1.15—still the lowest tax in the region (in 2008 the neighboring states of New Jersey taxed cigarette packs at $2.575 and Pennsylvania at $1.35)—making Delaware a favorite stop for out-of-state smokers.[8]

Delaware was not among the forty-four states that had brought suits against cigarette companies to compensate taxpayers for the publicly funded treatment of smoking-related illnesses. Delaware abstained from the litigation even though lung cancer deaths accounted for 31 percent of all Delaware cancer deaths in 2002–4, although the rate had declined. Reasons for Delaware's abstention were most likely related to its general conservatism with respect to governmental intervention in private affairs. Even though the state was a bystander, however, its authorities knew that Delaware's share of any settlement was all but guaranteed.

While Delaware did not join the original group of state attorneys general in suing the tobacco industry, it nevertheless shared the largesse of payments as a signer of the ultimate tobacco settlement—the November 1998 "Master Settlement Agreement" that committed the tobacco industry to pay forty-six states approximately $206 billion over twenty-five years; the four remaining states settled their lawsuits separately. Delaware's share of the settlement amounted to nearly $30 million annually in payments from the tobacco companies, scheduled to total $840 million by 2025. In December 2004 it was revealed that Delaware was one of only three states (also Maine and Mississippi) that had kept its promise to fight tobacco use, and to work on the health effects of smoking, with the money it received from tobacco companies.[9]

Carper's successor, Democratic governor Ruth Ann Minner (2001–9), had a personal incentive to tackle the problem, as she had lost her husband to cancer some years before. Armed with additional recent evidence that secondhand smoking imperiled nonsmokers as well, she appointed a cancer study council as one of her first acts as governor in January 2001. Governor Minner's Advisory Council on Cancer Incidence and Mortality followed its predecessors by emphasizing tobacco usage as a leading cause of cancer. But, unlike her predecessors, Minner broke new ground by moving to ban smoking in most indoor public places in Delaware.

A bill to ban such smoking was first introduced in the Delaware Senate in April 2001, and actually passed the Senate in May, but failed to pass in the House during the 2001 session. Carried over to the 2002 session, the House finally passed the bill in May 2002, followed shortly by approval of the Senate and Governor Minner's signature, effective November 27, 2002. Since November 2002 Delaware has had one of the most comprehensive smoke-free air laws in the country. The "Clean Indoor Air Act" prohibits smoking in most indoor public places in Delaware, including restaurants, bars, casinos, workplaces, libraries, and schools.[10]

Passage of Delaware's Clean Indoor Air Act was not easy by any means. Ranged against cleaner-indoor-air action was the tobacco industry and Delaware's three powerful casinos—Dover Downs, Delaware Park, and Midway Slots—that contributed video-lottery (slot machine) revenue accounting for approximately 7 percent of the state's total revenue in 2007. Although not as organized and powerful as tobacco companies and the casinos, Delaware's many small bar and tavern owners also opposed the smoking ban.

The governor's signature did not end the matter. After passage of the Clean Indoor Air law, the casinos and bars led a campaign during the 2003 legislative session to repeal portions of the law. They were initially successful in lobbying some legislators to support legislation that would exempt certain venues from the smoking ban, including taverns, taprooms, racetracks, and gambling facilities, but this attempt was defeated in the state Senate. A second attempt to weaken the law would have fined the individual smoker rather than the business where the smoking occurred, making it nearly impossible to enforce the law. This bill passed the state House of Representatives with thirty-eight legislators voting in favor and three absent, but it was defeated in the Senate by a vote of thirteen to six.

In a September 2003 issue of the *Wilmington News Journal*, columnist Ron Williams wrote: "If you suspected the nicotine-stained hand of Big Tobacco in Delaware during the debate over the Clean Indoor Air Act, you were correct several times over." Citing a Washington-based study, Williams noted that since 2000 a total of $70,290 from the tobacco industry and its allies had been contributed to forty-nine of Delaware's sixty-two state legislators.[11]

Given the power, effort, and access of the special interests opposed to the smoking ban, the question arises as to what explains their failures to defeat or weaken the Clean Indoor Air Act either before or after it became law. The answer is the grassroots campaign in support of passing and preserving the law, led by the so-called IMPACT (Initiative to Mobilize for the Prevention of Tobacco Use) of the Delaware Tobacco Prevention Coalition. IMPACT was an organized and dedicated coalition of tobacco control and prevention advocacy organizations, doctors groups, legislators, and other concerned Delawareans. The core organizations of the coalition were the "Big Three"—the American Lung Association of Delaware, the American Cancer Society, and the American Heart Association—which already had databases of the names of hundreds of potential Delaware volunteers, letter-writers, and phone-callers. Other members of the coalition were some seventy-five organizations including civic groups such as the United Way and the Parent Teachers Association, other health-related organizations such as state government agencies, doctors' groups, environmental groups, church groups, voters groups such as the League of Women Voters, and youth organizations—all nonprofit organizations (not one corporate or for-profit organization was included). Key to the coalition's success was its overarching strategy—it kept its focus on health. Its message was simple and never varied—"Second-hand smoke causes disease and death!"[12]

The coalition's success may also be attributable to the fact that Delaware public opinion was supportive of the indoor smoking ban. A mid-2003 survey, conducted by the University of Delaware's Center for Applied Demography and Survey Research, found that less than 25 percent of adult Delawareans were smokers, and more than 91 percent of nonsmokers as well as 71 percent of smokers agreed that people should be protected from secondhand smoke.[13] Subsequent annual surveys from 2004 to 2007 confirmed the 2003 findings.

Revenues from the video lottery initially dropped about 10 percent but fully recovered by the second year after the institution of the smoking ban.

POLITICS OF NONPROFITS

Reportedly, there were over one thousand nonprofits in Delaware in 2007, a large number for such a small state. Private giving, charitable enterprise, and philanthropy in Delaware constitute a long and well-established tradition spawned mostly by the munificence of prominent du Pont family members.[14]

Delaware governments have partnered with many for-profit nongovernmental entities (e.g., corporations and other business organizations) for initiating and implementing publicly funded programs and projects, such as those related to public education reform.[15] Delaware's small size has enhanced the roles of nonprofits, however, and has fostered close relations between grant seekers and donors. Indeed, Delaware's private sector surpasses its public sector in the delivery of human services, and government human services in Delaware are either functions of the state government or the private sector, or both partnering together. Some state-supported human services are contracted out to nonprofits, rather than being administered by what otherwise would be a larger state bureaucracy. Approximately 8 percent of the expenditures of the state's largest government agency, the Department of Health and Social Services, is allocated to the private sector.

Delaware state government expenditures for fiscal year 2007 totaled $3,025 million, of which $365.1 million were for "grants" and $289.5 million were for "contractual services." In other words, by adding the latter two figures, a total of $654.6 million, or roughly more than 20 percent of the state's total budget, comprised projected disbursements to the private sector (for-profits and nonprofits).

One theme of this book has been that, since Delaware is such a small state, the responsibility for most important government services lies in the state government, and the local governments offer few services compared with local governments in larger and more populous states. In fact, Delaware's state legislature appropriates more money for nonprofits than for municipalities. Nonprofits may receive state government money, without being designated by name in appropriations of the legislature, simply by receiving contracts from state agencies. Nonprofits may also lobby for state funding by securing nonprofit designation by name in the state budget and general appropriations, the legislature's joint grant-in-aid bill, and the legislature's joint bond bill. Designation by name in a state agency's budget as a line item provides the greatest security for a nonprofit, as its designation is likely to reappear annually, such as in the budget of the Department of Health and Social Services, which accounts for approximately one-fourth of annual state spending. Distribution of funding in an annual grant-in-aid bill may include a specific grant by name to a nonprofit, for nonprofit services. Likewise, the bond bill may also designate a nonprofit by name, but only for a capital project. A three-fourths vote of the General Assembly is required for allocations directly to named private entities.

Nonprofits must often compete with one another for state funds. Much of their political activity and lobbying focuses on the General Assembly's joint finance committee (which handles grants-in-aid) and its joint bond bill committee, because whatever is decided by these committees (consisting of leaders of both houses and both major political parties) usually becomes law; these "pork-barrel" bills are always the last considered before adjournment and their passage is assured by virtue of "logrolling" (i.e., "you vote for my bill and I'll vote for yours"). The grants-in-aid to 482 nonprofits legislated by the General Assembly in fiscal year 2007 totaled $50 million, the distribution of which included, among others, 358 community services organizations, 60 volunteer fire companies, 46 senior centers, and 7 veterans organizations.[16]

Delaware nonprofits that receive federal funding are subject to public disclosure and financial reporting requirements imposed by the Internal Revenue Service. The state requires each state-funded nonprofit be audited. Contracts with nonprofits for services are monitored and subject to audit. Otherwise, nonprofits are seldom monitored or held accountable for state grant funds they receive. A rare exception was Governor Minner's 2007 executive order that all sixty Delaware volunteer fire companies be audited. Another exception was the nonprofit Schwartz Center for the Arts in Dover.

The Schwartz Center was constructed in 1904 as the Dover Opera House and was expanded by George M. Schwartz in 1923 into a movie theater known as the Capital Theater. It closed in 1982 and reopened in October 2001 as the Schwartz Center for the Arts after an extensive modernization and expansion funded in part by various state government grants-in-aid. According to tax returns for fiscal 2002, the center still had a surplus of more than $540,000, after which it experienced serious financial difficulties, prompting the resignations of its executive director and several board members, changes to members of its executive committee, and an investigation by the state auditor.

The state auditor's 2004 examination was broader than the state money involved, because, explained the auditor, "The state funds are so intermingled with a lot of the other funds, to some degree it would be pretty hard to distinguish between them." The auditor found a combination of cost overruns, booking shows that lost money, and poor internal controls. In addition, he found that the initial refurbishing was projected a little over $2 million, but actually cost over $8 million. "There was too much debt," he concluded, "that put pressure on the fund-raising side of the operation."[17]

The Delaware Association of Nonprofit Agencies (DANA), formed in 1986, speaks for more than 225 charitable and community-based institutions throughout Delaware, representing the entire spectrum of the nonprofit sector. DANA is committed to helping Delaware nonprofits link with public and private grant-makers, and to serving other common interests of nonprofits. Massive federal government funding cuts in the late 1990s, followed by a national economic recession, adversely affected every nonprofit in the state and became DANA's principal concern. Its executive director in November 2003 lamented, "We're being hit in all areas."[18]

DANA members in 2003 accounted for more than $500 million in annual operating budgets and employed over twelve thousand people. DANA itself, however, is not a funding agency. Delaware's principal nongovernmental fundraiser is the United Way of Delaware (UWD)—the DuPont Company's traditional charitable cause—comprising sixty full-member nonprofits and fifty-two affiliate nonprofits. Decreased giving associated with the economic recession prompted UWD to reverse past practice by lowering its fundraising goal for 2003 to $28.3 million, compared with the 2002 target of $30 million. Nevertheless, UWD raised $29.3 million by February 2004, or 102 percent of its goal.[19]

Another major nongovernmental fundraiser for nonprofits is the Delaware Community Foundation (DCF), founded in 1986. DCF, with assets of about $230 million in 2006, managed over five hundred charitable funds established by donors. The foundation invests and administers these funds, then distributes the income as grants to many Delaware nonprofits.[20]

Political power consists of the capacity to acquire and allocate resources. In this sense, the political activity of a nonprofit may consist of competition with other nonprofits to acquire scarce or limited resources. A nonprofit's political activity, on the other hand, may also be directed toward establishing linkages, interdependencies, and cooperation with other nonprofits with similar goals and interests in order to maximize resources. Making available affordable housing in Delaware provides an example.

The federal Community Reinvestment Act (CRA) of 1977, as amended, is intended to thwart the discriminatory practice of "red-lining" or "predatory lending" by banks and other lending institutions, which involves denying credit or mortgages to low-income and minority applicants, by encouraging lenders to meet their credit needs for acquiring affordable housing.[21] To ensure such equal access for underserved populations of Delaware, the nonprofit Delaware Community Reinvestment Action Council (DCRAC) was established in 1987 as a watchdog.[22] Delaware banks, in turn, formed in 1994 the Delaware Community Investment Corporation (DCIC) to fulfill their obligations under CRA. DCIC comprised thirty-six member banks in 2004 that, by pooling their assets and shared risks, were able to channel their capital for affordable housing projects, including multifamily rental developments, a day care center, seventeen group homes, and a nursing home facility.[23]

Meanwhile, from 1993 to 2006 DCF partnered with the University of Delaware's Center for Community Development and Family Policy (UD/CCDFP; later renamed the Center for Community Research and Service) and the Delaware State Housing Authority (DSHA) to establish and operate the nonprofit Housing Capacity Building Program (HCBP). In 1997 DCIC also joined as a partner. The main goal of HCBP was to develop a stronger system to sustain more low- and moderate-income Delawareans in affordable homes by making "capacity building grants" to Delaware housing-related nonprofit organizations. DCIC contributed 10 percent annually of its net revenue to HCBP, and the assets of the now defunct HCBP were managed by DCF as one of its five hundred charitable funds.[24]

Accordingly, a complex cooperative network—of nonprofit institutions, profit-making banks, the federal government, and the Delaware state government—has existed to encourage affordable housing in Delaware by providing equal access to housing-related credit and capital. Nevertheless, housing discrimination in the state has continued to be a problem. A 2003 University of Delaware study found that "with respect to lending, African Americans' applications for mortgages are rejected considerably more frequently than those of Whites with comparable incomes. Hispanics fare somewhat better than Blacks, but not as well as Whites."[25]

INFLUENCE OF THE MEDIA

In their 1993 study of interest group politics in Delaware, Johnson and Pika commented that "citizen activism is not ordinarily at high levels in Delaware." They pointed to the small number of media outlets as a partial explanation for "public quiescence," and noted that Delaware constituted only 8 percent of the Philadelphia television market, "which devotes only limited attention to Delaware news." Their study quoted one observer as follows: "In Delaware, we're hurt by the fact that as far as the General Assembly is concerned, you really only have two players, two newspapers. . . . That isn't a great universe from which to draw investigative reporters. . . . In other states, the press would be much more heavily into it, and they would create the scandals or the questions which lead to groups like Common Cause requesting hearings or investigations or changes in the law."[26]

Delaware's small population explains the small number of media outlets. There are a number of periodicals and small town newspapers, but only two newspapers of consequence—the *Wilmington News Journal* and the *Delaware State News*. The latter is published in Dover and, though it claimed in 2003 to be "the dominant daily newspaper in downstate Delaware," its weekday circulation was only 17,966, with Sunday at 29,199.[27] On the other hand, the *Wilmington News Journal* ranked ninety-third among the top hundred newspapers in the nation with the largest circulations, reporting in 2006 its weekday paid average circulation to be 134,865.[28]

The *Wilmington News Journal* has engaged increasingly in investigative reporting about public policy issues in Delaware, especially in recent years. For example, few could doubt the significant influence of the *Wilmington News Journal* series in 2005 and 2006 on health issues in the state prison system. The series publicized high rates of inmate deaths from HIV/AIDS, mistreatment of cancerous tumors, the spread of flesh-eating bacteria, and suicide. Accordingly, a special civil rights team from the U.S. Department of Justice launched an ongoing investigation of Delaware's Department of Correction concerning the quality of medical and mental health services inside Delaware prisons.

In 2003 there were sixteen radio stations in Delaware, half of which claimed to be news outlets, and fifteen television stations broadcasting into the state.[29]

CONCLUSION

We sense that linkages between private and public sectors of power are comparatively closer in Delaware than in other states, primarily because of Delaware's small size, tradition, and political culture. Delaware's small size and population breed intimacy among bureaucrats, legislators, lobbyists, politicians, nongovernmental entities, and the citizenry.

Regardless of political loyalties, interdependency and collegiality exist to an extent that nongovernmental influence in the governing process is ubiquitous and public-private distinctions are blurred. Given the absence of ideological political barriers, Delaware allows wide latitude for the influence of special interests, to which the small size of the state also contributes.

CHAPTER TWELVE

Sprawl, Pollution, and Health

Like other states, Delaware is challenged by multiple policy problems, as discussed in the book *Governing Delaware: Policy Problems in the First State* (2000). This chapter focuses selectively on three major policy and political problems affecting the quality of life of Delawareans: sprawl, pollution, and health. These persistent problem areas are exacerbated by Delaware's rapid population growth in recent years.

The degree of connection between sprawl, pollution, and health is open to debate wherever they coexist. There is little question that sprawl, however defined, may lead to higher emissions from automobiles, since sprawl tends to increase trip lengths. Construction on suburban land sites may lead to more runoff, but at the same time pollution from farm activities will be reduced. The degree to which these examples affect health is open to question. Clearly, emissions from automobiles may adversely affect those with asthma, but on the other hand, sprawl spreads out these emissions. Many would say that pollution and health problems are more likely related to industry. Typical sprawl does not usually include the sprawl of industry. Indeed, sprawl tends to move people away from industrial sites.

In other words, the interconnectedness of sprawl, pollution, and health is complex and is not amenable to simple answers. Accordingly, we refrain from ascribing as yet unproved causal relationships between them.

Although Delaware is a very small state with a population about the size of Indianapolis, it nevertheless has the seventh highest density among the states, and its population growth rate between 1990 and 2000 was the fourth highest among the states east of the Mississippi River. Delaware's population growth has multiple sources, but there are essentially two major drivers. First, economic expansion has generated jobs that need to be filled. Second, people from outside the state are retiring to Sussex County mainly because of the beach areas and low taxes. All of this puts pressure on keeping agricultural land.

Both air pollution and water pollution in Delaware are major issues. Unfortunately, they are not just internal problems. Delaware is located in the middle of a megalopolis with through-traffic galore. Delaware's portion of the Delaware River is subject to pollution from Pennsylvania and New Jersey as well as Delaware.

Pollution is a complex problem. There are many causes and kinds of ubiquitous pollution in Delaware.[1] For example, Delaware's eastern coast along the Delaware River and Bay is intermittently threatened by oil spills of tankers bound to or from regional refineries, as happened in December 2004. One can also point to the fifteen hazardous "Superfund" waste sites still listed in the state in 2004 by the federal Environmental Protection Agency (EPA). During the previous decade, six such sites had been delisted, and—of the remaining fifteen—there were eleven categorized as "construction completed," meaning that all physical remediation efforts were in place by 2005. Our concern in this chapter, however, is restricted to the problem of Delaware's compliance with the federal Clean Air Act of 1970 and the Clean Water Act of 1972, along with their amendments, aimed at stiffening federal air and water pollution standards.

Several health issues also are prominent. Some of them relate to the diverse population, some to the number of in-migrants, and all to non-obvious solutions.

This chapter examines some salient effects and policy dimensions of these quality-of-life problems in Delaware.

PROBLEM OF SPRAWL

The problem of managing growth is largely in Delaware's unincorporated areas. Until the 1960s the state did not have the necessary tools, and the county governments were not structured to undertake the task. Although forty-one of the forty-eight states had authorized zoning by 1932, Delaware counties were not authorized to zone until the 1950s, or to establish planning commissions until the 1960s. Accordingly, local zoning preceded local planning in Delaware, regardless of the facts that planning gives direction for zoning, and that, as University of Florida professor Sydney Carter noted, "zoning without direction is worth nothing at all" because "zoning is a tool only that must be used with a plan in order to have meaning."[2] Moreover, the planning profession had prescribed zoning that separated residential properties from commercial properties and that helped create sprawl and increase traffic.

The General Assembly in 1961 created a state planning office as a central staff agency in the governor's office to encourage municipalities and counties to develop comprehensive land-use plans. However, the administration of Republican governor Pete du Pont abolished the office in 1977 and reassigned planners to various state agencies. The General Assembly enacted in 1978 the Land Use Planning Act, authorizing state participation in local planning decisions.[3]

Soon after passage of the Financial Center Development Act (FCDA) in 1981, a new economic development office, later named the Delaware Economic Development Office, or DEDO, was created. Specifically, DEDO's charge was to help retain and expand existing businesses, recruit new firms, and help new business start-ups. A 1991 study concluded: "The state has been weak in . . . land use policy . . . [and] has a history of yielding to development interests. . . . County and local planning agencies have operated independently with the state assuming a subordinate advisory role. The absence of land use planning initiatives at the state level is in marked contrast to the state's extensive involvement in economic development measures which . . . have had significant effects on land use."[4]

Regardless of political posturing and rhetoric about managing growth, during the administrations of Republican governor Mike Castle (1985–1993) and Democratic governor Tom Carper (1993–2001), Delaware lacked sustained commitment to enforceable land-use planning, largely because Delaware is a conservative state with not much interest in activist government. The typical Delawarean was more interested in personal issues. He or she wanted a house on a large lot, opposed traffic congestion, but still wanted a faster way to the beach. Delaware's mostly flat topography and permeable soil made it easy to construct a single-family house on a lot of one-half to two acres almost anywhere in the state, with merely a septic tank for sewage disposal where a sewer line was unavailable.

Although "sprawl" is a very elusive and complex term defying easy definition, according to a 2004 book entitled *Place Matters*, sprawl is defined as "a land development pattern that spreads residential units over a large area. A classic example is the single-family home built under three-acre minimum-lot zoning. Sprawl also encompasses the separation of residential from commercial land uses, the absence of clustered development or town centers, and reliance on the automobile." Moreover, sprawl is related to urban decline. A 1995 University of Delaware study found continuation of a seventy-year trend of Delaware's population moving from more-dense to less-dense areas—marked prominently by Wilmington's 37 percent population loss since 1940—thus producing a chain-reaction, domino-effect, "suburban sprawl." According to the study: "The process is continuous and dynamic. As a household relocates to lower density, the households who preceded the new resident to that area begin to lose the feeling of the low density they had chosen in earlier years and eventually correct this situation by moving to lower density. Thus the sprawl continues."[5]

As in most of the Northeast, farmland is rapidly disappearing in Delaware as it is replaced by housing developments. A University of Delaware economist warned in 1991 that one-third of the state's 1945 farmland had already been developed and that half the remainder would not be farmable by the end of the century unless the state undertook measures to keep current farmland from being developed. A result was enactment of the Delaware Agricultural Lands Preservation Act, creating a state foundation to pay farmers to preserve their land from development. At least two hundred acres must be available for a farmer to qualify for the program. Some farms are preserved for a period of ten years and others in perpetuity. According to the state department of agriculture, a total of 129,163 acres had been preserved by 2008, including 64,830 acres that had been permanently protected, at a total cost of $67.4 million.

In March 1996 the state had paid an average of $1,313 per acre in its first round of such purchases, and $933.84 in the second round. Some wealthy farmers became richer by pledging to keep their land in agriculture. Leading the list in the second round in 1996 were the five farms owned by a state legislator who received over $1 million for agreeing not to develop his prime farmland.[6]

New Castle County's 1996 comprehensive land-use plan called for farmers' land preservation applications to be reviewed by the state foundation, the county's planning board, and the New Castle County Farmland Preservation Advisory Board chaired by Democratic county councilman J. Christopher Roberts from Odessa in southern New Castle County. Councilman Roberts faced heavy criticism for his family's plan to convert its 170 acres among Delaware's most fertile land into a housing development. "How can he be chairman of the agricultural board," asked a neighboring farmer, "and be building these houses at the same time?" Regardless of the criticism, the Democratic Party named Roberts to be its candidate for a September 1997 special election to fill an unexpired term for the state's fastest growing state House of Representatives district, located in southern New Castle County. Roberts was unsuccessful. In July 2002 a federal indictment alleged he had accepted a $5,000 bribe from an intermediary of a development consultant in October 1998 for assistance in gaining approval of a 283-home New Castle County subdivision. Roberts pleaded guilty to a lesser charge of tax violation, and signed a plea agreement to cooperate with the local U.S. attorney's office in its ongoing investigation of alleged illegal activities in New Castle County government. Roberts lost his county council seat in a 2002 Democratic primary.[7]

Sprawl is in the eye of the beholder. Delawareans are generally not "city" people. According to surveys, only about 5 percent of the residents aspire to live in a city. As the population has grown, largely in the unincorporated areas, people have increasingly chosen to live in subdivisions. In the 1960s and 1970s, when much of the original growth spurt happened, sewers were being largely funded by the federal government. In the most recent period these costs have had to be borne within the state. As costs to the state have risen, and politicians have wished to avoid any real tax increases, pressures have mounted to utilize existing capacity. However, buyers of new homes can always "vote with their feet." They do not have to live where they are directed. At the same time, developers who own, or have options on, the land are more than willing to accommodate these buyers. Thus, there will be development in areas without adequate public infrastructure—sewers, water, and perhaps transportation. If one government, such as a county, tries to restrict this activity, a town will fill the void by annexation. If a county is too restrictive, buyers will jump to another county or even across a state line. This is the Delaware experience at present.

The administration of Democratic governor Ruth Ann Minner, beginning in 2001, attempted to exert a measure of control over sprawl by launching the "Livable Delaware" initiative. By using a comprehensive "carrot-and-stick" strategy, the state ostensibly would attempt to direct new growth to areas where the state and local governments were most prepared in terms of existing infrastructure. The program had modest success by 2005. The conflicting goals of state, county, and local governments, however, were difficult to coordinate, and the General Assembly appeared more likely to respond to unhappy constituents.

PROBLEM OF AIR POLLUTION

The federal Clean Air Act of 1970 authorized the federal Environmental Protection Agency (EPA) to establish national air quality standards for seven pollutants that threaten human health and welfare, including ozone, the main component of smog. In 2003 Delaware was out of compliance with two of the seven standards—ozone and PM2.5 (particulate matter less than 2.5 micrometers). Ozone levels are determined by the weather (hot and dry is high, and cool and wet is low), levels of NO (nitrous oxides), and levels of VOC (volatile organic compounds). Delaware, of course, cannot control the weather, and it does not have absolute control over emissions that create ozone, because the emissions are regional in nature, as is ozone itself.

Current programs focus on automobile gasoline vapors, power plants, and chemical plants. From 1995 to 2005, ozone levels were declining nationally and in EPA Region 3, which contains Delaware. The decline in Delaware was such that by 2005 its ozone level was only slightly above the standard. In 2003 Delaware was out of compliance on two days of that year with one standard and on seven days with another standard. Its number of noncompliance days, while still unacceptable, was nevertheless declining. The state was supposed to be in compliance by 2005, but that did not happen. Delaware's ozone levels were indistinguishable from levels of nearby counties in Maryland, Pennsylvania, and New Jersey within the region. In 2006 there were no days in Delaware in which the one-hour ozone standard was exceeded, but there were six days that exceeded the eight-hour standard. Nevertheless, the trend was downward.

The second area of Delaware's noncompliance has been PM2.5 respirable particles that are very fine. Both local and regional sources contribute to these concentrations in Delaware. The sources tend to be power plants, natural sources, and urban pollution that can be transmitted long distances. Overall, PM2.5 concentrations have been falling in the United States. However, in the Northeast of the country there has been a slight rise in recent years. Within Delaware, Kent and Sussex Counties met the standard, but New Castle County did not. In 2006, however, New Castle County met both standards, as did Kent and Sussex. New Castle County's levels are lower than those found in the nearby counties of Baltimore, Philadelphia, and Camden.[8]

While Delaware is well within compliance of the Clean Air Act for sulfur dioxide, individual companies still must come into compliance. Consider the case of Premcor, which was Delaware's sole oil refinery abutting the Delaware River—previously known as Motiva and now known as Valero. It is safe to say that no pollution site in Delaware has been the subject of more complaints and violations through the years than this refinery. On November 30, 2004, Delaware's state Department of Natural Resources and Environmental Control (DNREC) approved the largest air pollution control agreement in the state's history, whereby Premcor would spend an estimated $200 million to upgrade its smokestack and abide by a new production cap. DNREC estimated that the agreement would reduce sulfur dioxide emissions by almost thirty thousand tons, or 97 percent of Premcor's then current sulfur dioxide output (Premcor was sold to Valero in 2005).[9]

Releases of toxic chemicals into the air in Delaware have been decreasing in recent years. These releases are largely acid gases (hydrochloric and sulfuric). Because of its small population, and hence lesser emissions than in more populous states, Delaware in 2003 ranked thirty-fifth among the states in toxic air emissions, and thirty-eighth for toxic emissions related to cancer. Many different companies that generate toxic releases in Delaware were controlled by state permits. The two largest were public utility power plants in New Castle County and Sussex County. Premcor was a distant third, along with Invista (Seaford), Daimler-Chrysler (Newark), Formosa Plastics (Delaware City), and General Motors (Wilmington). A slightly different list is generated when one considers HAPs (hazardous air pollutants). It is interesting to note that Premcor accounted for less than 7 percent of emissions of HAPs, while the two public utility power plants in New Castle County accounted for 68 percent of such emissions.[10]

Dealing with air pollution issues is not simple in view of the fact that these companies involved have significant effects on Delaware's economy, particularly with respect to employment and incomes. Generally, Delaware claims it tries to balance environmental and economic issues. Obviously, however, many environmental organizations have a different perspective.

PROBLEM OF WATER POLLUTION

Almost immediately after the November 2004 elections, the *Wilmington News Journal* published an unprecedented example of investigative journalism by two of its premier reporters in a front-page, four-day series of what was called "Delaware's Troubled Waters" under these banner headlines: "State's Premier Waters Are Rank with Sewage"; "Danger in the Water, but Little Is Done"; "Growth Smothers Sussex County Bays"; and "Wastewater Problems Require Costly Solutions." Delaware clearly has a problem with the condition of its waterways—an even more complex problem than that posed by air pollution.[11]

Waterways can have a variety of uses—fish and wildlife; recreation; public water supply; industry; and agriculture. A waterway that is impaired for one use may be fine for another. There are many sources of impairment in Delaware—agriculture, natural sources, municipalities, land disposal, off-farm animal holding areas, on-site treatment systems, construction, industry, land development, and unknown sources. The types of contamination in the state are many, including nutrients, organic materials, pathogens, suspended solids, metals, and pesticides.

The best source for evaluating contemporary Delaware waterways is the

2002 water quality assessment data reported to the U.S. Environmental Protection Agency (EPA).[12] With respect to the category of rivers, streams, and creeks, there are about 2,500 miles within seven watersheds in Delaware. The news is not favorable for either humans or fish. For all practical purposes, none of these watercourses were found safe for either recreation or fishing, and only 37 percent were safe for fish and wildlife propagation. Almost all this category of waterways, however, was safe for public water supply, industrial use, and agriculture. Pathogens, nutrients, and organic materials were the prime contaminants of impairment of these waterways, with pathogens accounting for most of the problems. Agriculture, natural sources, and municipal-generated wastes were the dominant sources of impairment, with agriculture accounting for twice as much as any other source. Industrial point-source pollution accounted for 105 miles of the 2,500 total miles reported.

The EPA category of Delaware lakes, ponds, and reservoirs followed a different pattern. Of roughly three thousand acres, almost all of these waterways were found suitable for public water supply and industrial and agricultural use. About 77 percent was even usable for fish and wildlife propagation. The bad news was that 95 percent of these acres were not safe for recreation. Pathogens were by far the most significant contaminant for impairment, and once again the major sources for impairment were agriculture, natural sources, and municipalities.

Finally, bays and estuaries were basically usable only by industry, largely because nutrients and pathogens precluded other uses. Fortunately for Delaware, its coastal shorelines merited a green light for all uses.

Industry, as well, contributes to the problem of water pollution in Delaware, although its culpability is minor compared to other sources. By far the largest industry discharges are from the Perdue chicken processing plant in Georgetown of Sussex County. Of 916,000 pounds of chemical releases to Delaware waters in 2003, Perdue accounted for fully one-third. About one-quarter was contributed by Invista in Seaford of Sussex County, and another one-third by Premcor in New Castle County. The dominant chemicals for all three were nitrate compounds that added to the nutrients problem in Delaware's waterways. Premcor, however, released a more complex array of chemicals than the other two.

Premcor represented a problem with respect to a relatively small, but significant, amount of carcinogens released to the water. Of a total of 10,000 pounds of carcinogens released in 2003, Premcor released a majority, including 5,400 pounds of benzene and 1,700 pounds of nickel. DuPont Company's Edgemoor power plant in New Castle County, while releasing smaller but still significant amounts of chromium (750 pounds) and nickel

(1,100 pounds), ranked first in the nation for off-site transfer (i.e., transfer to other locations for disposal) of dioxin and dioxin-like compounds.

It appears apparent that very little is likely to improve the current situation in Delaware waterways until non-point pollution is reduced. Plans currently in place rely on management practices. Manure storage structures, poultry composts, and other animal waste systems are being installed on a cost-sharing basis to control animal wastes. The impact on nutrient reduction, however, is not yet clear. A more productive strategy would appear to be modifying land adjoining impaired streams and ditches. Such strategies include developing grassy strips, restoring wetlands, planting hardwood trees, and maintaining permanent wildlife habitats.[13]

Chicken manure runoff has always represented a vexing water pollution problem in Delaware, since more than 250 million broilers are produced annually, with a sizeable impact on the economy of Sussex County and the state as a whole. In 2004 more than 35,000 tons of excess manure was transported to areas with lower risks of water pollution.

Runoff from municipalities and urban areas in general also has been a challenge. The strategy being implemented has been the planting of trees, because they reduce runoff especially of particulate matter from industrial and agricultural areas.

While these programs will help, it will be a long journey to markedly improve Delaware's waterways. Delaware and New Jersey rank third and fourth respectively among the states with regard to the percentage of surface water with impaired or threatened uses. Sussex County is in the worst shape in Delaware, with Kent and New Castle Counties trailing significantly. Given the amount of construction and associated water pollution problems in Sussex County, Delaware's ranking is unlikely to improve soon. Certainly, Delaware is not helped by the fact that New Castle County is downstream from nearby Delaware County in Pennsylvania, which has an even worse record than Sussex County.

PROBLEM OF HEALTH

Health-related issues are usually near the top of Delaware's public agenda, because the topic is politically sensitive. Leading the way are the problems of cancer, infant mortality, health disparities, and diabetes. Also, the city of Wilmington has been grappling with a spate of homicides precipitated by drug wars in the city. These have spawned a sense of helplessness and cries for action by the state and city governments, and have become an issue of public health.

Table 1. Delaware Health Rankings, 2006, 2005, 1990

Measure	State Rankings			Measurement		
	2006	2005	1990	2006	2005	1990
Prevalence of Smoking (% of population)	25	39	39	20.6	24.3	31.8
Motor Vehicle Deaths (per 100,000,000 miles)	21	25	33	1.4	1.5	2.6
Prevalence of Obesity (% of population)	19	11	47	23.5	21	14.4
High School Graduation (% of incoming ninth graders)	36	40	36	73	62	71
Violent Crime (offenses per 100,000 population)	44	42	27	632	568	432
Lack of Health Insurance (% without health insurance)	20	29	13	13	14.5	9.1
Infectious Disease (cases per 100,000 population)	46	45	42	31.5	30.8	48.9
Children in Poverty (% of persons under age 18)	18	17	1	14.2	13	8.6
Immunization Coverage (% of children ages 19–35 mon.)	11	9	–	84.2	86	–
Occupational Fatalities (per 100,000 workers)	16	19	17	4.6	4.9	8.7*
Per Capita Public Health Spending ($ per person)	8	8	–	246	246	–
Adequacy of Prenatal Care (% of pregnant women)	15	20	–	80.3	78.1	–
Poor Mental Health Days (in previous 30 days)	17	44	–	3.1	3.8	–
Poor Physical Health Days (Days in previous 30 days)	16	21	–	3.4	3.4	–
Cardiovascular Deaths (per 100,000 population)	29	27	32	315.5	321	417
Cancer Deaths (per 100,000 population)	37	34	50	210.8	210	223
Infant Mortality (per 1,000 live births)	37	40	41	7.6	8.1	11.6
Premature Death (years lost per 100,000 population)	34	30	33	8083	7901	8916
Overall	30	33	30	–	–	–

Source: United Health Foundation, 2006.
*Data may not be comparable.

The 2006 edition of *America's Health Report* accorded Delaware an overall ranking of thirtieth among the fifty states. Produced by the United Health Foundation in cooperation with the prestigious American Health Association and authoritative Centers for Disease Control and Prevention and other federal agencies and national associations, this edition represented the sixteenth and most comprehensive and comparative state-by-state analysis of health status.[14] These rankings combined individual measures of personal behaviors, community environment and health policies with resultant health outcomes into one comprehensive view of the health of each state. Table 1 shows Delaware's rankings for the years 2006, 2005, and 1990 according to these factors.

In examining these rankings, one should note that it is not always better for a state to be ranked first than last, because in some cases being ranked first means that the state had the highest score, whereas in other cases a ranking of first means it had the lowest score. In other words, rankings are slippery numbers to deal with, but at the extremes they probably mean something. Thus, rankings between sixteen and thirty-five may be meaningless because of inherent imprecisions in the measures, whereas rankings above sixteen may be useful to consider, as are those below thirty-five.

Delaware ranked relatively high in 2006 on access to health insurance (twentieth), children in poverty (eighteenth), occupational fatalities (sixteenth), per capita public health spending (eighth), and adequacy of prenatal care (fifteenth). For the most part, these rankings reflect that Delaware is a relatively high income state.

On the other hand, Delaware trailed badly in 2006 in a number of areas: high school graduation (thirty-sixth), violent crime (forty-fourth), infectious disease (forty-sixth), cancer deaths (thirty-seventh), infant mortality (thirty-seventh), and premature death (thirty-fourth). We choose to focus on three of these categories for the reason that the first two categories are subject to significant measurement error (largely because of measurement and reporting issues).

Infectious disease, primarily from HIV/AIDS, represents a serious problem in Delaware. In a report issued in 2005 it was noted that in Delaware the disparity between whites and blacks had increased from a factor of 8.23 times in the 1993–97 interval to 15.56 in the 1998–2002 period. The overall U.S. disparity ratio in 2002 was 8.65. Disparity is measured as the black/white rate; thus the HIV rate in Delaware was fifteen times higher for blacks than for whites. Most of this problem seemed to be related to intravenous drug use. This disparity likely was part of the reason for the black homicide rate being nearly four times that of whites (3.94)—a ratio below that of the

United States, which was 5.67. HIV mortality among blacks in Delaware was the fourth leading cause of death, accounting for 4.7 percent of all deaths. The percentage of black males dying from HIV (6.1 percent) was double that for black females (3 percent), whereas the proportion of whites was .35 percent.[15] Nearby states within the I-95 corridor—Maryland, New Jersey, and New York—were ranked forty-eighth, forty-fifth, and fiftieth respectively, indicating that HIV/AIDS is not just a Delaware problem.

Delaware's cancer death rate is a source of great consternation. Governor Ruth Ann Minner, as we have noted, formed a task force to examine the problem and to propose some actions she could take. A cancer consortium was put in place to help follow through on the recommendations of the task force. By mid-2005 two measures had been legislated: Delaware's Clean Indoor Air Act (discussed in chapter 11), and an increase in the cigarette tax. It is still too early to measure any potential impact on lung cancer from these two actions.

Other cancer-related actions are oriented toward improving screening, public education, and better health care access. One problem, however, is the system's inability to associate any particular solution with a measurable reduction in the rate. In 2006 Delaware was ranked thirty-seventh among the states in the incidence of cancer deaths, and yet was only 4.5 percent above the median rank of twenty-five. While the spread from bottom to top was an increase of 51.5 percent, there was no definitive reason for the difference. Delaware, for example, is a high income state with excellent access to health insurance. It was ranked twenty-fifth in the prevalence of smoking, and eighth in public health spending. One of the difficulties in sorting out policy responses is that only 48.3 percent of the people residing in the state have lived there for their entire lives, compared with 77.7 percent in Pennsylvania and 65.3 percent in New York. To the extent some type of exposure was at fault, where and when that occurred can not be ascertained. In fact, even looking back to five years before the 2000 census, 14 percent of current Delaware residents had lived in another state. This leads to a disquieting conclusion that Delaware could take the policy steps it deems necessary, but whether these steps would change the numbers demonstrably is another question.

Infant mortality has been the focus of another task force of the administration of Governor Minner. Delaware was ranked thirty-seventh in this category as well. The state has approximately 11,000 live births per year, and 100 die within the first year, of whom 80 do not survive even one month. In order to reach the U.S. median rate, 23 fewer babies would have to die out of the 11,000 born. Roughly two-thirds of Delaware babies who die within the first year weigh less than 1,500 grams, which means the risk of their dying is 130 times greater than a child born with a weight of at least

2,500 grams. All premature babies are either born in, or are quickly transferred to, a tertiary care hospital where they can receive the most advanced medical care available. There are issues such as "ART" (advanced reproductive therapy), which can tend to produce large plural births with low birth weights and higher risks of infant mortality. Many of the women who have chosen this option have been higher-income, well-educated suburbanites who have reached an advanced age where such assistance is required. There are serious issues as to the degree of "wanted-ness" of the child and difficult circumstances in which the mothers live. Drinking, smoking, and lack of prenatal care are also issues.[16]

Given the facts that Delaware has had good rankings in child poverty, access to health care, and access to prenatal care, it is difficult to determine why the state should find itself in its infant mortality predicament. There are racial disparities in infant mortality (2.41), prenatal care (2.19), and low birth weight (1.95), but even taken together they do not explain Delaware's overall poor ranking.[17]

Regardless of Delaware's negative rankings in these three areas, life expectancy for white men and white women in the state is essentially the same as that for the nation as a whole. Both black men and black women in Delaware, moreover, have longer life expectancies than in the nation as a whole.

CONCLUSION

The preceding discussion of the three policy areas serves to illustrate several dimensions of governance and politics in Delaware. First, the state's "individualistic political culture" and traditional conservatism are alive and well. Second, there are areas where the goals of governmental entities are in conflict and thus change occurs at a snail's pace, which, of course, is quite in accord with the first observation. Third, even within the government there is a healthy competition between executive departments (e.g., environmental control and economic development), which forces compromise and balance. Fourth, the tradition has been that when the heat is too hot in the kitchen, give the job to a task force, which deflects the heat and calms the political waters, and maybe the task force will come up with a good idea after the next election.

Even in areas where the federal government has evinced an interest (e.g., EPA, FHWA) the tendency in Delaware is to drag political feet in the hope that the situation will change or an easy solution will be forthcoming. Simply put, there is rarely a rush to regulate in Delaware. And this is unlikely to change in the foreseeable future, unless a crisis must be faced.

Epilogue

After the 2006 legislative session ended in June, political activity within the state shifted from the General Assembly toward the off-year November elections. Once again, most incumbent state legislators were reelected, and including popular Democratic state treasurer Jack Markell, who won by garnering 70.5 percent of the vote—the highest among candidates for statewide offices.

The 2006 contest for attorney general was wide open, dwarfing federal contests whereby Democratic senator Tom Carper and Republican representative Mike Castle easily won reelection. Three-term Republican attorney general Jane Brady's unexpected resignation the previous year to accept a superior court judgeship paved the way for Republican candidate Ferris W. Wharton—assistant U.S. attorney and long-time deputy attorney general—to face Democrat Joseph R. "Beau" Biden III in Delaware's showcase race of 2006. Democratic governor Minner's appointment of Brady to achieve the constitutionally mandated bipartisan composition of the superior court was dubbed "the deal" by some pundits because it opened contention to the post of attorney general by Beau Biden. Although Wharton, fifty-three, had much more experience than thirty-seven-year-old Biden, who had been practicing law for only ten years, Biden was the namesake son of his famous father—U.S. Senator Joseph R. Biden Jr. The younger Biden handily defeated Wharton to become attorney general.

On the national scene, meanwhile, Delaware's Senator Biden was feverishly campaigning to become the Democratic Party's candidate for the 2008 presidential election. By late July 2007, however, his fundraising for the prior three months brought him only $2.45 million, ranking him sixth among eight Democratic candidates, far behind front-runners Senator Barack Obama of Illinois, who had raised $33 million, and Senator Hillary Rodham Clinton of New York, who had raised $27 million. As we have noted, Biden was among the first aspirants to withdraw from the race. Prior to the Democratic Party's national convention in Denver in late August 2008, presidential candidate Obama named Biden his running mate for vice president. Amidst the pride felt by many Delawareans was the prospect of the state losing considerable clout in the U.S. Senate—whoever would succeed Biden in that body—by virtue of the loss of his seniority and the chairmanship of important senate committees.

The General Assembly in 2007 made progress by finally reforming Delaware's workers compensation law and by passing laws that established tougher standards for tracking sex offenders and helping victims of child abuse to obtain justice. Also enacted were controversial bills establishing collective bargaining rights for public employees and expending $13 million for the purchase by the state of a Bank of America building in downtown Wilmington. The latter bill was passed in the closing minutes of the session without any public discussion.

A number of important highway projects were delayed for another year for lack of money, although lawmakers agreed to various vehicle taxes and fees, including an increase of I-95 tolls from $3 to $4. Moreover, the state's cigarette tax was increased by 60 cents to $1.15 per pack.

The 2007 legislature never voted on important bills in one or both chambers, including toughening or expanding the Freedom of Information Act, reforming the law pertaining to mandatory minimum sentences, creating health insurance pools for small businesses, and permitting stem-cell research.

In June 2007 State Treasurer Jack Markell announced his bid to defeat Lieutenant Governor John Carney in the upcoming September 2008 Democratic primary for governor, which figured to dominate 2008 elections to statewide offices. Carney had been already endorsed by Governor Minner to be her successor and was generally accepted as the Democratic Party's anointed gubernatorial candidate. Meanwhile, well-known Alan B. Levin was eyeing a bid to become in 2008 the Republican candidate for governor. Levin, chairman of the state chamber of commerce and former head of his family's drug store business, would be a formidable candidate, according to Democrats Markell and Carney. However, Levin surprisingly chose not to run. The Republicans finally settled on former judge Bill Lee of Sussex County as their nominee; Governor Minner had narrowly defeated Lee in her 2004 bid for reelection.

At this writing, Delaware's politics and policy nexus in 2008 featured the spirited contest for the governorship between Lieutenant Governor Carney and Treasurer Markell leading up to the Democrats' September 9 primary, and the General Assembly's efforts to meet the new challenges of an incipient nationwide recession plus conflicts over a proposed offshore wind farm, an eminent domain issue, and health information dissemination.

The run-up to the Carney versus Markell Democratic Party primary was highlighted by both candidates announcing detailed policy positions with little difference between them, until the unprecedented revelation that Carney was being funded by the party to pay for radio ads. Although the party had endorsed Carney at its convention, the party shattered its pre-primary neutrality according to critics by funding Carney's ads. Markell insisted that Carney repay such money, because he was spending money donated to defeat Republicans—not to defeat one Democrat against another.

As was the case for other legislative bodies throughout the nation, Delaware's General Assembly was beset with revenue shortages in 2008 that forced belt-tightening expenditure reductions of many programs. Such action was not in the aggregate very controversial: it had to be done for the legislature to achieve the balanced budget required by the Delaware constitution. For example, the gross receipts tax cut won by business in 2005 was essentially repealed, but business was able to obtain a sunset provision to have the tax cut restored in 2012.

In 2008 the General Assembly and the Delmarva Power Company of Delaware finally reached a conclusion to the prolonged struggle that followed the 59 percent increase in electricity prices caused by the General Assembly's previous deregulation of the electric power industry. The General Assembly sought to force Delmarva Power to sign a wind power purchase contract with another private company—Bluewater Wind LLC. The plan called for sixty large wind turbines to be built by Bluewater nearly twelve miles offshore from Rehoboth Beach in federal waters. Raising constitutional issues was establishment of a special committee of four entities, whose membership included state executive branch representatives as well as the state controller general representing the legislative branch, which was unable to take final action. A conflict ensued within the General Assembly involving determined citizens and lobbyists, supported by the *Wilmington News Journal*, who wanted "green energy" regardless of the cost. The six months of conflict was finally settled when Delmarva Power voluntarily signed a drastically downsized wind power purchase contract with Bluewater, minus most costly provisions. Acceptance of these changes by the General Assembly and Bluewater doubtlessly was influenced by Delmarva's suspension of its lawsuit and business objections to an involuntary contract. Remaining was the question whether this nation's first offshore wind farm would in fact be built given the uncertainty of financing. Also unresolved were the necessity of having a back-up carbon-producing gas plant and the question of how much Delaware businesses not using the wind power would nevertheless end up having to pay.

The 2008 legislature was also confronted by a heated dispute between South Wilmington landowners and the city of Wilmington, which had threatened to use its power of eminent domain to take over private property, including a scrap yard, lumber yard, and auto repair shop, for waterfront development. The General Assembly overwhelmingly passed a bill, with only one dissenting vote, that provided tough restrictions on Delaware government entities to take private property by eminent domain. Governor Ruth Ann Minner vetoed the bill, claiming it could restrict the state's ability to preserve beach property or other costly uses. Curiously, by virtue of an eleven to nine vote in the Senate, the legislature failed to override the veto. Unanswered was the question why so many legislators initially approved the measure but yet failed to support the override.

Another noteworthy action of the 2008 General Assembly resulted in Delaware establishing the nation's first statewide health information exchange system featuring a classic Delaware public-private partnership with fifty-fifty cost sharing. The fully operational system, connecting an estimated half of Delaware physicians in 2008, permits direct transmission of test results from hospitals, labs, and other test providers to the doctors who ordered the tests. Previous test results had been transmitted by mail, couriers, and proprietary electronic means.

Politics in 2007 and 2008 continued to emphasize the inherent conservatism of Delaware public affairs, most influenced by the saliency of a business/employment public posture, enforcement of public finance safeguards against insolvency, and a suspicious eye toward government regulation. However, caution in overemphasizing Delaware's conservative inclinations is appropriate in light of two unique nationally significant firsts that may be characterized as radical departures from conservative public policy, as reflected by the Coastal Zone Act of 1971 and the Clean Indoor Air Act of 2002.

With regard to the distribution of government functions in Delaware, in 2007 and 2008 there was no reversal in the seventy-five-year trend of local governments transferring major functions to the state government. Economies of scale in this small state continued to ordain that the state government administer the more important functions of government. This phenomenon has resulted in narrowly focused local governments compared with their counterparts in other states. The most significant functions still administered at Delaware's local levels concerned planning and zoning functions, but jurisdictional overlap of creeping sprawl was creating an opening for even these development concerns to yield increasingly—albeit reluctantly—to state government oversight and control.

We have observed, too, that within Delaware's state government, the leadership role of the governor in general had increased relative to that of the legislature. Both the executive and judicial branches had become more prominent than in the past. Still, successful political behavior in Delaware continued to require executive-legislative cooperation, business-friendly political actors and parties, bipartisan and consensus decision-making, and a generally quiescent electorate that was disposed to support incumbents.

"Change," however, became the mantra during the 2008 election season in Delaware when, to the dismay of party leaders, incumbent Lieutenant Governor John Carney was narrowly defeated by State Treasurer Jack Markell in a spirited Democratic Party primary. Markell then easily defeated former judge Bill Lee in the governor's race. Meanwhile, Senator Joe Biden had become the nation's vice president–elect when the Obama-Biden ticket carried the general election. Regardless that Carney became an odds-on favorite to fill out the two remaining years of Biden's seat in the U.S. Senate, lame-duck governor Ruth Ann Minner appointed Ted Kaufman, Biden's longtime chief of staff. Perhaps more important for Delaware from a historical perspective was the smashing victory for the Democrats in the General Assembly by which they gained firm control of both houses for the first time in many years.

As the twenty-first century has progressed, one overarching characteristic of Delaware stands out in retrospect, and that is the relative stability pervading Delaware public affairs.

Change comes slowly in Delaware public policy. Extreme solutions to problems are avoided. Radical reformers remain on the fringes. Accordingly, a climate of predictability is likely to remain a hallmark of the government and politics of Delaware.

Notes

1. DELAWARE IN TRANSITION

1. Paul Dolan, *The Government and Administration of Delaware* (New York: Thomas Y. Crowell Co., 1956), 4.

2. See, e.g., Maureen Moakley and Elmer Cornwell, *Rhode Island Politics and Government* (Lincoln: University of Nebraska Press, 2001), 2.

3. See John A. Munroe, *History of Delaware*, 3rd ed. (Newark: University of Delaware Press, 1993), 19. Munroe's *History* forms the basis for much of the historical content of this chapter and book, and is generally regarded as the most authoritative and comprehensive history of Delaware.

4. Munroe, *History of Delaware*, 48.

5. For population data in this section, see "2000 Census of Population and Housing: Delaware," in *Profiles of General Demographic Characteristics, 2000* (Washington DC: U.S. Dept. of Commerce, issued May 2001); William W. Boyer, *Governing Delaware: Policy Problems in the First State* (Newark: University of Delaware Press, 2000), 24–26, and sources cited; and Aron Pilhofer, "Delaware Up 18% in Census," *Wilmington News Journal*, December 19, 2002.

6. Carol E. Hoffecker, *The Changing Look of Delaware* (Newark: University of Delaware Library, Special Collections Department, 2001), 2.

7. Division of Soil and Water Conservation, "Managing Nonpoint Source Pollution from Agriculture," *Delaware Coastal Programs* (Dover: Delaware Department of Natural Resources and Environmental Control, 2002), 1.

8. Bureau of Economic Research, *Annual Delaware Economic Report, 1994–95* (Newark: University of Delaware, 1996), C-1, C-6.

9. See "Wilmington Area Top Employers," *Wilmington News Journal*, March 18, 2001, Business Section; Munroe, *History of Delaware*, 103–6; "To 14th,"

Wilmington News Journal, April 26, 1995, B7; Neil Cornish and Maureen Milford, "Changing the Guard," *Wilmington News Journal*, October 1, 1995, A1; and "DuPont World's 22nd Biggest, Fortune Reports," *Wilmington News Journal*, July 9, 1991, B8.

10. Leslie A. Pappas, "Best in the Business: Manufacturing," *Wilmington News Journal*, March 17, 2002.

11. International Trade Administration, *Delaware Export Benefits* (Washington DC: U.S. Department of Commerce, August 2001).

12. See, e.g., Victor Greto, "Winning the Biotech Battle," *Wilmington News Journal*, December 26, 2004, A1, A6.

2. POLITICAL CULTURE OF THE "FIRST STATE"

1. See, e.g., Gabriel A. Almond and Sydney Verba, *The Civic Culture: Political Attitudes and Democracy in Five Nations* (Princeton NJ: Princeton University Press, 1963); and Almond and Verba, eds., *The Civic Culture Revisited* (Newbury Park CA: Sage Publications, 1989).

2. Daniel E. Elazar, *American Federalism: A View from the States*, 3d. ed. (New York: Harper & Row, 1984), chap. 5, see also sources cited at 143n.1.

3. Elazar, *American Federalism*, 122–33; see esp. Elazar's map, "Dominant Political Culture, by State," 135.

4. See, e.g., Nicholas Verchaver, "Who's the King of Delaware?" *Fortune*, May 1, 2002.

5. Information about incorporations in Delaware is available from the Delaware Division of Corporations, Delaware State Government, Dover.

6. Article 9, section 5 of the Delaware Constitution of 1897 provides that "No foreign corporation shall do any business in this State . . . without having an authorized agent or agents in the State upon whom legal process may be served."

7. See A. Gilchrist Sparks III and Donna L. Culver, "Corporations Article IX," in *The Delaware Constitution of 1897: The First One Hundred Years*, ed. Harvey Bernard Rubenstein, Randy J. Holland, et al. (Wilmington: Delaware State Bar Association, 1997), 159–65.

8. See Joseph T. Walsh and Thomas J. Fitzpatrick Jr., "Judiciary Article IV," in Rubenstein et al., eds., *Delaware Constitution of 1897*, 129.

9. See Sydney B. Silverman, "An Outsider Looks at Chancery," *Delaware Lawyer* 13, no. 2 (1995): 17; and "Tax Laws Are Not the Only Reason," *Wilmington News Journal*, July 28, 1991, N7.

10. See: U.S. Chamber Institute for Legal Reform, "Lawsuit Climate 2008: Where Does Your State Rank?" http://www.instituteforlegalreform.com/states// lawsuitclimate2008/index.cfm (accessed August 11, 2008); and Forbes

Magazine, "The Best State for Business," http://www.forbes.com/business/2008/07/30/virginia-georgia-utah-biz-cz_kb_0731beststates_table.html (accessed August 11, 2008).

11. See Title 8, *Delaware Code*, chap. 5; and State of Delaware, Department of State, Division of Corporations, "How to Calculate Franchise Taxes," http://corp.delaware.gov/frtaxcalc.shtml (accessed August 9, 2008).

12. *Delaware Fiscal Notebook, 2001 Edition*, 126.

13. Quoted by Ron Williams, "Credit Card Business Isn't Very Pretty," *Wilmington News Journal*, November 26, 2004, A20.

14. See Ted Griffith, "Credit Card Scrutiny, Complaints Intensify," *Wilmington News Journal*, September 17, 2004, A1, A2; and Hank Stuever, "Just One Word: Plastic—Why We Owe Our Souls to Wilmington, Delaware," *Washington Post Magazine*, June 16, 2002.

15. See, e.g., Governor's Strategic Economic Council, *Report and Recommendations—Finance* (Dover: State of Delaware, 2002), 7; and Jeff Montgomery, "Corps, Pa. Announce Deal on Dredging," *Wilmington News Journal*, June 24, 2008, D11.

16. 64 *Del. Laws* c 461; HB 724, August 13, 1984.

17. Quoted by Ted Griffith, "Reinforced Delaware Tax Shelter Designed to Add Jobs," *Wilmington News Journal*, November 22, 2004, A1. See also Joseph N. Distefano, "Delaware's Holding Power," *Wilmington News Journal*, January 22, 1996, A1, A6, A7.

18. Edward C. Ratledge, *Delawareans' Attitudes toward Economic Growth: Survey Results* (Newark: University of Delaware, Center for Applied Demography & Survey Research, November 16, 1998), 21.

3. DELAWARE IN THE FEDERAL SYSTEM

1. See John Kincaid, "The Competitive Challenge to Cooperative Federalism: A Theory of Federal Democracy," in *Competition among States and Local Governments: Efficiency and Equity in American Federalism*, ed. Daphne A. Kenyon and John Kincaid (Washington DC: Urban Institute Press, 1991), 89–90.

2. "Delaware Slots Bracing for Pennsylvania Threat," *Dover NewsZap*, July 7, 2003, available at CasinoMan.net, http://www.casinoman.net/gambling-news/article/delaware-slots-bracing-for-pennsylvania-threat.1699.asp (accessed August 7, 2008).

3. *Delaware Code*, Title 29, chap. 50, subchapter I-B.

4. Celia Cohen, *Only in Delaware: Politics and Politicians in the First State* (Newark DE: Grapevine Publishing, 2002).

5. See, e.g., Trif Alatzas, "AstraZeneca Picks Delaware," *Wilmington News Journal*, April 30, 1999, A1, A7; and "Del. Went All Out for Company," *Wilmington New Journal*, May 2, 1999, A1, A10.

6. Ruth Ann Minner, "Delaware Held Up during Recession," *Wilmington News Journal*, October 22, 2003, A15; see also, Progressive Policy Institute, "Overall Scores," The 2002 State New Economy Index, http://www.neweconomy index.org/states/2002/overall_rank.html (accessed August 7, 2008).

7. Only from 1813 to 1823 was Delaware entitled to two members of the U.S. House of Representatives.

8. See Carol E. Hoffecker, *Honest John Williams: U.S. Senator from Delaware* (Newark: University of Delaware Press; London: Associated University Presses, 2000).

9. In 1989 Biden shared this distinction with the simultaneous campaigning by former Governor Pete du Pont, who briefly sought the Republican presidential nomination.

10. Russell W. Peterson, *Rebel with a Conscience* (Newark: University of Delaware Press; London: Associated University Presses, 1999), 144–45.

11. See Russell Peterson, "A History," *Delaware State News*, June 27, 1992, 5.

12. Peterson, *Rebel with a Conscience*, 191–94.

13. See Philadelphia District, U.S. Army Corps of Engineers, *Delaware River Main Channel Deepening Project*, http://www.usace.army.mil/cw/hot_topics/ ht_2003/del_riv_chan.pdf (accessed August 7, 2008).

14. Quoted by Robert Long, "Dredging: Boon or Boondoggle?" *Wilmington News Journal*, May 10, 1999, A5.

15. See, e.g., Green Delaware, *Alert 115*, November 29, 2001; League of Women Voters of Greater Dover, "Delaware River Dredging Statement," *Dover Voter*, January 2002, 4; "Stronger Opposition," *Wilmington News Journal*, June 14, 2000; and Jim Walsh and Jeff Montgomery, "Delaware River Dredging Plan on Hold," *Wilmington News Journal*, April 23, 2002.

16. See House Bill No. 111, 142nd General Assembly of Delaware, 2003; and Delaware Department of Transportation, *FY 04–09 Financial Plan 9-15-03.xis*, September 2003.

17. Quoted by J. L. Miller, "Governors Want to Keep Guard Control," *Wilmington News Journal*, August 21, 2006, A5.

18. Jeff Montgomery, "State to Fight Rollback of Clean Air Rules," *Wilmington News Journal*, August 29, 2003; Christopher Drew and Richard A. Oppel Jr., "Senators and Attorneys General Seek Investigation Into E.P.P. Rules Change," *New York Times*, November 7, 2003, A17, and "Lawyers at E.P.A. Say It Will Drop Pollution Cases," *New York Times*, November 6, 2003, A1.

19. See "JFC Approves Spending Plan for Tobacco Funds," *Wilmington News Journal*, May 30, 2003.

20. See Delaware Development Office, *Carper Administration Third-Year Progress Report* (Dover: State of Delaware, 1995).

21. Thomas R. Carper, Governor, *State of the State Address*, January 21, 1999, introduction.

22. Title 29, *Delaware Code*, chap. 39.

23. See, e.g., *Hines v. Davidowitz*, 312 U.S. 52 (1941).

24. See Information Technology and Innovative Foundation, "The 2007 State New Economy Index," http://www.itif.org/index.php?id=30 (accessed August 7, 2008).

25. Office of Trade and Economic Analysis, U.S. Department of Commerce, "State Exports to the World," *Export America*, September 2001, 30–33; and Foreign Trade Division, U.S. Census Bureau, "Total U.S. Exports via Delaware to Top 25 Countries," http://www.census.gov/foreign-trade/statistics/state/data/de.html (accessed August 8, 2008).

26. Quoted by Jane Brooks, *Wilmington News Journal*, March 16, 1996, E4. See also Hoffecker, *Honest John Williams*, 45.

27. Information provided by the University of Delaware Center for International Studies and the Office of Foreign Students and Scholars.

4. THE CONSTITUTION

1. See Maurice A. Harnett III, "Delaware's Charters and Prior Constitutions," in Rubenstein et al., eds., *Delaware Constitution of 1897*, 23–24. Much of this chapter is dependent on this monumental work.

2. See Munroe, *History of Delaware*, 121–23.

3. Munroe, *History of Delaware*, 147–53.

4. Henry R. Horsey, Henry N. Herndon Jr., and Barbara MacDonald, "The Delaware Constitutional Convention of 1897," in Rubenstein et al., eds., *Delaware Constitution of 1897*, 66.

5. Quoted by Horsey et al., "Delaware Constitutional Convention," 67.

6. Quoted by Henry R. Horsey and William Duffy, "The Supreme Court of Delaware until 1951: The 'Leftover Judge System,'" Delaware State Courts, http://courts.state.de.us/Courts/Supreme%20Court/?history2.htm (accessed August 8, 2008).

7. Munroe, *History of Delaware*, 47.

8. Delaware Constitution of 1776, art. 23.

9. Ralph Moyed, "Legislature Is Bad Enough, Mob Is Worse," *Wilmington News Journal*, April 10, 1996, A10.

10. *State v. Bender*, 293 A.2d 551, 553 (Del. 1972).

11. William T. Quillen, "Amendments and Conventions Article XVI," in Rubenstein et al., eds., *Delaware Constitution of 1897*, 209.

12. See *Opinions of Justices*, 330 A2d 764 (Del. Sup. Ct. 1974); Elbert N. Carvel and Henry L. Winslow, "Constitutional Revision Commission of 1968–69," in

Rubenstein et al., eds., *Delaware Constitution of 1897*, 225; and Paul Dolan and James R. Soles, *Government of Delaware* (Newark: University of Delaware, 1976), 19.

5. POLITICAL PARTIES AND ELECTIONS

1. Munroe, *History of Delaware*, 142–43.
2. Quoted by Munroe, *History of Delaware*, 147.
3. Munroe, *History of Delaware*, 148, 150.
4. Munroe, *History of Delaware*, 153.
5. Gregory S. Franseth, L. Rebecca Johnson Melvin, and Shiela Pardee, "The End of an Era in Delaware: The Practical Politics of Willard Saulsbury, Jr.," in *Collections* 11 (Newark: University of Delaware Library Associates 2003): 1–27, at 13.
6. Roger A. Martin, "Delaware Failed in its Chance to Give Women the Right to Vote," *Wilmington News Journal*, August 6, 1995, H1.
7. See Carol E. Hoffecker, "Delaware's Woman Suffrage Campaign," *Delaware History*, 2, no. 3 (1983):149–67.
8. See Cohen, *Only in Delaware*, 10–12.
9. Thus, Republican-announced candidate for the U.S. Senate John Williams knew "that he must go to Wilmington to receive the blessing of the state party's real leader, Frank du Pont, T. Coleman du Pont's son" (Hoffecker, *Honest John Williams*, 62).
10. Dolan, *Government and Administration of Delaware*, 29.
11. Cohen, *Only in Delaware*, 36.
12. Note, however, that from 1967 to 1969, Republicans controlled the House of Representatives, while the Senate was evenly split, with nine seats held by Republicans and nine by Democrats.
13. Dolan and Soles, *Government of Delaware*, 27–28.
14. Janet B. Johnson and Joseph A. Pika, "Delaware: Friends and Neighbors Politics," in *Interest Group Politics in the Northeastern States*, ed. Ronald J. Hrebenar and Clive S. Thomas (University Park: Pennsylvania State University Press, 1993), 71.
15. See James Phelan and Robert Pozen, *The Company State: Ralph Nader's Study Group on Delaware* (New York: Grossman, 1973), xi. Similarly, see also Gerald Colby Zilg, *Du Pont: Behind the Nylon Curtain* (Englewood Cliffs NJ: Prentice-Hall, 1974); and Gerald Colby, *Du Pont Dynasty* (Secaucus NJ: Lyle Stuart, 1984).
16. *Roman v. Sincock*, 377 U.S. 695 (1964).
17. *Delaware Code Annotated* (rev. 1974), title 29, sec. 801–4.
18. Alicia Nichols, "State Gets 'D-' in Disclosure," *The Review*, September 26, 2003, A2.

19. See "Campaign Financing and Disclosure Act of 1990," *Delaware Code*, title 15, chap. 80.

20. See Celia Cohen, "Campaign Finance Reform Pursued," *Wilmington News Journal*, March 17, 1990, A3; Public Citizen, *Report Concerning Total Campaign Receipts Received by Members of the U.S. House of Representatives and the U.S. Senate* (Washington DC: Public Citizen's Congress Watch, 1997), 2; Carl Weiser, "For Biden, Funding Is Greener Elsewhere," *Wilmington News Journal*, March 24, 2002, A1, A9; and Joseph A. Pika, "The 2000 Delaware Senate Race," *Election Advocacy: Soft Money and Issue Advocacy in the 2000 Congressional Elections* (Provo UT: Brigham Young University, Center for the Study of Elections and Democracy, 2001), 51–61, esp. table 18.4.

21. Public Law No. 107-155, March 27, 2002. For Biden's presidential campaign autobiography, see Joe Biden, *Promises to Keep: On Life and Politics* (New York: Random House, 2007).

22. See Maureen Milford, "MBNA to Tighten Corporate Costs," *Wilmington News Journal*, March 9, 2004, A1, A5.

23. See "Common Cause, "Bankruptcy Legislation Enters Final Stages; MBNA Hedges Its Bets," *Common Cause News*, April 20, 2000; Christopher H. Schmitt, "Tougher Bankruptcy Laws—Compliments of MBNA?" *Business Week*, February 26, 2001; and editorial, "MBNA's Foray in Campaign Finance Makes Case for Reform," *Wilmington News Journal*, March 15, 1995, A8.

24. Jennifer Brooks, "Bank of America Buys MBNA—MBNA Generous to Politicians, Especially GOP," *Wilmington News Journal*, July 2, 2005, A7; and Aron Pilhofer and Jonathan D. Epstein, "MBNA Bankrolls Delaware Politics," *Wilmington News Journal*, November 4, 2000, A1, A2. See also Steven Weiss, Center for Responsive Politics, "Money Talks," Capital Eye, March 4, 2005, http://www.opensecrets.org/capital_eye/inside.php?ID=159 (accessed August 9, 2008).

25. Johnson and Pika, "Delaware," 61, 62; and David Mark, *Going Dirty: The Art of Negative Campaigning* (Lanham MD: Rowman and Littlefield, 2006), 177–80.

26. Cohen, *Only in Delaware*, 363.

27. Patrick Jackson, "Del.'s Primary Didn't Lure Many Candidates," *Wilmington News Journal*, January 4, 2004, B5–B6.

28. Erin Kelly, "Castle One of Top Republican Rebels," *Wilmington News Journal*, January 12, 2004, B3.

29. Celia Cohen, "All of Delaware Will Miss Him," *Delaware Grapevine*, December 21, 2003, http://www.delawaregrapevine.com/dec03stories/12-03%20roth%20service.htm (accessed August 9, 2008).

30. See Cohen, *Only in Delaware*, 3–4; Chip Guy and Patrick Jackson, "A Return

Day for the Hardy," *Wilmington News Journal*, November 5, 2004, A1, A3; and Mark, *Going Dirty*, 178.

31. Letter from Ralph Nader to the Steering Committee of the U.S. Green Party and the Presidential Exploratory Committee of the Green Party, December 22, 2003, in the Green Party of Delaware, *The Green Diamond* 3, no. 46 (December 27, 2003), http://gpde.us/GreenDiamond/Vol_3/Vol_3_Issue_46.htm (accessed August 9, 2008).

6. THE GOVERNOR AND ADMINISTRATION

1. Dolan and Soles, *Government of Delaware*, 63.

2. See Dolan, *Government and Administration of Delaware*, 72–74.

3. See William B. Chandler III and Pierre S. du Pont IV, "Executive Article III," in Rubenstein et al., eds., *Delaware Constitution of 1897*, 101–5.

4. *Opinions of the Justices*, 290 A2d 645 (1972).

5. For elaboration of Levinson's political career, see Boyer, *Governing Delaware*, 81–84.

6. William W. Boyer, introduction to Charles P. Messick, *An Adventure in Public Personnel Administration* (Newark: University of Delaware, 1973), x.

7. See Antoinette Thomas Gregory Neville, "The Impact of Public Employee Unionism on the Merit System: The Case of New Castle County, Delaware" (M.A. thesis, University of Delaware, 1976), 33; and Marion C. Stewart, "The Intergovernmental Personnel Act of 1970 and Its Implementation in Delaware" (M.A. thesis, University of Delaware, 1972), 23–49.

8. Kenneth E. Thorpe, New Castle County personnel director, to Dr. Edward B. Shils, February 13, 1967, as quoted in Neville, "Impact of Public Employee Unionism," 24.

9. Dolan, *Government and Administration of Delaware*, 139–46.

10. See "Report of Governor's Merit System Study Committee To: Governor Charles L. Terry, Jr.," typescript, May 20, 1966, Delaware Public Archives, 11; and *Delaware Code Annotated*, title 29, chap. 59.

11. See Boyer, *Governing Delaware*, 113–14.

12. See Christopher L. Perry, *Russell W. Peterson, Governor of Delaware, 1969–1973*, Oral History Series no. 3 (Wilmington: Delaware Heritage Commission 1999), 55–56; and Governor's Task Force on Reorganization of the Executive Branch of Government, *Final Report on Cabinet Departments* (Dover DE: State of Delaware, 1970), 13.

13. Among other later changes was the addition in 1976 of a new Department of Correction, headed by a commissioner appointed by the governor. Also, the governor's administrative control was further strengthened in 1997 when the position of state superintendent of public instruction, who had been appointed

by the state board of education (headed by the board's president), was replaced by the position of secretary of education, appointed by the governor.

14. Quoted by Cohen, *Only in Delaware*, 190.

15. Peterson, *Rebel with a Conscience*, 122.

16. See Ned Davis, *Charles L. Terry: Governor of Delaware, 1965–1969*, Oral History Series no. 4 (Wilmington: Delaware Heritage Commission, 2000), 32–33, 94; and Munroe, *History of Delaware*, 229, 255.

17. See Perry, *Russell W. Peterson*, 74–120.

18. Roger A. Martin, *A History of Delaware through Its Governors, 1776–1984* (Wilmington DE: McClafferty Printing, 1984), 539.

19. See Roger Martin, *Sherman W. Tribbitt, Governor of Delaware, 1973–1977*, Oral History Series no. 2 (Wilmington: Delaware Heritage Commission, 1998).

20. For elaboration of du Pont's tenure as governor, see Larry Nagengast, *Pierre S. du Pont IV, Governor of Delaware, 1977–1985*, Oral History Series (Dover: Delaware Heritage Commission, 2006).

21. For elaboration of Carper's takeover of the Democratic Party in New Castle County, see Boyer, *Governing Delaware*, 65–68.

7. THE GENERAL ASSEMBLY

1. For a history of the General Assembly see Carol E. Hoffecker, *Democracy in Delaware: The Story of the FirstState's General Assembly* (Wilmington DE: Cedar Tree Books, 2004), a book the assembly commissioned to celebrate its three-hundredth anniversary.

2. See, e.g., Hoffecker, *Democracy in Delaware*, chap. 5.

3. Munroe, *History of Delaware*, chap. 9, esp. p. 145; and Hoffecker, *Democracy in Delaware*, 109–11.

4. See, e.g., Munroe, *History of Delaware*, 175–80; Hoffecker, *Democracy in Delaware*, 121–26; and Franseth, Melvin, and Pardee, "The End of an Era in Delaware," *Collections* 11:12–14.

5. Carol E. Hoffecker, "Delaware Woman Suffrage Campaign," *Delaware History*, 20, no. 3 (1983): 149–67; and Martin, "Delaware Failed in Its Chance," H1.

6. See Boyer, *Governing Delaware*, 48–49.

7. See Boyer, *Governing Delaware*, 133

8. Cohen, *Only in Delaware*, 313.

9. Hoffecker, *Democracy in Delaware*, 259.

10. See *Opinions of the Justices*, 245 A.2d 172 (Del. Sup. Ct. 1968); and editorial, "Private-Sector Workers Are the New Minority in General Assembly," *Wilmington News Journal*, September 20, 1996, A14.

11. See: "The Freedom of Information Act," *Delaware Code Annotated*, title 29, chap. 100, at www.delcode.state.de.us (accessed August 9, 2008); M. Jane Brady, Attorney General, et al., *Delaware Freedom of Information Act: Policy Manual*, at www.state.de.us/attgen/civil/foia.htm (accessed August 9, 2008); J. L. Miller and Patrick Jackson, "With Millions at Stake, Critical Decisions in Del. Made in Secret," *Wilmington News Journal*, January 9, 2005, A1, A7; and editorial, "Bill to Shed Light on the Legislature Isn't Likely to Go Very Far," *Wilmington News Journal*, May 3, 2005, A10.

12. Editorial, "Avoids Public," *Wilmington News Journal*, July 31, 2005, A13. See also Al Mascitti, "Lawmakers Call It 'Epilogue Language,' But It's Just Plain Underhanded," *Wilmington News Journal*, June 21, 2005, B1; editorial, "Underhanded Trend of Secretive Legislation Deserves Condemnation," *Wilmington News Journal*, August 31, 2005, A12, and related articles on June 23, 2006, A1, A8, A14, B1, and B6.

13. See Hoffecker, *Democracy in Delaware*, 256–57; and J. L. Miller and Patrick Jackson, "Minner Cabinet Picks Met with Criticism," *Wilmington News Journal*, January 14, 2005, A1, A9.

14. See Tom Eldred, "Pro Tem's Influence Strong, Essential," *Dover Delaware State News*, June 18, 2002, 1, 3.

15. Hoffecker, *Democracy in Delaware*, 257.

16. Hoffecker, *Democracy in Delaware*, 259.

17. Alan Rosenthal, "The Scope of Legislative Reform," in *Strengthening the States: Essays on Legislative Reform*, ed. Donald G. Herzberg and Alan Rosenthal (Garden City NY: Doubleday, 1971), 8

18. Hoffecker, *Democracy in Delaware*, 258.

19. Quoted by Patrick Jackson, "Remapping Gets Push from Judge," *Wilmington News Journal*, March 29, 2002, B1.

20. See Patrick Jackson, "Lawmakers Adopt New District Map," *Wilmington News Journal*, April 19, 2002, A1, A17; and "Governor Oks New Districts," *Wilmington News Journal*, April 20, 2002, B1, B2.

21. See Frank Sims, "Letter to the Editor: You've Been Robbed," *The Green Diamond E-NewsLetter*, January 28, 2003; and Al Mascitti, "Unopposed Races Take Voters Out of the Assembly Contest," *Wilmington News Journal*, November 5, 2002, B1.

22. Dolan, *Government and Administration of Delaware*, 182.

23. See *Belton v. Gebhart*, 87 A.2d 862 (1952).

24. *Brown v. Board of Education of Topeka*, 347 U.S. 483 (1954).

25. See *Evans v. Buchanan*, 393 F.Supp. 428 (D. Del. 1975), affirmed by the U.S. Supreme Court, 423 U.S. 963 (1975). See also Jeffrey A. Raffel, *The Politics of School Desegregation: The Metropolitan Remedy in Delaware* (Philadelphia: Temple University Press, 1980).

26. See 72 *Delaware Laws* 287 (2000); *Delaware Code*, title 14, chap. 2, subchapter 2.

27. Ralph Moyed, "Only the Black Kids Got Bused in the Old Days," *Wilmington News Journal*, August 27, 2001.

28. "Our View: Neighborhood Schools," *Wilmington News Journal*, December 15, 2002, A12.

29. Quoted by Stephen Sobek, "School Plans Sparking Fears of Resegregation," *Wilmington News Journal*, November 25, 2001, A1, A9.

30. See Leland Ware, "Closed Doors in Housing Color Public Schools," *Wilmington News Journal*, June 2, 2004, A13.

31. Quoted in "What Important People Say about NANS," NANS: The National Association for Neighborhood Schools, http://www.nans.org/vip.shtml (accessed August 9, 2008).

32. *Ward T. Evans v. State of Delaware*, 2004 Del. LEXIS 545 (November 23, 2004).

33. 2005 Del. HB 31, 75 *Del. Laws* 1, Section 5403 (a).

34. *Ward T. Evans v. State of Delaware*, 2005 Del. LEXIS 138 (April 11, 2005).

8. COURTS, JUDGES, AND LAWYERS

1. Paul Dolan, "The Supreme Court of Delaware, 1900–1952," *Dickenson Law Review* 56 (1952), 166–76.

2. See Delaware Constitution of 1897, art. 4.

3. Delaware Constitution of 1897, art. 4, sec. 83.

4. See, e.g., Governor Ruth Ann Minner, "Executive Order No. 4 Ordering the Continuation of the Judicial Nominating Commission and Appointing New Members," State of Delaware: The Official Website for the First State, http://www.state.de.us/governor/orders/eo_4.shtml (accessed August 9, 2008).

5. William T. Quillen and Michael Hanrahan, *A Short History of the Delaware Court of Chancery—1792–1992* (Wilmington DE: Widener University School of Law, 1993), 11–12, at http://courts.delaware.gov/Courts/Court%20of %20Chancery/?history.htm (accessed August 9, 2008).

6. See Lauren A. Otten and Patricia C. Hannigan, "Preliminary findings in the 1992 Delaware Lawyer Satisfactory Survey," *Delaware Lawyer* 12, no. 3 (1993): 12–15, 35–36; and "Gender Bias Found in Del. Legal System," *Review*, September 15, 1995, A3.

7. For local news coverage of Moore's demise, see the following articles in the *Wilmington News Journal*: May 7, 1994, A3; May, 12, 1994, A18; May 15, 1994, A1; May 18, 1994, A1, A9; May 19, 1994, A1, A14; and May 20, 1994, A1, A7. For national news coverage, see, e.g., Karen Donovan, "Shareholders' Advocates Protest Justice's Removal," *National Law Journal*, June 6, 1994,

B1; "The Controversial Del. Court Nomination," *National Law Journal*, July 11, 1994, A17; Dianna B. Henriques, "Top Business Court under Fire: Critics Say Politics Is Hurting Delaware Judiciary," *New York Times*, May 23, 1995, D1, D8; and John Close, "When Moore Is Less," *Counsel Magazine*, November 1995, 105, 108.

8. Quoted by Jerry Hager, "Berger Takes Her Seat on State Supreme Court," *Wilmington News Journal*, July 23, 1994, A7.

9. Quillen and Hanrahan, *A Short History*, 24. See also Maureen Milford, "Chancery Court Strives to Stay on Top," *Wilmington News Journal*, June 2, 2005, B7, B10.

10. Carol Hoffecker, *Federal Justice in the First State: A History of the United States District Court for the District of Delaware* (Wilmington: Historical Society for the United States District Court for the District of Delaware, 1992), 171.

11. William L. Cary, "Federalism and Corporate Law: Reflections upon Delaware," *Yale Law Journal* 83, no. 4 (1974), 668.

12. E. Norman Veasey, "I Have the Best Job in America," *Delaware Lawyer* 13, no. 4 (1995), 21, 23; and "It Is Time to Give Credit," *Delaware Lawyer* 12, no. 4 (1994), 6.

13. Editorial, "Distinguished Record," *Wilmington News Journal*, April 7, 2004, A12.

14. Cary, "Federalism and Corporate Law," 701.

15. Editorial, "Talk of Federal Corporate Oversight Challenges Delaware," *Wilmington News Journal*, December 17, 2004, A16.

16. For an overview, see "Common Law," *Wikipedia: The Free Encyclopedia*, http://en.wikipedia.org/wiki/Common_law (accessed August 9, 2008).

17. See, e.g., Michael Hanrahan, "The Development of the Delaware Court of Chancery As a Corporate Forum," *Delaware Lawyer* 2, no. 3 (1984), 34–37.

18. Richard C. Kiger, "The Continuing Importance of the English Common Law," *Delaware Lawyer* 6, no. 2 (1987), 110.

19. Report of the Convention's Committee on the Bill of Rights as quoted by Rodman Ward Jr. and Paul L. Lockwood, "Bill of Rights Article I," in Rubenstein et al., eds., *Delaware Constitution of 1897*, 85.

20. Dolan, *Government and Administration of Delaware*, 23.

21. Joseph T. Walsh and Thomas J. Fitzpatrick Jr., "Judiciary Article IV," in Rubenstein et al., eds., *Delaware Constitution of 1897*, 128.

9. STATE-LOCAL RELATIONS

1. See, e.g., Joseph F. Zimmerman, "Developments in State-Local Relations, 1990–91," in *The Book of the States, 1992–93* (Lexington KY: Council of State Governments, 1992), 29:630.

2. Population estimates for the year 2007 in this section are from the Population Division of the U.S. Census Bureau and are consonant with those estimates of the Delaware Population Consortium's *Annual Population Projections*, Version 2007.0.

3. Edward C. Ratledge, *State Growth and Development: Delawareans' Views on Issues and Public Policy Options* (Newark: University of Delaware Center for Applied Demography and Survey Research, 1995), 23.

4. *Delaware Code Annotated*, title 22, chap. 3, sec. 301–3.

5. *City of Trenton v. State of New Jersey*, 262 U.S. 182, 187, 43 S. Ct. 534, 537 (1923).

6. Dolan, *Government and Administration of Delaware*, 332.

7. See *Delaware Code Annotated*, title 22, chap. 8, sec. 802, 811, for relevant provisions; and Antoinette T. Eaton and Peter Ross, *A Guide for Delaware Municipal Charter Review* (Newark DE: University of Delaware, Public Administration Institute, 1990), 13.

8. Jeffrey A. Raffel, Jerome R. Lewis, Deborah A. Auger, and Kathryn G. Denhardt, "Delaware," in *Home Rule in America: A Fifty-State Handbook*, ed. Dale Krane, Platon N. Rigos, and Melvin B. Hill Jr. (Washington DC: CQPress, 2001), 87.

9. Eaton and Ross, *Guide for Delaware Municipal Charter Review*, 14 n.1.

10. See Delaware Education Improvement Commission, *Empowering Schools for Excellence: Final Report and Recommendations* (Dover DE: The Commission, 1995), 26 and appendixes F and J.

11. Chip Guy, "Eastern Sussex Residents Want Louder Voice in County Council," *Wilmington News Journal*, August 4, 2004, A1, A6.

12. Sussex County Council, Agenda, September 18, 2007.

13. Molly Murray, "Millville May Not Be Tiny for Long," *Wilmington News Journal*, September 27, 2004, A1, A5.

14. Al Mascitti, "Downstaters Are Thriving on Subsidies from Up North," *Wilmington News Journal*, February 27, 2003, B1.

15. Quoted by Molly Murray, "Sussex to Allow Clustered Housing," *Wilmington_News Journal*, August 4, 2004, B1, B2 at B2.

16. Quoted by Bruce Pringle, "Sussex Groups Grow, but Clout Lagging," *Wilmington News Journal*, January 2, 1994, A7.

17. Quotes from Melissa Tyrrell, "State's Newest Growth Area: Smyrna," *Wilmington News Journal*, September 28, 2004, A2.

18. See Mike Finney, "The Turning of Smyrna: A Former Town Nestled Next to an Expressway Will See Its Population Double in Three Years," *Wilmington News Journal*, August 18, 2003, E1, E3.

19. Harry F. Themal, "What's the Legacy of Greenhouse as NCCo Executive?" *Wilmington News Journal*, May 6, 1996, A10.

20. See John Taylor, "Enlarge New Castle County Council," *Wilmington News Journal*, February 17, 1991, B12; editorial, "Larger County Council and Widened State Role Needed to Curb Sprawl;" *Wilmington News Journal*, May 8, 1996, A10; and Robert Moore, "NCCO Council Wins Approval to Expand," *Wilmington News Journal*, July 2, 1996, A1.

21. See speech by Tom Gordon, http://www.co.new-castle.de.us/Executive/ 2004Address/Budget%20Speech%202004.htm (accessed August 10, 2008).

22. Quotes are from "Wilmington Cannot Keep Limping along on Limited Revenue," *Wilmington News Journal*, March 23, 2002; and Adam Taylor, "Wilmington Scores Political, Fiscal Win," *Wilmington News Journal*, July 2, 2003.

10. PUBLIC FINANCE

1. See Paul Dolan, *The Organization of State Administration in Delaware* (Baltimore: Johns Hopkins University Press, 1950), 111; *Report of the Delaware State Survey Commission* (Dover: State of Delaware, 1920), 9–5; and 32 *Delaware Laws* 26 (1921).

2. See, e.g., Boyer, *Governing Delaware*, 62.

3. Boyer, *Governing Delaware*, 126–28.

4. Delaware Department of Finance, *Delaware Fiscal Notebook: 2004 Edition*, November 24, 2003, 53–54.

5. Jonathan Chait, "Rogue State: The Case against Delaware," *The New Republic*, August 19 & 26, 2002, 20–23.

6. Chait, "Rogue State," 22, 23.

7. "Forecasts for Management Decisionmaking," *The Kiplinger Letter* 80, no. 9 (February 28, 2003), at http://special.kiplinger.com/Kletter/letter030228.html (accessed August 10, 2008).

8. "The Government Performance Project: The Way We Tax—Delaware," Governing.com, February 2003, at http://www.governing.com/gpp/2003/gp3de.htm (accessed August 10, 2008).

9. Editorial, "Gov. Minner for Second Term," *Wilmington News Journal*, October 17, 2004, A16.

10. All data related to revenues and expenditures in this chapter are from the Delaware Department of Finance, especially from its annual editions of the *Delaware Fiscal Notebook*.

11. See *Delaware Code Annotated*, title 29, sec. 4803(g); and Castle, "Balanced Budget Secures Future," *Wilmington News Journal*, December 8, 1996, G4.

12. See *State Rankings 2007: A Statistical View of the 50 United States* (Lawrence KS: Morgan Quinto Press, 2007) 246, 268.

13. For more information, see, e.g., Suzanne C. Moore, "Putting State Finances under the Microscope," *Delaware State Chamber of Commerce Business Journal* 1, no. 10 (1995), 12–13.

14. See *Delaware Constitution of 1897*, art. 3, sec. 21; and *Delaware Code Annotated*, title 29, chaps. 11 (controller general), 27 (treasurer), 29 (auditor), 63 (budget director), 83 (secretary of finance).

15. See Celia Cohen, "Tax Cut a Proven Road to Del. Re-election," *Wilmington News Journal*, May 19, 1996, B1; and Eva Tahmincioglu, "Delaware Wins Fiscal Plaudits," *Wilmington News Journal*, September 7, 1995, B7.

16. Quotes from Trif Alatzas, "Coalition Seeks Corporate Tax," *Wilmington News Journal*, December 3, 1996, A1; and Joseph N. Distefano, "Business Cool to Surcharge on State Tax," *Wilmington News Journal*, December 3, 1996, B10.

17. Beth Miller, "Minner Survives Toughest Contest: Wilmington, NCCO Voters Give Second term to Governor," *Wilmington News Journal*, November 3, 2004, A1, A7.

18. See discussion of the joint finance and bond bill committees by Hoffecker, *Democracy in Delaware*, 250–52, 256–57.

19. William M. Remington, "Delaware's Tax System in a Digital Age," *Delaware Lawyer* (Fall 2004): 19.

11. NONGOVERNMENTAL INFLUENCE AND PARTICIPATION

1. Kim Rogers Burdick, "A Folklorist Looks at Lobbyists" (unpublished analytical paper submitted in partial fulfillment for the degree of Master of Public Administration, University of Delaware, 1989), 15, 16, 24, 29.

2. Janet B. Johnson and Joseph A. Pika, "Delaware: Friends and Neighbors Politics," in *Interest Group Politics in the Northeastern States*, ed. Robert J. Hrebenar and Clive S. Thomas (University Park PA: Pennsylvania State University Press, 1993), 61.

3. Johnson and Pika, "Delaware," 67, 73, 79–80.

4. Johnson and Pika, "Delaware," 81, 85, 91.

5. Roger A. Martin, *Memoirs of Twenty-two Years in the Delaware State Senate* (Wilmington DE: Roger A. Martin, 1995), 92–94.

6. See, e.g., editorial, "Our View," *Wilmington News Journal*, 7 September 2003, A14.

7. See *Scorecard: The Pollution Information Site* (New York: Environmental Defense, 2004), at http://scorecard.org/env-releases/hap/state.tcl?fips_state _code=10#sources (accessed August 10, 2008).

8. Federation of Tax Administrators, "State Excise Tax Rates on Cigarettes," January 1, 2005, http://www.taxadmin.org/fta/rate/tobacco.pdf (accessed August 10, 2008).

9. See National Association of Attorneys General, *Master Settlement Agreement*, http://www.naag.org/backpages/naag/tobacco/msa/msa-pdf/1109185724 _1032468605_cigmsa.pdf/download (accessed August 10, 2008); and Hiran

Ratnayake, "Del. Makes Good on Promise to Fund Anti-tobacco Fight," *Wilmington News Journal*, December 3, 2004, A1, A15.

10. See "Clean Indoor Air Act," *Delaware Code*, Title 16, chapter 29. Note that Delaware's first clean indoor air law was passed in 1994; however, it was weak and mainly designated smoking areas within certain venues. Moreover, it explicitly preempted more stringent local ordinances except for Wilmington and Dover.

11. Ron Williams, "Big Tobacco Spread Money around Dover," *Wilmington News Journal*, September 9, 2003, A10.

12. Chris Bostic, "Tobacco Policy Trend Alert—Clean Indoor Air: The Delaware Campaign Model," report for the American Lung Association, January 2003.

13. Edward C. Ratledge, *Tobacco Attitudes and Media Survey—2003* (Newark: University of Delaware, College of Human Services, Education and Public Policy, Center for Applied Demography & Survey Research, 2003).

14. Dolan, *Government and Administration of Delaware*, 221.

15. See, e.g., Boyer, *Governing Delaware*, 195–98; and Kathryn G. Denhardt, Megan M. Manlove, Amy B. Droskoski, and Consuella M. Barbour, "The Delaware Experience with Privatization Initiatives," in *Competition and Privatization Options: Enhancing Efficiency & Effectiveness in State Government*, ed. Jeffrey A. Raffel, Deborah A. Auger, and Kathryn G. Denhardt (Newark: University of Delaware, Graduate College of Urban Affairs and Public Policy, Institute for Public Administration, 1997), 41–51.

16. Bill No. 400, 143rd General Assembly, June 30, 2003.

17. Quotes from J. L. Miller, "State Will Audit Schwartz Center," *Wilmington News Journal*, February 20, 2004, B1; and Bill Potter, "Schwartz Probe Continues: Audit Goes to Attorney General," *Delaware State News*, May 19, 2004. See also related articles in *Delaware State News*, February 19 and 25, 2004.

18. Quoted by Mike Chalmers, "Charities Dealing with Less," *Wilmington News Journal*, November 27, 2003, A1, A9.

19. Information provided by United Way of Delaware, Wilmington.

20. See Delaware Community Foundation, "Facts and Figures," http://www.delcf .org/About_2_1.htm (accessed August 13, 2008).

21. See Community Reinvestment Act, "Background and Purpose," http://www .ffiec.gov/cra/history.htm (accessed August 13, 2008).

22. See Delaware Community Reinvestment Action Council: Your Fair Lending Advocate in Delaware! http://www.dcrac.org/ (accessed August 13, 2008).

23. Delaware Community Investment Corporation, *Report to Members* 10, no. 4 (January 2004).

24. Information provided by the Center for Community Research and Service, University of Delaware, Newark.

25. Leland Ware and Steven W. Peuquet, *Delaware Analysis of Impediments to Fair Housing Choice* (Newark: University of Delaware, School of Urban Affairs & Public Policy, Center for Community Research and Service, 2003), 2.

26. Johnson and Pika, "Delaware," 69, 70, 71.

27. See *Delaware State News*, http://www2.newszap.com/profiles/Delaware/DelawareStateNews/ (accessed August 13, 2008).

28. See Audit Bureau of Circulations, "Reader Profile: Top 100 Newspapers in the United States," March 31, 2008, http://www.infoplease.com/ipea/A0004420.html (accessed August 12, 2008).

29. Delaware Radio Stations, http://www.rockhawk.com/Delaware.htm (accessed August 13, 2008).

12. SPRAWL, POLLUTION, AND HEALTH

1. For an overview of pollution in Delaware, see, e.g., Boyer, *Governing Delaware*, chap. 10.

2. Professor Sydney Carter of the University of Florida, quoted in Ernest R. Bartley and William W. Boyer, *Municipal Zoning: Florida Law and Practice* (Gainesville: University of Florida, Public Administration Clearing Service, 1950), 10. See also Dolan and Soles, *Government of Delaware*, 236, 238.

3. *Delaware Code Annotated*, title 29, chap. 92.

4. Devona E. G. Williams, "Quality of Life for Whom: The Case in the State of Delaware" (Ph.D. dissertation, University of Delaware, 1991), 145–46, 160.

5. See George Galster et al., " Wrestling Sprawl to the Ground: Defining and Measuring an Elusive Concept," *Housing Policy Debate* 12, no. 4 (2001), 681–718; Peter Dreier, John Mollenkopf, and Todd Swanstrom, *Place Matters: Metropolitics for the Twenty-first Century*, 2nd ed. (Lawrence: University Press of Kansas, 2004), 59; and Edward C. Ratledge, *State Growth and Development: Delawareans' Views on Issues and Policy Options (A Preliminary Report)*, (Newark: University of Delaware, Center for Applied Demography and Survey Research, 1995), 24.

6. See *Delaware Code Annotated*, title 3, chap. 9; Jane Brooks, "7,100 Farmland Acres Preserved," *Wilmington News Journal*, November 26, 1996, B7; and "Delaware Farmers Move to Preserve 10,000 Acres," *Wilmington News Journal*, January 24, 1997, B12.

7. See Terry Spencer, "Preservation Leader Seeks to Sell Farmland," *Wilmington News Journal*, July 23, 1996, A1, A4; Terry Spencer, "State Official Fears Roberts' Land Sale Will Start a Trend," *Wilmington News Journal*, July 23, 1996, A5; Robert Moore, "9th District Rivals Detail Fund Raising," *Wilmington News Journal*, September 9, 1997, B1, B6; Robert Moore, "Cathcart Narrowly Upsets Roberts," *Wilmington News Journal*, September 14, 1997, A1, A7; and

Mary Allen, "Roberts Enters Guilty Plea," *Wilmington News Journal*, November 25, 2003, A1, A4.

8. See Department of Natural Resources and Environmental Control, *Delaware Annual Air Quality Report, 2003*, doc. no. 40-0-02-204 (Dover: State of Delaware, 2003); U.S. Environmental Protection Agency, *The Ozone Report: Measuring Progress through 2003*, no. 454/K-04-001 (Research Triangle Park NC: EPA, 2004); and U.S. Environmental Protection Agency, *The Particle Pollution Report: Current Understanding of Air Quality and Emissions through 2003*, no. 454-R-04-002 (Research Triangle Park NC: EPA, 2004).

9. See Jeff Montgomery, "State Approves Upgrade for Premcor," *Wilmington News Journal*, December 1, 2004, B1; and the Premcor Refining Group, Inc., *Memorandum: Phase II of the Application for Permits to Construct a Refinery Pollution Control Upgrade Project (PCUP) at the Premcor Refining Group, Inc.'s Delaware City Refinery*, February 7, 2005.

10. See Delaware Department of Natural Resources and Environmental Control, *Delaware Toxics Release Inventory, 2003 Data Summary* (Dover DE: March 2005); and Center for Applied Demography and Survey Research, University of Delaware, TRI Explorer Geography Report, http://www.epa.gov/triexplorer/geography.htm (accessed August 9, 2008).

11. See the issues of the *Wilmington News Journal* for November 7–10, 2004; and Jaqueline D. Savitz et al., *Dishonorable Discharge: Toxic Pollution in Delaware Waters* (Washington DC: Environmental Working Group, September 1996).

12. U.S. Environmental Protection Agency, "Water Quality Assessment Data for the State of Delaware Year 2002," April 1, 2005, http://oaspub.epa.gov/waters/w305b_report_v2.state (accessed August 14, 2008).

13. See Delaware Department of Natural Resources and Environmental Control, *Delaware's Nonpoint Source Program, 2004 Annual Report* (Dover: Delaware Department of Natural Resources and Environmental Control, Division of Soil & Water Conservation, 2005); and Delaware Department of Natural Resources and Environmental Control, *Strategic Plan, Fiscal Years 2003–2005* (Dover: Delaware Department of Natural Resources and Environmental Control, 2001).

14. See United Health Foundation, "Snapshot: Delaware," in *America's Health Rankings—2006 Edition*, p. 40, http://www.unitedhealthfoundation.org/ahr2006/2006ahr.pdf (accessed August 14, 2008).

15. Eric Jacobson, John Jaeger, and Edward C. Ratledge, *Health Disparities in Delaware—2004* (Newark: University of Delaware, Center for Applied Demography and Survey Research, 2005), 28.

16. See Edward C. Ratledge and Roberta C. Gibson, *Summary Statistics from the 2000 Prams Survey* (Newark: University of Delaware, Center for Applied Demography and Survey Research, 2001).

17. Racial disparities are measured as the black rate/white rate. For example, a disparity of 2.0 indicates the black rate is twice the white rate.

Suggested Sources for Further Reading

Delaware's small size and sparse population help explain the paucity of research related to its government and politics, as compared to populous states with multiple and highly differentiated public affairs research institutions. Accordingly, one is compelled to rely on limited resources in Delaware, many of which are associated with faculty and staff of the University of Delaware.

PRINCIPAL INSTITUTIONAL SOURCES

Among institutional sources are studies related to the university's College of Human Resources, Education and Public Policy—notably its School of Urban Affairs and Public Policy, its Institute for Public Administration, and its Center for Applied Demography and Survey Research. In addition, the university's Department of History and Department of Political Science and International Relations are sources of significant studies. The holdings of Delaware's principal library, the University of Delaware's Morris Library, are electronically available.

Pertinent documents and information regarding Delaware state and local governments and agencies are available on the Internet and through their Web sites. Likewise, related federal government sources and data are available online. Government documents are also available in Dover at the Delaware Legislative Council Research Library and the Delaware State Law Library.

Delaware's sole statewide daily newspaper, the *Wilmington News Journal*, is the principal source for contemporary news of Delaware government and politics, as well as a source for occasional investigatory reporting.

The following studies and sources are not exhaustive, but are selective and illustrative, available for the guidance of students and citizens for further study of Delaware government and politics.

DELAWARE HISTORY

The best bibliography covering the period from the earliest printed material about Delaware—including histories, reference works, and serial publications—through the year 1960 is *A Bibliography of Delaware through 1960* (Newark: University of Delaware Press, 1966), compiled from four principal libraries: Public Archives (Dover), Historical Society of Delaware (Wilmington), Wilmington Institute Free Library, and the University of Delaware (Newark). In addition, the Historical Society of Delaware publishes a semiannual journal, *Delaware History*.

The Delaware Public Archives contains a collection of historical records dating from the seventeenth century to the present, including documents, maps, sound and audio recordings, and more than fifty thousand historical photographs.

The so-called "Delaware Collection," housed in the Special Collections Department of the University of Delaware Library, contains manuscripts and archival sources that span nearly two centuries of Delaware politics, including the congressional and personal papers of U.S. Representative Thomas Carper and U.S. Senators J. Allen Frear, George Gray, Willard Saulsbury Jr., and John Williams.

The most comprehensive history of Delaware, authored by the late University of Delaware history professor emeritus John A. Munroe, and now in its fourth edition, is *History of Delaware* (Newark: University of Delaware Press, 2001). As a guide for further historical research, the bibliographical essay at the end of Munroe's book is especially useful.

DELAWARE GOVERNMENT AND POLITICS

The most pertinent of previous studies, listed in the order of their years of publication, are listed here.

The Government and Administration of Delaware (New York: Thomas Y. Crowell Co., 1956), authored by the late University of Delaware political science professor Paul Dolan, relates political and administrative arrangements to Delaware's political and social patterns of the mid-twentieth century.

Government of Delaware (Newark: University of Delaware, 1976), coauthored by Paul Dolan and his colleague at the University of Delaware, political science professor James R. Soles, analyzes the structure and practices of Delaware's state government.

History of Delaware through Its Governors, 1776–1984 (Wilmington DE: McClafferty Printing, 1984), authored by former state senator Roger A. Martin, is a biographical directory of the governors of Delaware as well as a chronicle of its political history.

Memoirs of Twenty-two Years in the Delaware State Senate (Wilmington, 1995), also written by Roger A. Martin, describes what it was like to serve in Delaware's state senate.

The Delaware Constitution of 1897: The First One Hundred Years (Wilmington: Delaware State Bar Association, 1997), coedited by Harvey B. Rubenstein, Randy J. Holland, and others, commemorates the centennial of the Delaware Constitution of 1897 by articulating the legal practices of Delaware's organic structure and the evolution of complex legal issues inherent in Delaware's constitution.

Governing Delaware: Policy Problems in the First State (Newark: University of Delaware Press, 2000), by University of Delaware political science professor emeritus William W. Boyer, is a comprehensive policy analysis of the governance of Delaware that focuses on its political culture and public policy problems at the turn of the century.

Only in Delaware: Politics and Politicians in the First State (Newark: Grapevine Publishing, 2002), authored by journalist Celia Cohen, is a chronological analysis of the individuals and forces that have shaped modern Delaware politics.

Democracy in Delaware: The Story of the First State's General Assembly (Wilmington DE: Cedar Tree Books, 2004), written by University of Delaware history professor emeritus Carol E. Hoffecker, is the tricentennial commemoration commissioned by Delaware's General Assembly that reconstructs its long history.

Index

Nevada Politics and Government: Conservatism in an Open Society
By Don W. Driggs and Leonard E. Goodall

New Jersey Politics and Government: Suburban Politics Comes of Age, second edition
By Barbara G. Salmore and Stephen A. Salmore

New York Politics and Government: Competition and Compassion
By Sarah F. Liebschutz, with Robert W. Bailey, Jeffrey M. Stonecash,
Jane Shapiro Zacek, and Joseph F. Zimmerman

North Carolina Government and Politics
By Jack D. Fleer

Oklahoma Politics and Policies: Governing the Sooner State
By David R. Morgan, Robert E. England, and George G. Humphreys

Oregon Politics and Government: Progressives versus Conservative Populists
By Richard A. Clucas, Mark Henkels, and Brent S. Steel

Rhode Island Politics and Government
By Maureen Moakley and Elmer Cornwel

South Carolina Politics and Government
By Cole Blease Graham Jr. and William V. Moore

West Virginia Politics and Government
By Richard A. Brisbin Jr., Robert Jay Dilger, Allan S. Hammock,
and Christopher Z. Mooney

West Virginia Politics and Government, Second Edition
By Richard A. Brisbin Jr., Robert Jay Dilger, Allan S. Hammock,
and L. Christopher Plein

Wisconsin Politics and Government: America's Laboratory of Democracy
By James K. Conant

Back from Boot Hill

After finding himself in a coffin, on the way to Boot Hill, Clay Tulane wants answers.

As he pieces together the story of how he got there with the help of local townsfolk Miss Winona and the boy Pocket, he finds himself drawn into a violent stuggle against local landowner, Marsden Rockwell, and his bunch of hired guns.

Tulane has more personal reasons, however, for seeking a final confrontation with the notorious killer, Lonnie Spade. As tension mounts and battle lines are drawn, Tulane's search for the truth throws up as many questions as answers. What is the real reason Rockwell and his Bar Nothing outfit want to take over the neighbouring Pitchfork L, and is it connected with the mystery of the strange mesa known as Sawn-Off Mountain?